Praise for *Why the Jews?*

"I have now read twice the book by Dennis Prager and Joseph Telushkin, *Why The Jews?* Without a doubt, it is one of the most thought-provoking books on this theme: clear, persuasive, and considered. In seeking to study the origin and course of Jew-hatred, the authors have traversed history and psychology, religion and current affairs. In a short span, they have ranged over two thousand years, every geographic region, and every manifestation of a phenomenon that is both all-pervasive and apparently indestructible. This is a provocative book. It is also a disturbing one. But there can be no doubt that it should be read by every person disturbed by prejudice, and indeed by every prejudiced person."

—Professor Martin Gilbert, Oxford University,
official biographer of Winston Churchill, author of
Churchill: A Life, and *The Holocaust, A History*

"The wisest, most original and provocative book on the subject I have ever read."

—Rabbi Harold Kushner, author of
When Bad Things Happen to Good People

"A learned and wise book. It should of course be read by Jews who know what the tragedy of antisemitism has meant to them in our time. But it should also be read by non-Jews lest ignorance and indifference again be accomplices to crime."

—Martin Peretz, former editor, *The New Republic*

"The theory that Jewish values are the root of antisemitism regardless of time and locale is presented with utter clarity and cogent argument. This book deserves the widest attention. It offers a solution to antisemitism that is both inescapable and memorable."

—Rabbi Gunther Plaut, President, Central Conference
of American Rabbis, and author of
The Torah—A Modern Commentary

BY DENNIS PRAGER

Think a Second Time

Happiness Is a Serious Problem: A Human Nature Repair Manual

Still the Best Hope: Why the World Needs America's Values to Triumph

The Ten Commandments: Still the Best Moral Code

BY JOSEPH TELUSHKIN

Jewish Literacy: The Most Important Things to Know About the Jewish Religion, Its People, and Its History

Jewish Humor: What the Best Jewish Jokes Say About the Jews

Jewish Wisdom: Ethical, Spiritual, and Historical Lessons from the Great Works and Thinkers

Words That Hurt, Words That Heal: How to Use Words Wisely and Well

Biblical Literacy: The Most Important People, Events, and Ideas of the Hebrew Bible

The Book of Jewish Values: A Day-by-Day Guide to Ethical Living

The Ten Commandments of Character: Essential Advice for Living an Honorable, Ethical, Honest Life

A Code of Jewish Ethics, volume 1, You Shall Be Holy

A Code of Jewish Ethics, volume 2: Love Your Neighbor as Yourself

Hillel: If Not Now, When?

Rebbe: The Life and Teachings of Menachem M. Schneerson, the Most Influential Rabbi in Modern History

WHY
THE
JEWS?

**THE REASON FOR ANTISEMITISM, THE MOST
ACCURATE PREDICTOR OF HUMAN EVIL**

DENNIS PRAGER and
JOSEPH TELUSHKIN

TOUCHSTONE
New York London Toronto Sydney New Delhi

TOUCHSTONE
An Imprint of Simon & Schuster, Inc.
1230 Avenue of the Americas
New York, NY 10020

This Touchstone edition 2016

TOUCHSTONE and colophon are registered trademarks of Simon & Schuster, Inc.

For information about special discounts for bulk purchases,

please contact Simon & Schuster Special Sales:

1-866-506-1949 or business@simonandschuster.com

Designed by Ruth Lee-Mui

10   9   8   7   6   5   4   3   2   1

The Library of Congress has cataloged the 2003 edition as follows:

Prager, Dennis, 1948–
    Why the Jews? : the reason for antisemitism / Dennis Prager and Joseph Telushkin.
        p.   cm.
    Includes bibliographical references and index.
    1. Antisemitism. 2. Antisemitism—History. I. Telushkin, Joseph, 1948– II. Title.
DS145.P484 2003   305.892'4—dc21   2003050719

ISBN 978-0-7432-4620-0 (pbk)
ISBN 978-1-4165-9123-8 (ebook)

TO
RAOUL WALLENBERG

IT WAS JUDAISM THAT BROUGHT THE CONCEPT OF A GOD-GIVEN
UNIVERSAL MORAL LAW INTO THE WORLD . . . THE JEW CARRIES THE
BURDEN OF GOD IN HISTORY [AND] FOR THIS HAS NEVER BEEN FORGIVEN.
—The Reverend Edward H. Flannery,
National Conference of Catholic Bishops

CONTENTS

PREFACE

ASK ALMOST ANYONE—Jew or non-Jew, scholar or layperson— why Jews have been hated so deeply and for so long, and you are likely to be told that people need scapegoats, or that Jews are affluent, or that antisemitism is yet another sad example of racism or religious bigotry, or that antisemites are simply sick. In fact, you are likely to be given every reason for antisemitism except, amazingly, that it is a response to anything distinctly Jewish.

We devoted seven years to writing this book to counteract this dejudaization of Jew-hatred, this universalization of a unique phenomenon. Until recently and throughout their history Jews have believed that they are hated because Judaism made them different and challenging, not because they were rich, or convenient scapegoats, or but another bullied minority, or for any other reason unrelated to their being Jews.

The purpose of this book is to substantiate this age-old Jewish understanding of antisemitism. We intend to refute modern attempts to deny the distinctly Jewish reasons for Jew-hatred and its contemporary manifestation, anti-Zionism. The historical record clearly indicates, we believe, that Jew-hatred is unique. The very word *Jew* continues to arouse passions as does no other religious or national name. Why this hatred? Why this passion? That is the subject of our inquiry.

But this book is not only an explanation of this unique hatred, as important as that is. There is another, equally important reason for this book. When non-Jews understand Jew-hatred, they will understand that hatred of the Jews serves as mankind's early warning system of great evil. Antisemites begin with Jews. But they never end with Jews. Putting aside moral considerations, non-Jews need to fight Jew-hatred for their own sake. Antisemites—Nazis and Islamist terrorists, to take just two recent examples—have persecuted and murdered far more non-Jews than Jews.

Understand Jew-hatred and you begin to understand the hatred that is the most accurate predictor of human evil—antisemitism.

INTRODUCTION TO THE 2016 EDITION

INTRODUCTION TO THE 2016 EDITION

U NDER NORMAL CIRCUMSTANCES, authors are very pleased to have a second edition—let alone a third—of their book published.

But these are not normal circumstances. Indeed, there is no small measure of sorrow for us that *Why the Jews?* is being published in a third edition—not as the first edition was, as a historical study, but as a source of contemporary concern. Seventy years after the Holocaust, there are powerful forces that again want to destroy Jews.

This is not what we expected. When *Why the Jews?* was originally published in 1983, we wrote the book because we believed antisemitism was profoundly misunderstood, not because of any particular danger to the Jews. Now, a little over three decades later, Jew-hatred continues to be misunderstood, and Jews are in grave danger.

The most obvious objects of Jew-hatred are the residents of Israel, the only country in the world whose right to exist is challenged, and, as David Harris of the American Jewish Committee, has noted, "the only UN member state that has been targeted for annihilation by another UN member state [Iran]."

Iran has repeatedly called for the annihilation of Israel and has devoted great efforts to developing nuclear weapons that it hopes will eventually enable it to accomplish that goal. And lest anyone believe that Iran's antagonism is only against Israel and Zionism—and therefore somehow not antisemitism—it has even sponsored conferences on Holocaust denial.

Nor is Iran alone in isolating the one Jewish state for opprobrium. Israel has been the subject of more hostile resolutions at the United Nations General Assembly than all the other 192 UN member states combined, a fact even more confounding given that it is surrounded by among some of the worst human rights violators in the world.

There is no explanation for the worldwide antipathy to Israel other than its being the world's only Jewish state. Of course some criticisms of Israel are legitimate. Yet there is no explanation other than antisemitism for why Israel has become the pariah among the world's nations—just as the Jewish individual was among the European nations.

Moreover, hatred for the Jews in the second decade of the twenty-first century is not at all confined to the Jews of Israel.

Jew-hatred in Europe, fueled by the rapid growth of radical Muslims in Europe, has so increased that the *Atlantic* featured a cover story in 2015 asking "Is It Time for the Jews to Leave Europe?"[*]

Some of the statistics from that article:

- England. The Community Security Trust in England recorded 1,168 antisemitic incidents in 2014, by far the highest number ever recorded. A survey of British Jews revealed that more than half fear that Jews have no future in Great Britain.
- Belgium. In May 2014, four people were shot to death by a French Muslim at the Jewish Museum in Brussels.
- Holland. A 2003 survey found that 74 percent of Dutch citizens felt Israel was the greatest threat to world peace, greater than Iran and North Korea. All this animosity in a country that was home to the Holocaust's most famous victim, Anne Frank. And in 2006, the Arab European League, a "civil rights organization" based in the Netherlands (and Belgium), published a cartoon featuring a shirtless Hitler in bed with a frightened dark-haired girl. "Write this in your diary, Anne," Hitler tells her.

[*]Jeffrey Goldberg, "Is It Time for the Jews to Leave Europe?" *The Atlantic*, April 2015.

- Denmark. In 2015, a Jew guarding a Copenhagen synagogue where a Bat Mitzvah was taking place was murdered by a Danish-born Muslim. In the aftermath of a number of anti-Jewish incidents in Denmark, Rabbi Jair Melchior, head of the Danish Jewish community, told a reporter from Reuters: "It's not a dangerous antisemitism. It's spitting, cursing, things like that," a particularly sad declaration of what Melchior felt Jews who wanted to remain in Denmark need to learn to endure.

  At about the same time, a Danish imam urged Muslims to murder Jews: "Count them and kill them to the very last one. Don't spare a single one of them. Make them suffer terribly." Seventy-two years after the citizens of Denmark organized to save the Jews from the Nazis, we find a Danish cleric exhorting Muslims in Europe to resume Hitler's work.

- Sweden. In Malmo, Chabad rabbi Shneur Kesselman, the only Jew in the city who dresses in an identifiably Jewish manner (kippah, long beard), has been the victim of over a hundred attacks. "People throwing bottles from their car," Kesselman recalled in an interview with Jeffrey Goldberg, the author of the *Atlantic* cover story, "and someone backing up their car in order to hit me." Kesselman and his wife do not venture out as a couple—much as some parents do not fly together—for fear of being murdered and leaving their children orphans.

- Germany. In 2014, a synagogue in Wuppertal was firebombed by two Palestinian-Germans. Arguably as bad, a German judge denied that the attack was an act of antisemitism, but rather ascribed it to a desire to bring "attention to the Gaza conflict."

- France. France's 475,000 Jews constitute less than one percent of the country's population. Yet in 2014, according to the French Interior Ministry, Jews were the targets of 51 percent of all racist attacks in France.

  In Toulouse, in 2012, a French Muslim attacked a Jewish school, killed a thirty-year-old rabbi and his two sons, ages three and six, and then chased down an eight-year-old Jewish girl and shot her to death.

In January 2015, a French Muslim murdered four Jews at a kosher supermarket in Paris.

A month earlier, Muslim robbers broke into a Jewish home, demanding exorbitant sums of money (telling the occupants that they knew they were rich because they were Jewish) and raped a nineteen-year-old woman in the apartment.

It is becoming increasingly common for French Jews living in neighborhoods in proximity to Muslim areas to remove mezuzot from their doors.

- Hungary. The Jobbik Party, the third-largest party in Hungary, lists anti-Zionism as one of its core values, and calls on the Hungarian government to draw up a list of Jews in Hungary who might constitute a "national security risk."

  In Erpatak, the mayor hung the Israeli prime minister in effigy, and announced that he "opposes the efforts of Freemason Jews to rule the world."

- Turkey. Turkey's Islamist president Recep Tayyip Erdogan has routinely compared Israel to the Nazis—or worse. For example: "Those who condemn Hitler day and night have surpassed Hitler in barbarism."

- India. To draw but one example from outside of Europe, in November 2008, Rabbi Gavriel and Rivka Holtzberg, the couple who ran the Chabad House in Mumbai, were murdered, along with four other Jews, by Muslim terrorists from Pakistan.

There are many who claim that it is Israel's presence on the West Bank that prompts this violence against Jews in Europe and elsewhere. But Goldberg cited a different reason culled from conversations with Jew-haters throughout Europe: "I did not hear critiques of Israel's occupation policies. I heard, instead, complaints about the Jews' baleful influence in the world."

That it is Jews generally, not just Israel, whom Jew-haters regard as the enemy was made clear some years earlier when the Islamist murderers of *Wall Street Journal* reporter Daniel Pearl made him declare before slitting his throat on camera, "My father is a Jew, my mother is a Jew, and I am a Jew."

Likewise Hassan Nasrallah, the leader of Hezbollah, has declared that if only all the Jews would gather in Israel, "it will save us the trouble of going after them worldwide."

And what of the Unites States? Jews have never lived in a country other than Israel in which they have been treated as well as in the United States. Both of us have long regarded as alarmist those who, in the aftermath of any anti-Jewish incident, exaggerated the amount of Jew-hatred in America, or who predicted an imminent outbreak of anti-semitic attacks.

The United States has been uniquely open to Jews and to Juda-ism, a fact exemplified—to cite but one example—by Senator Joseph Lieberman's nomination as the Democratic Party candidate for vice-president in 2000. As was noted at the time, the fact that Lieberman was a religiously observant Jew who wouldn't campaign on Saturday because he observed the Jewish Sabbath actually increased his popu-larity.

A 2014 Pew Study showed that Jews, Catholics, and evangelical Christians were the three most positively regarded religious groups in the United States, with Jews coming out, by a small margin, on top. Jews received a warm, positive rating from 63 percent of Americans, which is particularly striking given that there are more than ten times as many Catholics and ten times as many evangelical Christians in the United States as there are Jews (Jews make up less than 2 percent of the Amer-ican population).

Nevertheless, for the first time, we see antisemitism as a potential and mounting threat to the well-being of American Jews.

American Jews have commonly associated antisemitism with Chris-tianity (primarily because of the Jewish historical experience in Europe) and with the political Right (again, primarily because of the Jewish experience in Europe). That situation has shifted. Christians in America (particularly evangelicals) are among Israel's most steadfast supporters. The same applies to the political Right.

Hostility to Jews—or at the very least to Jewish well-being—is now primarily located on the political Left, in particular in universities and among left-wing activist groups, including some mainstream Protestant churches. The critique of the Jewish community leveraging its wealth for malevolent self-serving purposes is a reprise of one of the most damaging anti-Jewish stereotypes, and is far more believed by left-wing students at secular universities than by any other students.

This hostility manifests itself not as traditional antisemitism—hatred of all Jews—but as singling out one country among the world's two-hundred-plus countries for particular hatred—the Jewish country, Israel—and its Jewish supporters.

The most widespread expression of Israel-hatred is the BDS (Boycott, Divestment, and Sanctions) movement, which is devoted to forging an economic, academic, and cultural boycott of Israel. Some BDS supporters, including many of its Jewish supporters, naively believe that BDS is opposed to Israel only because of its control over the West Bank, an opposition that will end when a Palestinian state is in existence. But the movement's leadership has repeatedly made it clear that BDS's goal is to maintain a complete boycott of Israel and, in the words of Omar Barghouti, the movement's founder, to "end Israel's existence as a Jewish state."

Over these past years, resolutions calling for the boycott of Israeli academic institutions have been passed by the American Studies Association, the American Anthropological Association, and the Modern Language Association. In the past three years, the number of colleges that have considered BDS resolutions to boycott Israel has doubled in each year, while "Israel apartheid weeks" are organized at an ever-increasing number of American and European universities each year. Incidents directed at individual Jews are also becoming more common at some of the most prestigious American universities. At Stanford University, a Jewish woman running in a student government election solicited the support of representatives of the Students of Color Coalition. She was asked, "Given your Jewish identity, how would you vote on divestment [from Israel]?" a question irrelevant to a student government election, but very relevant to those whose goal it is to marginalize Jewish students on campus.

A friend whose son was applying to college was warned by his college admissions adviser to remove mention of the Labor Zionist camp he had attended. As the adviser told him, "It is not going to help you to have the word *Zionist* on your application." It is very unlikely that the adviser would have similarly advised a student not to mention that he or she was involved in pro-BDS activities.

In case it needs to be clarified, we are well aware that one can be critical, even highly critical, of Israeli policies without being antisemitic or even anti-Israel. But libeling Israel or working to economically strangle the Jewish state are different matters entirely. Those who equate Israel with the Nazis, or accuse Israel of engaging in genocide against the Palestinians, are no different from the medieval Christians who perpetrated the infamous blood libel, the charge that Jews murder Christian children in order to drink their blood for religious purposes.

The contemporary equivalent of the blood libel is the "genocide" libel against Israel, a charge often made by BDS activists. Just as the blood libel was spread with the goal of bringing about the destruction of Jewish communities (tens of thousands of Jews were murdered because of the blood libel), so too the genocide libel is spread with the goal of bringing about the destruction of the State of Israel. (For the record, the Palestinian population in Israel has increased sevenfold since Israel's creation in 1948.)

Given the long and universal history of antisemitism, Jews have accepted that a certain level of antisemitism will exist even in a generally friendly society. How then can one assess whether antisemitism is reaching a dangerous level? A key test is this: When a person is exposed as an antisemite, does it raise or lower that person's status in society? In the mid-1980's, it was revealed that the black activist Jesse Jackson, who was then pursuing the Democratic nomination for president, had made some antisemitic remarks to a black journalist. Jackson felt the need to go to a synagogue and apologize for his comments. A few years later, Patrick Buchanan, a leading conservative figure in the Republican Party, made antisemitic remarks and, when called on them, refused to apologize. Buchanan was subsequently marginalized.

As long as being exposed as an antisemite injures one's status in American society, America will remain a country in which Jews continue to prosper. However, if being exposed as one who works to harm Israel—let alone aids those who seek to destroy it—or to otherwise harm the Jewish people—does not lower the regard in which that individual is held, the Jewish community will be in trouble.

Given that anti-Israel hostility is increasing and inevitably affects Jews' welfare outside of Israel—including, potentially, that of the Jews of the United States and, even more so, the Jews of Europe—there is cause for concern. Enough concern, as we noted above, to prompt a reissue of this book.

We do believe, however, that the more people come to understand Jew-hatred, antisemitism, and anti-Zionism, the more people will come to oppose it.

The Jews, as we repeatedly show in the book, are the proverbial canary in the mine, whose death warns the miners of toxic fumes. Jews die at the hands of those who will murder countless others in addition to the Jews. Therefore moral non-Jews who do not confront antisemites are doomed to be their victims. Antisemites start with Jews but never end with them.

Had the world confronted Hitler and the Nazis over their antisemitism in the 1930s, not only the six million Jews would have been saved, but an additional fifty-five million people who were killed in World War II. So, too, the world essentially ignored Palestinian Muslim terror (no Palestinian Christians were suicide bombers) against the Israelis—and now far more non-Jews and even Muslims have been slaughtered by Islamist terror groups. Indeed, today it is Christians who are the most persecuted minority throughout the Middle East and much of Africa, a fact generally ignored by the media.

However many people read the first edition of *Why the Jews?*, we could only wish that far more had done so. They would have understood that those who want Israel destroyed, and who send young people to blow themselves up in order to murder as many Jews as possible, are humanity's problem as much as the Jews' problem. For to understand antisemitism is to understand the role of this tiny people as the lightning rod for evil in every culture in which they have lived. That was the reason for the book in 1983. This is the reason for reissuing it a generation later.

WHY THE
JEWS?

PART ONE

WHY THE JEWS?
THE EXPLANATION

ONE
Why Jew-Hatred Is Unique

H ATRED OF THE JEW has been humanity's greatest hatred. While hatred of other groups has always existed, no hatred has been as universal, as deep, or as permanent as antisemitism.[1]

The Jews have been objects of hatred in pagan, religious, and secular societies. Fascists have accused them of being Communists, and Communists have branded them capitalists. Jews who live in non-Jewish societies have been accused of having dual loyalties, while Jews who live in the Jewish state have been condemned as "racists." Poor Jews are bullied, and rich Jews are resented. Jews have been branded as both rootless cosmopolitans and ethnic chauvinists. Jews who assimilate have been called a "fifth column," while those who stay together spark hatred for remaining separate. Hundreds of millions of people have believed (and in the Arab world many still do) that Jews drink the blood of non-Jews, that they cause plagues and poison wells, that they secretly plot to conquer the world, and that they murdered God.

The *universality* of antisemitism is attested to by innumerable facts, the most dramatic being that Jews have been expelled from so many of the European and Arab societies in which they have resided. Jews were expelled from England in 1290, France in 1306 and 1394, Hungary between 1349 and 1360, Austria in 1421, numerous localities in Germany between the fourteenth and sixteenth centuries, Lithuania in 1445 and 1495, Spain in 1492, Portugal in 1497, and Bohemia and Moravia in 1744–45. Between the fifteenth century and 1772, Jews were not allowed into Russia; when finally admitted there, they were restricted to one area, the Pale of Settlement. Between 1948 and 1967, nearly all the Jews of Algeria, Egypt, Iraq, Syria, and Yemen fled these countries, fearing for their lives.

The *depth* of antisemitism is evidenced by the frequency with which hostility against Jews has gone far beyond discrimination and erupted into sustained violence. In most societies in which Jews have lived, they have at some time been subjected to beatings, torture, and murder solely because they were Jews. In the Russian Empire during the nineteenth and early twentieth centuries, mass beatings and murders of Jews were so common that a word, *pogrom*, was coined to describe such incidents.[2] And these pogroms were viewed by their antisemitic perpetrators as being of such significance that they were equated with the saving of Russia.[3]

On a number of occasions even beating and murdering Jewish communities was not deemed sufficient. Antisemitic passions have run so deep that only the actual annihilation of the Jewish people could solve what came to be called by antisemites the "Jewish Problem." The basic source of ancient Jewish history, the Bible, depicts two attempts to destroy the Jewish people, that by Pharaoh and the Egyptians (Exodus 1:15–22) and that of Haman and the Persians (book of Esther). While it is true that the historicity of these biblical accounts has not been proven or disproven by nonbiblical sources, few would dispute the supposition that in ancient times attempts were made to destroy the Jews.[4] Indeed, the first recorded reference to Jews in non-Jewish sources, the Mernephta stele, written by an Egyptian king about 1220 B.C.E., states, "Israel is no more."

Jewish writings from the earliest times until the present are replete with references to attempts by non-Jews to destroy the Jewish people.

Psalm 83:5 describes the enemies of the Jews as proponents of genocide: "Come, and let us cut them off from being a nation, that the Name of Israel may no more be remembered." Just how precarious Jews have viewed their survival is reflected in a statement from the ancient, and annually recited, Passover Haggadah; "In every generation they rise against us in order to annihilate us."

On three occasions during the last 350 years, annihilation campaigns have been waged against the Jews: the Chmelnitzky massacres in eastern Europe in 1648–49, the Nazi German destruction of Jews throughout Europe between 1939 and 1945, and the attempt to eradicate the Jewish state by its enemies.[5]

For various reasons, the Chmelnitzky massacres are today not well known among Jews and are virtually unknown among non-Jews; perhaps the Holocaust tends to overshadow all previous Jewish suffering. Yet without denying the unique aspects of the Nazi Holocaust, there are a number of significant similarities between it and the Chmelnitzky massacres. In both instances, all Jews, including infants, were targeted for murder; the general populaces nearly always joined in the attacks; and the torture and degradation of Jews were an integral part of the murderers' procedures. These characteristics are evidenced by the following contemporaneous description of a typical Chmelnitzky massacre:

Some of [the Jews] had their skins flayed off them and their flesh was flung to the dogs. The hands and feet of others were cut off and they were flung onto the roadway where carts ran over them and they were trodden underfoot by horse. . . . And many were buried alive. Children were slaughtered in their mothers' bosoms and many children were torn apart like fish. They ripped up the bellies of pregnant women, took out the unborn children, and flung them in their faces. They tore open the bellies of some of them and placed a living cat within the belly and left them alive thus, first cutting off their hands so that they should not be able to take the living cat out of the belly . . . and there was never an unnatural death in the world that they did not inflict upon them.[6]

The *permanence* (as well as depth) of antisemitism is attested to by the obsessive attention given to the "Jewish Problem" by antisemites throughout history. At one time or another nearly every major country that has had a large Jewish population has regarded this group, which never constituted more than a small percentage of its population, as an enemy. To the Roman Empire in the first century, the European Christian world for over fifteen centuries, the Nazi Reich, the Soviet Union, and to the Arabs and much of the Muslim world, the Jews have been or are regarded as an insufferable threat.

Jews have been perceived as so dangerous that even after their expulsion or destruction, hatred and fear of them remain. The depiction of Jews as ritual murderers of young Christian children in Chaucer's "Prioress's Tale" in *The Canterbury Tales* one hundred years after all Jews had been expelled from England attests to the durability of antisemitism. So does the characterization of Jews as usurers who wish to collect their interest in flesh in Shakespeare's *The Merchant of Venice*, three hundred years after the Jews' expulsion.[7] A more recent example was Poland in 1968, when for months the greatest issue for Polish radio, television, and newspapers was the "Unmasking of Zionists in Poland." Of the thirty-three million citizens of Poland in 1968 then under Communist rule, the Jews numbered about twenty thousand or less than one-fifteenth of 1 percent.[8]

How are the universality, depth, and permanence of antisemitism to be explained? Why such hatred and fear of a people who never constituted more than a small minority among those who most hated and feared them? Why, nearly always and nearly everywhere, the Jews?

Many answers have been offered by scholars. These include, most commonly, economic factors, the need for scapegoats, ethnic hatred, xenophobia, resentment of Jewish affluence and professional success, and religious bigotry. But ultimately these answers do not explain antisemitism; they only explain what factors have *exacerbated* it and caused it to erupt in a given circumstance. None accounts for the universality, depth, and persistence of antisemitism. In fact, we have encountered virtually no study of this phenomenon that even attempts to offer a universal explanation of Jew-hatred. Nearly every study of antisemitism consists almost solely of historical narrative, thus seeming to indicate that no universal reason for antisemitism exists.

We reject this approach. To ignore or deny that there is an ultimate cause for antisemitism contradicts both common sense and history. Antisemitism has existed too long, and in too many disparate cultures, to ignore the problem of ultimate cause and/or to claim that new or indigenous factors are responsible every time it erupts. Factors specific to a given society help account for the manner or time in which antisemitism erupts. But they do not explain its genesis—why antisemitism at all? To cite but one example: the depressed economy in Germany in the 1920s and 1930s helps to explain why and when the Nazis came to power, but it does not explain why Nazis hated Jews, let alone why they wanted to murder every Jew. Economic depressions do not explain gas chambers.

The very consistency of the passions Jews have aroused demands a consistent explanation. Ancient Egyptians, Greeks, and Romans, medieval and many modern Christians and Muslims, and Nazis and Communists have perhaps only one thing in common: they have all, at some point, counted the Jews as their enemy, often their greatest enemy. Why?

Among Jews, this question has been posed only in the modern era. Until the modern age, Jews never asked, "Why the Jews?" They knew why. Throughout their history, Jews have regarded Jew-hatred as an inevitable consequence of their Jewishness. Contrary to modern understandings of antisemitism, the age-old Jewish understanding of antisemitism does posit a universal explanation for Jew-hatred: Judaism, meaning the Jews' God, laws, peoplehood, and claim to being chosen. The historical record, as we shall show, confirms the traditional Jewish view that the Jews were hated because of Jewish factors. Modern attempts to dejudaize Jew-hatred, to attribute it to economic, social, and political factors, and universalize it into merely another instance of bigotry, are as opposed to the facts of Jewish history as they are to the historical Jewish understanding of antisemitism.

Antisemites have not hated Jews because Jews are affluent—poor Jews have always been as hated; or strong—weak Jews have simply invited antisemitic bullies; or because Jews may have unpleasant personalities—genocide is not personality-generated; or because ruling classes focus worker discontent onto Jews—precapitalist and noncapitalist societies such as the former Soviet Union, other Communist states, and various Third World countries, have been considerably more antisemitic than capitalist societies. Antisemites have hated Jews because Jews are Jewish. Christian antisemites ceased hating rich Jews when they became Christians. Muslim antisemites embrace Jews who convert to Islam. The same has held true for virtually all other antisemites except the Nazis, whom we shall discuss later.

What about Judaism has provoked anti-Jewish hostility? There are four answers.

1. For thousands of years Judaism has consisted of four components: God, Torah, Israel, and Chosenness; that is, the God introduced by the Jews, Jewish laws, Jewish peoplehood, and the belief that the Jews are God's chosen people. Jews' allegiance to any of these components has been a major source of antisemitism because it not only rendered the Jew an outsider, but more important, it has often been regarded by non-Jews as challenging the validity of their god(s), law(s), national allegiance, and/or national worth.

   By affirming what they considered to be the one and only God of all humankind, thereby implying illegitimacy to everyone else's gods, the Jews entered history—and have often been since—at war with other people's most cherished beliefs. The antisemites also hated the Jews because the Jews lived by their own all-encompassing set of laws. And because the Jews also asserted their own national identity, Jews intensified antisemitic passions among those who viewed this identity as threatening their own nationalism.

2. As if the above were not enough, Judaism has also held from the earliest times that the Jews were chosen by God to achieve this mission of bringing the world to God and His moral law (i.e., ethical monotheism). This doctrine of the Jews' divine election has been a major cause of antisemitism.

3. From its earliest days, the *raison d'être* of Judaism has been to change the world for the better (in the words of an ancient Jewish prayer recited daily, "to repair the world under the rule of God"). This attempt to change the world, to challenge the gods, religious or secular, of the societies around them, and to make moral demands upon others (even when not done expressly in the name of Judaism) has constantly been a source of tension.

4. As a result of the Jews' commitment to Judaism, they have led higher-quality lives than their non-Jewish neighbors in almost every society where they have lived. For example, Jews have nearly always been better educated; Jewish family life has usually been more stable; Jews aided one another more than their non-Jewish neighbors aided each other; and Jewish men have been less likely to become drunk, beat their wives, or abandon their children. As a result of these factors, the quality of life of the average Jew, no matter how poor, was higher than that of a comparable non-Jew in the same society (see Chapter 4).

This higher quality of life among Jews, which, as we shall show, directly results from Judaism, has, as one would expect, provoked profound envy and hostility among many non-Jews.

Since Judaism is the root cause of antisemitism, Jews, *unlike victims of racial or ethnic prejudice,* could in almost every instance of antisemitism, except Nazism, escape persecution. For thousands of years and until today, Jews who abandoned their Jewish identity and assumed the majority's religious and national identity were no longer persecuted.*

For these reasons, Jews have always regarded antisemitism as a response, however immoral, to Judaism. Thus, most Jews until the modern

---

*There is one apparent exception to this rule, the Marranos and Conversos of Spain. In the fourteenth and fifteenth centuries, Jews who converted to Christianity in Spain were not easily accepted into Catholic society. But this was overwhelmingly due to the circumstances of the Jews' conversions. The Christian hierarchy was reluctant to accept these Jewish converts as genuine Christians because it knew that they had converted under threats of expulsion or death, and therefore the sincerity of the Jews' Christianity was questioned.

era, and most religious Jews to this day, would describe Jews murdered by antisemites not as victims of ethnic prejudice but as having died *al kiddush hashem,* that is, as martyrs sanctifying the name of God before the world.

Once one understands why Judaism has precipitated antisemitism, the unique universality, depth, and permanence of Jew-hatred also become understandable. It takes infinitely more than economic tensions or racial prejudice to create the animosity that often has involved the torturing of children and the murdering of entire communities. Only a people representing a threat to the core values, allegiances, and beliefs of others could arouse such universal, deep, and lasting hatred.

That is why totalitarian regimes, secular and religious, inevitably are antisemitic. Totalitarian regimes by definition aim to control the totality of their citizens' lives and can therefore tolerate no uncontrolled religious or national expressions, both of which are part of Judaism. Once the Jewish roots of antisemitism are recognized, the only solutions to the "Jewish Problem," as far as antisemites are concerned, are obvious. The Jews must either convert, be expelled, or murdered. In the 1880s, the Russian czar's procurator of the Holy Synod and architect of Russian government policy at the time, Constantine Pobedonostev, is said to have offered precisely this advice: One-third of the Jews living in the Russian Empire should be converted to Christianity, one-third should be expelled, and one-third should be put to death.[9]

In fact, for the last two thousand years, this has repeatedly been the chronological order of antisemitic acts. First, attempts would be made to convert the Jews. When the Jews refused, they were often expelled. And when even expulsion failed to solve the "Jewish Problem," there remained one "Final Solution," which is precisely the name the Nazis gave to their plan to annihilate the Jews.

It is also clear that antisemitism is *not* ethnic or racial prejudice, though it obviously shares certain features with them. Haters of Jews persecuted them for the same reasons Romans persecuted Christians, Nazis tortured members of the Resistance, and Communist regimes imprison dissidents. In each instance, the group is persecuted because its different beliefs represent a threat to the persecuting group. This hatred must be understood as being very different from a racial or ethnic prejudice.

Blacks in America, for example, have been discriminated against because of the physical fact of their blackness, not because of specific black ideas or beliefs. Hatred of blacks is racial prejudice. Blacks cannot stop being black. But in dictatorships, dissidents can stop being dissenters, and a Jew has always been able to, and in general still can, stop being a Jew.

Even the major exception to this rule, Nazi antisemitism, confirms the Jewish basis of antisemitism. The Nazis simply maintained that Jews could never really become non-Jews. They believed that no matter how much Jews may consciously attempt to appear and behave like non-Jews, they nevertheless retain the values of Judaism. Nazi anti-Jewish "racism" emanated from a hatred of Judaism and what Jews represent. Nazi racism is *ex post facto;* first came the antisemitism, then came the racist doctrine to explain it.

Antisemitism is, therefore, as Jews have always regarded it: a response to Jews. The charges often made by antisemites—that Jews poison wells, drink human blood, plot to take over the world's governments, or control world finance—are hallucinatory. But the roots of antisemitism are not. The real reasons antisemites hate Jews and the accusations they make against them are rarely the same. This is hardly uncommon. When people harbor hatreds, individually or communally, they rarely articulate rationally the reasons for their hatred.

We should not be so naive as to regard all antisemitic accusations as the reasons for the antisemitism. For example, the modern belief that economic factors cause antisemitism, besides confusing exacerbating factors with causes, grants the accusations of antisemites far too much credence. It is analogous to the efforts of some fine historians to determine the historical accuracy of the Christian claim that the Jews killed Jesus, because Christian antisemites called Jews "Christ killers," as if proving one way or another would have ended Christian antisemitism. It is also analogous to the tireless efforts of other fine historians to decipher the exact number and circumstances of Arabs displaced during the founding of Israel, as if those who single out Israel from all other countries to support efforts to destroy it do so because six hundred thousand Arab refugees were created in 1948.

The questions for those wishing to understand the roots of antisemitism are not whether some Jews helped execute a fellow Jew two thousand years ago, or how great a role Jews played in the German economy, or how many Arabs fled Israel in 1948. The questions are why, to begin with, people hate Jews, and then invent reasons to do so.

The answer is Judaism, its distinctiveness and its challenges, and we have offered four reasons why this is so. In the pages that follow, we pursue a more detailed analysis of these reasons.

TWO

Antisemitism: The Hatred of Judaism and Ethical Monotheism

JUDAISM CONSISTS OF FOUR COMPONENTS: God, Torah (laws and teachings), Israel (Jewish nationhood), and Chosenness. Throughout Jewish history, the Jews' affirmation of one or more of these components has challenged, even threatened, the gods, laws, and cultures of non-Jews among whom the Jews have lived.

THE JEWS CARRY THE BURDEN OF GOD IN HISTORY

Judaism's first component asserts that the God who revealed himself to the Jews is the one and only God, that any other gods, and everything else that is worshiped, is false, and that this God makes moral demands upon every person and judges every person and nation. These ideas, known as ethical monotheism, have generated animosity against the Jews ever since they introduced them to the world.

In the ancient world, every nation but the Jews worshiped its own gods and acknowledged the legitimacy of others' gods. The Jews declared that the gods of the non-Jews were nonsense: "They have mouths but cannot speak, eyes but cannot see, ears but cannot hear" (Psalms 115:5–6).

There is but one God and he had revealed himself through the Jews. One need not be a theologian or historian to understand why these doctrines bred massive anti-Jewish resentment.

The Jews' belief in God threatened more than their neighbors' gods. It challenged many of their fundamental values. "It was Judaism," wrote the Reverend Edward H. Flannery of the National Conference of Catholic Bishops, "that brought the concept of a God-given universal moral law into the world"; willingly or not, "the Jew carries the burden of God in history [and] for this has never been forgiven."[1] The world to which the Jews have introduced God and His moral demands has often resented this theological and moral challenge. It is little wonder that hatred of the Jew became, as Father Flannery wrote, "the greatest hatred in human history."

A basic element of antisemitism is, therefore, a rebellion against ethical monotheism, against the "thou shalts" and "thou shalt nots" introduced by the Jews in the name of a supreme moral authority. This point has been forcefully stated by the late non-Jewish social psychologist Ernest van den Haag:

Fundamental to [antisemitism] . . . though seldom explicit and conscious, is hostility to the Jewish belief in one God, a belief to which antisemites very reluctantly converted and which they never ceased to resist. Antisemitism is one form this resistance takes. Those who originated this burdensome religion—and yet rejected the version to which the Gentiles were converted—easily became the target of the resentment. One cannot dare to be hostile to one's all-powerful God. But one can be to those who generated Him, to whom He revealed Himself and who caused others to accept Him.

The Jewish God is invisible and unrepresentable; even unmentionable, a power beyond imagination, a law beyond scrutiny. He is universal, holding power over everybody and demanding obedience and worship from all. Nonetheless, He entered history and listened to, argued with and chose the Jews—and the Jews alone. . . . No wonder they are the target of all those who resent His domination. . . .

Most unpleasant, their invisible God not only insisted on being the one and only and all-powerful God—creator and lord of everything and the only rightful claimant to worship—He also developed into a moral God. . . .

The Jews have suffered from their own invention ever since; but they have never given it up, for it is, after all, what makes the Jews Jewish.[2]

From the earliest times, as van den Haag has noted, the Jews have suffered for representing, even when not embodying, obedience to God, and for denying the validity of the non-Jews' gods. Jewish opposition to Roman gods, for example, was unique and notorious. The fourth-century Roman emperor Julian attacked the Jews for "striving to gratify their own God [while] they do not at the same time serve the others." A first-century emperor, Caligula, was outraged at the Jews because they were the only people in the Roman Empire who refused to place his statue in their Temple. When a delegation of Jews came to meet with him, Caligula complained: "So you are the enemies of the gods—the only people who refuse to recognize my divinity, and yet you worship a god whose name you dare not pronounce." When the Jewish group protested that the Jews had already brought three sacrifices on the emperor's behalf to their Temple in Jerusalem, Caligula rightly noted, "Yes, you make a sacrifice *for* me, but not *to* me."[3]

Yet it was the Jews' God, not the Romans' gods, that ultimately prevailed in Rome. In the fourth century, the Roman Empire adopted the God of the Jews when Christianity became the Roman religion. This proved to be no blessing for the Jews, however. For the church created the most virulent form of antisemitism prior to Nazism—and the root cause, again, as it was with the Romans, was the Jews' understanding of God.

While the church adopted the Jews' God, it also posited the divinity of a first-century Jew, Jesus of Nazareth. To the Jews, however, belief in Jesus' divinity compromised monotheism. This denial alone would have sufficed to provoke early Christian antisemitism, just as the Jews' denial of Roman gods had provoked Roman hostility. But the Jews' denial of Jesus' divinity was far more threatening to the nascent church than their denial of Roman divinities was to Rome. For Jesus was a Jew, he directed his message to the Jews (Matthew 15:24), and all religious claims made for him were based on Jewish sources. Yet the Jews rejected the divine and messianic claims made for or by him. The Jews' monotheism, which dictated this denial, has been the single most important factor in Christian antisemitism.

Belief in the God introduced by the Jews continued to spread. In the seventh century, on the Arabian peninsula, a second offshoot of Judaism, Islam, arose. Islam, like Judaism, denied the divinity of Jesus, asserting the divinity of no one but Allah (Arabic for God). This rendered the Jews' situation under Islam somewhat easier, but the Jews incurred ongoing Muslim hatred for denying the divinity of Muhammad's message, particularly since Muhammad had wanted the Jews to validate his message and convert to Islam.

With the decline of religion in the West beginning in the eighteenth century, and with the rise of nationalism, the Jews remained objects of hostility—now both for their adherence to the national component of Judaism as well as for their religious beliefs.

Two of the three most virulent forms of modern antisemitism have been secular. Both Nazism and communism have sought to destroy the God, as well as the national identity, of the Jews. The Nazis' ultimate aim was to destroy the mortal threat posed by monotheism's God-based morality to their race/nation–based morality. Hitler declared that his mission in life was to destroy the "tyrannical God of the Jews" and His "life-denying Ten Commandments."[4] In 1936, a Nazi official, a supreme group leader named Schultz, speaking at a meeting of the National Socialist Confederation of Students, made this very point: "We cannot tolerate that another organization is established alongside of us that has a different spirit than ours. We must crush it. National Socialism in all earnestness says: 'I am the Lord thy God, thou shalt have no other gods before me.'"[5] Because of the threatening nature of their religion, the Jews, who through both Judaism and Christianity had introduced monotheism, had to be destroyed.

Communist regimes also perceived monotheism's threat. Communist party members agreed with their religious opponents that one can either be true to God or to the party, but not to both. The moment one believes in God, one has an external standard by which to judge the government. This is why a person who advocated belief in God in the Soviet Union, for example, risked incarceration.

Though affirmation of God's existence was not widespread among the early Soviet Jewish dissidents, they did deny the proclaimed truths of communism, just as their ancestors had challenged the deities of ancient Rome or the divinity of Jesus. One of the best-known Soviet Jewish protest songs contained the words *"Nye boyusa nikovo Krome boga odnovo"* (I fear no one, Except God, the only one). The denial of the non-Jews' gods was as much an operative principle among Soviet Jewish dissidents, and a cause of antisemitism, as it was among Jews in the Hellenic, Roman, and Christian worlds.

But affirmation of God, and the concomitant denial of other gods, is only the first of the four components of Judaism. The other three, Jewish law, Jewish nationhood, and chosenness, exemplified and reenforced the Jews' otherness and further provoked antisemitism.

JEWISH LAW AS SOURCE OF ANTISEMITISM

Had the Jews only believed differently from their non-Jewish neighbors, they would not have made as profound an impact as they have upon the non-Jewish world and, consequently, would not have generated as much hostility. The component of Judaism that concretized the Jewish challenge is Jewish law, which put the Jews' beliefs into action.

The first aim of Jewish law is to have the Jew express his affirmation of God and denial of other gods in daily actions.* Much of Jewish law emanates from these two considerations: eight Torah laws deal with the public affirmation of God's existence, and fifty-one legislate the denial of other gods. These laws also compel Jews to make public their distinctive beliefs. It is not enough for a Jew to acknowledge monotheism privately; his belief in God and denial of other gods must be expressed

---

*The singular male pronoun is being used solely for convenience.

in public. Maimonides, the preeminent codifier of Jewish law, legislated in the twelfth century that "[Jews] are in duty bound to proclaim this true religion to the world, undeterred by fear of injury from any source. Even if a tyrant tries to compel us by force to deny Him, we must not obey, but must positively rather submit to death; and we must not even mislead the tyrant into supposing that we have denied Him while in our hearts we continue to believe in Him."[6]

But Jewish law legislates far more than monotheism. The 613 laws ascribed to the Torah and the oral legal tradition ultimately codified in the Talmud legislate every aspect of the Jew's life. The laws of monotheism ensured that Jews put their different beliefs into practice, while the Jews' social laws ensured that they put their different ethical values into practice. The third area of Jewish law, the laws of sanctity and ritual, further ensured that Jews act and even dress and eat differently from their non-Jewish neighbors. Any group acting so differently from the majority culture is bound to elicit some hostility.

Kashrut, the dietary laws, is the best-known example of Jewish laws that separated Jews from their neighbors. By fully observing these laws, a Jew could eat little at his non-Jewish neighbor's home. Kashrut, which may be characterized as Judaism's compromise with vegetarianism, restricted the Jew to eating only certain species of animals and fish.[7] And a Jew couldn't even eat the permitted meat and fowl of his non-Jewish neighbor, for Kashrut also mandated that permitted animals had to be killed in a specific Jewish manner that minimized the animal's pain, hastened its death, and ensured that none of its blood be consumed. This in turn meant that Jews could not hunt, a common mode of obtaining food, and a highly popular sport, among many non-Jews. Finally, Kashrut did not permit eating meat and milk products together.[8]

Jews' observance of the many laws of the Sabbath also increased their distinctiveness and separation. One day each week, the Jews would retreat further from their non-Jewish neighbors and act even more differently from them. They refused to work, travel, cook, play musical instruments, plant, engage in business, touch money, or attend public events.[9] Instead, they would spend the day with their families and with fellow Jews in prayer, study, song, and conversation. On the Sabbath, even more than on other days, the Jews appeared to live in their own world.

But the Jews have not lived in their own world. They have not physically removed themselves from society as have, for example, the Amish in America. On the contrary, Jews have tended to immerse themselves in society while maintaining their own way of life. Had the Jews removed themselves from society, or been social failures, while adhering to their distinctiveness, they would have provoked far less hostility. Precisely because they have lived among non-Jews, and often prospered while maintaining their separate beliefs and practices, the Jews and their practices have provoked such antipathy.

From the time of their earliest writings, Jews have understood the separatist and challenging nature of their laws and the resentment they can engender. In the biblical book of Esther, the Persian king plans to destroy the Jews because t hey are "dispersed among the peoples in all provinces of [the] kingdom, *and their laws are different from those of everybody else*" (Esther 3:8; emphasis ours).

In the Christian world, Jewish law, along with the Jews' rejection of Jesus, was the major source of contention between nascent Christianity and its mother religion. Judaism holds that one is "put right" with God through performing the good deeds of the law. But according to Paul, this belief is irreconcilable with Christian salvation.[10] "For if a person could achieve salvation through good works [the law], then Christ would have died in vain" (Galatians 2:21). Therefore, according to Paul, "we conclude that a man is put right with God only through faith and not by doing what the law commands" (Romans 3:28), and furthermore, "Christ redeemed us from the curse of the law" (Galatians 3:10).

The Jews' insistence on the continuing validity of their law was consequently seen by many Christians as a denial of salvation through faith in Christ, and it was often attacked in church literature. A typical example appears in the medieval church document *Epistle of Diognetus:* "But now, as to certain ridiculous matters that call for no discussion—such as their scruples in regard to meat, their observance of the Sabbath days, their vain boasting about circumcision, and the hypocrisy connected with fasting and the feasts of the new moon—I don't suppose you need any instruction from me. For how can it be other than irreligious to accept some of the things God has created for man's use and to reject others, as though some were created for a good purpose and others were useless and superfluous? . . . And is it not ridiculous to boast of a mutilation of the flesh as a sign of a chosen people, as though on account of this they were particularly loved by God? . . . Who would look on all this as evidence of religion, and not, rather, as a sign of folly?"[11]

Until the modern era, Jews observed Jewish law, and this differentiated them from their non-Jewish neighbors and increased anti-Jewish sentiments. Even today when most Jews have ceased strictly observing Jewish law, thousands of years of observance continue to influence most Jews' behavior. In general, Jews still have lower rates of intoxication and spouse beating, higher levels of education, greater professional success, commit much less violent crime, and engage in greater communal solidarity. All this has been due solely to millennia of adherence to Jewish law (see Chapter 4), and has provoked profoundly ambivalent reactions—from admiration, to envy, to hostility—from non-Jews.

JEWISH NATIONHOOD AS SOURCE OF ANTISEMITISM

The third component of Judaism is Israel, the biblical and historical name of the Jewish nation, and the name of the modern Jewish state.[12] Between 70 and 1948, Israel the nation (or "people," or "ethnicity"— regarding Jews, we are using the terms interchangeably) existed while Israel the state did not. To non-Jews and even to many Jews, the peoplehood of the Jews is usually the most perplexing aspect of Judaism.

This confusion is understandable. For one thing, one normally associates a national group with a land and a state, yet for nearly two thousand years the Jews lived without their state and most Jews lived outside their land. A second source of confusion is that the Jews constitute the only group in the modern Western world that is both an ethnic group and a religion. For both these reasons, Jews are unique, a uniqueness that often renders the Jews suspect in the eyes of others.

But as perplexing, unique, and even discomfiting as it may be, the Jew is a member of both the Jewish people and the Jewish religion, and this has been so since the beginning of Jewish history. To deny that nationhood is a component of Judaism is as untenable as to deny that God or Torah are components of Judaism. This is particularly evident today, since Jewish nationhood is the one component of Judaism with which both religious and committed secular Jews identify.

One group of Jews did attempt to eliminate the national component of Judaism. During the nineteenth and early twentieth centuries, Reform Jews in Germany and the United States, fearing that mention of Jewish peoplehood would arouse antisemitism, called for the elimination of Judaism's national component.[13] But even these radical Reformers never denied that nationhood had always been a part of Judaism; they simply wanted it removed. The attempt failed, because neither Jews nor Judaism can survive the denial of Jewish peoplehood.

Likewise, the Jewish people cannot survive the elimination of the religious components of Judaism. For the Jewish nation is defined by the Jewish religion. The only way a non-Jew can become a member of the Jewish nation is by converting to the Jewish religion. The Jews are, therefore, the only nation that an outsider can join irrespective of geographical considerations (for example, to become a Canadian, one must first live in Canada). As a consequence, the Jews are a transnational nation, and this too has been a significant source of antisemitism.[14]

The Jews' commitment to monotheism, Jewish law, and their doctrine of chosenness (discussed in Chapter 3)—i.e., commitment to the religious aspects of Jewish life—has been the primary cause of antisemitism in religious societies. In the modern age, however, when nationhood displaced religion as a supreme value, the Jews' nationhood, and since 1948 the Jews' state, have become added causes and the primary targets of antisemitism.

Jewish nationhood became an additional target of non-Jews' animosity the moment the modern age of nationalism began. Immediately following the French Revolution, in December 1789, during a discussion in the French National Assembly on granting French Jews equal rights, Count Stanislas de Clermont-Tonnerre declared: "The Jews should be denied everything as a nation, but granted everything as individuals. . . . There cannot be one nation within another nation."[15]

These fateful and prophetic words foretold much of the modern world's attitude toward the Jews. To be equal to non-Jews, the Jews would have to abandon their Jewish national identity; that was the price of emancipation.

In 1789, French Jews were told what virtually all European Jews would eventually hear: the price of individual emancipation is national extinction. In 1807, Napoleon convened a Sanhedrin (the name of the Jewish high court in ancient Jerusalem) of seventy-one leading rabbis and lay leaders. They were to disavow any commitment to Jewish nationhood and to declare that the only national identity of French Jews was French. Having little choice, they acceded to all of Napoleon's demands, except the sanctioning of intermarriage. (This, too, was prophetic. To this day many Jews adopt virtually every characteristic of the non-Jews among whom they live but oppose their children marrying a non-Jew.)

In the age of religion, the Jews were offered equality on the condition that they abandon their religion and convert to the majority religion. In the new age of nationalism, the Jews were offered equality on the condition that they abandon their national identity and adopt the majority's national identity only. In both ages, opponents of the Jews delivered the same message: cease being Jews.

Today, as in 1789, the refrain of the Jews' opponents is "The Jews should be denied everything as a nation, but granted everything as individuals." The Soviets said this, many of the Muslim and Arab opponents of Israel say this, the United Nations, when it delegitimized Zionism, said this. They all deny opposing Jews as individuals; they claim they want only to destroy Jewish nationhood. This is why they do not call themselves antisemites but rather "anti-Zionists."

The major difference between antisemites throughout Jewish history and today's anti-Zionists is only which component of Judaism, which aspect of Jewish distinctiveness, each found the most intolerable. For example, medieval Christian antisemites found the Jews' religious beliefs intolerable, and today's anti-Zionists loathe the Jews' national commitment.

Among the most ardent enemies of Judaism today is the Left.

Marxists, for example, are theoretically opposed to all religions. But from Marxism's earliest days, its adherents tended to be particularly anti-Jewish. Among other reasons: Judaism, unlike other religions, incorporates nationhood, while Marxist theory advocates the tearing down of national as well as religious allegiances. In practice, however, Marxist parties have been intensely nationalistic wherever they attained power, and the combination of chauvinistic nationalism with Marxist theory produced a particularly virulent strain of antisemitism. Neither could tolerate the Jews. Thus, for example, Soviet Jews who were committed to the God and Torah components of Judaism provoked antisemitism for Marxist reasons (quite aside from traditional Russian Orthodox antisemitism), while those who affirmed the national component of Judaism provoked Jew-hatred for Soviet nationalist (Russian, Ukrainian, Moldavian, etc.) as well as Marxist reasons. Thus, Soviet antisemitism was a reaction to every component of Judaism.

It is no wonder, then, that religious, national, and political extremism are each antisemitic, and when combined, intensely antisemitic. For these reasons (developed further in Chapters 9 and 11), the most potent expressions of Jew-hatred today are found in fundamentalist Islam and on the radical Left. With few exceptions, they have supplanted the Right and Christendom (except for Christianity's extreme Rightist and Leftist elements), one hopes, permanently. And for both Islam and the Left, Judaism's third component, nationhood, as embodied in the state of Israel and Zionism, elicits the greatest hostility.

What about the issue of Jewish "dual loyalty"? Does the fact of Jewish nationhood mean that Jews outside of Israel have more than one loyalty?

An answer is possible once we define the question. If we are asking whether Jews outside Israel are loyal to two governments, that of the country in which they reside and the government of Israel, the answer is no. Jews who affirm the national component of Judaism, both in fact and according to Jewish law (*dina dimalkhuta dina,* "the law of the land is the law," according to the Talmud), live as every other good citizen, in accordance with the laws of, and fully loyal to, the country in which they reside, presuming, of course, that the government is not a dictatorship and does not pass immoral laws (exceptions that would apply to all decent citizens).

But, it is often asked, how would American Jews react if war broke out between the United States and Israel?

In view of the fact that democracies do not go to war with one another, the only imaginable way in which the United States and Israel would find themselves at war would be if either country abandoned its democratic and other moral principles. In such an event, the individual, whether Jew, Christian, or atheist, would be obligated to follow the dictates of his moral values, which are (or should be) higher than all governments. Loyalty to any country should never mean supporting the country's policies when they are morally wrong.

But still, doesn't the fact of Jewish nationhood mean that committed Jews are theoretically members of two peoples—the Jewish people and the people among whom they reside? Yes, and in this respect Jews are unique. But as long as moral rather than nationalist values are held supreme, this should trouble no one. An American Jew, for example, is no less loyal an American because he has a special attachment to Ethiopian Jews. But if this fact in and of itself should provoke certain individuals to antisemitism, that, as Jews have repeatedly seen, is the price a Jew pays when nationalism becomes a god.

THREE

The Chosen People Idea as a Cause of Antisemitism

WE HAVE SEEN HOW THE Jews' affirmation of God, law, and nationhood has provoked antisemitism. But as much as any other Jewish belief, the belief that the Jews are the chosen people—that of all the nations in the world God chose them to be his messengers to humankind—has caused antisemitism, today even more than in the past. Since non-Jews first became aware of this doctrine—that is, from the time the Bible became known to non-Jews—chosenness has evoked envy and hostility.

The Jews' belief in chosenness did not necessarily have to evoke such hostile reactions among non-Jews. But because of the Jews' distinctive religion and particularly because of their generally higher quality of life, the doctrine of chosenness was never dismissed as an innocuous belief of an innocuous people. The Jews' profound influence on others and the comparatively high quality of their lives have caused non-Jews to take Jewish claims of chosenness very seriously.

The early church, for example, took chosenness so seriously that among the first beliefs it adopted was that the church had taken over divine election from the Jews. Thus, church leaders did not deny that the Jews had been chosen. On the contrary, they so believed in it that they appropriated the doctrine for themselves, calling the church the New Israel. And Islam reacted even more forcefully. The Koran did not deny the chosenness of Abraham; it simply declared Abraham a Muslim. Islam and premodern Christianity have had a love-hate relationship with the Jews' idea of chosenness. They loved and believed in the idea and hated the Jews for continuing to claim it for themselves.

It is not surprising that religions emanating from the Jews or from Judaism—and therefore, in their eyes, now in competition with it—would be hostile to Jewish chosenness. What is surprising is that antagonism toward Jewish chosenness continues to the present day. Two developments should have greatly reduced this antagonism. One is the general decline in religious belief among many non-Jews, who therefore should have come to regard the chosen people belief as at worst a pompous anachronism. The second is the decline of belief in chosenness among many modern Jews; and among those Jews who do continue to believe in chosenness, few ever make reference to it.

Yet, virtually every modern antisemitic movement has referred to Jewish chosenness. Even the Soviets, adopting an ideology that rejected all religious beliefs, often cited it. In 1973, they actually initiated a UN debate on the subject of the Jews as the chosen people. In his opening statement, the Soviet ambassador to the United Nations, Yakov Malik, declared: "The Zionists have come forward with the theory of the chosen people, an absurd ideology. That is religious racism."[1] Malik then challenged the Israeli ambassador to "prove to the world" that the Jews are the chosen people (October 21, 1973).

In America, according to a University of California Five-Year Study of Antisemitism in the United States, of the eighteen "potentially negative" beliefs Americans hold about Jews, the one with the widest acceptance (59 percent) is that "Jews still think of themselves as God's chosen people."[2]

Why does this belief arouse antisemitism? One reason is that antisemites have long portrayed the chosen people belief as a Jewish claim to innate superiority. Some have contended that the Jews' belief in their chosenness lies at the heart of their alleged attempt to take over the world. *The Protocols of the Elders of Zion*, perhaps the most widely distributed forgery in history and the best-known modern work of antisemitism, was based on this portrayal of chosenness.[3]

But one need not be an antisemite to misinterpret the chosen people concept and thus find it offensive. In the mid-1930s, at the very time the Nazis were passing antisemitic laws against the Jews of Germany, George Bernard Shaw, one of the most noted playwrights of the twentieth century, said that the Nazis, with their doctrines of racial superiority, were merely imitating the Jews' doctrine of chosenness.[4] In a similar vein, in 1971, *Religion in Life*, a liberal Methodist journal, wrote, "it is not surprising that Hitler retaliated against the chosen race by decreeing that it was not the Jewish but the Aryan race that was chosen."[5]

Reactions to the Jewish belief in chosenness have often been so negative that some Jews have called for elimination of this belief from Judaism, in much the same way as early Reform Jews called for the elimination of the nationhood component of Judaism because of the hostility it aroused. The most noted attempt at removing chosenness from Judaism was undertaken by Mordecai Kaplan, the founder of the small but influential Reconstructionist movement of Judaism. In 1945, Kaplan's movement published its first prayer book, which noted: "Modern minded Jews can no longer believe that the Jews constitute a divinely chosen people."[6] Kaplan explained that his movement's abandonment of this belief was "the best way . . . to answer the charge that the chosen people doctrine has been the model for theories of national and racial superiority."[7]

Given that chosenness is an integral belief of Judaism that arouses hostility, and one to which many Jews react defensively, it is important to explain it. For while a proper understanding of the doctrine will still elicit some antisemitic reactions, the moral onus will then clearly be on those who attack it rather than on the Jews who hold it.

Jewish chosenness has always meant that Jews have believed themselves to be chosen by God to spread ethical monotheism to the world and to live as a moral "light unto the nations" (Isaiah 49:6). *All other meanings imputed to Jewish chosenness are not Jewish.*[8] The Hebrew Bible, where the concept originates, neither states nor implies that chosen-

ness means Jewish superiority or privilege. The Bible repeatedly declares
that the Jews were not chosen because of any intrinsically positive qualities. Every nation is equal before God—"Are you not as the children of
Ethiopia to me, children of Israel?" states the prophet Amos (9:7). God
chose the Jews, "not because you are big; indeed you are of the smallest
nations" (Deuteronomy 7:7), but simply because they are descendants
of the first ethical monotheist, Abraham (Genesis 18:19). That is their
single merit.

Moreover, the Hebrews did something no other religion's Bible ever
did—they canonized their greatest critics. From the Torah's repeatedly
critical depictions of Jews and repeatedly positive depictions of non-Jews
(e.g., Noah, and the daughter of Pharaoh, see below), to the prophets'
relentless moral critiques of the Jewish people, the Hebrew Bible has not
a hint of belief in Jewish superiority. It believes only in the superiority of
God and His moral law.

Thus, the Jews' chosenness confers neither privilege nor superiority, only obligation and frequent suffering—"Since I have known only
you of all the peoples of the earth, I will visit upon you all your sins"
(Amos 3:2). The Jews are chosen only to complete the task of teaching
that there is only one God, and of living according to His laws. This
people either chose itself or, as the believing Jew holds, were chosen by
God, to make humanity aware of the Supreme Moral Being. This is in
fact what the Jews, often despite themselves, have done. British-Jewish
theologian Louis Jacobs discusses this in *A Jewish Theology:* "It becomes
obvious that [regarding Jewish chosenness] we are not discussing a
dogma incapable of verification but the recognition of sober historical
fact. The world owes Israel the idea of the one God of righteousness and
holiness. This is how God became known to mankind."[9]

There is an additional reason Jewish chosenness should never be
understood as a doctrine of racial superiority. By no accepted definition
of either Jew or race are the Jews a race. The Jewish people is composed
of members of every race; it is a nation defined by its religion, not its race.
Hence, anyone, of any race or nationality, can become a Jew *and thereby
chosen.* Whoever assumes the Jewish task becomes a member of the chosen people. Since everyone can become chosen, chosenness cannot be

racial. One might just as well speak of a race of ethical monotheists, or a Christian race. Jews are descendants of Abraham, a Mesopotamian. What rendered him a Jew were his beliefs, not his blood.

On innumerable occasions, Jewish literature—from the Bible to the Talmud to the most recent rabbinic writings—has emphasized that chosenness is a matter of values rather than of race. As noted, Jewish sources repeatedly portray Jews in negative ways (hardly the characteristic of people who consider themselves racially superior) and go out of their way to depict righteous non-Jews. To cite one dramatic instance, the first two chapters of the book of Exodus imply that it was a *Jew* who reported Moses' killing of an Egyptian slave-master to the Pharaoh, and states that it was an *Egyptian*, Pharaoh's daughter, who saved Moses' life when he was an infant.

The incorporation of the book of Ruth into the Bible demonstrates how Judaism and chosenness are not ethnically based. Ruth, born a pagan, chose to become a Jew, and is so highly regarded that the Jewish tradition has awarded her the distinction of having the future Messiah descend from her. That Ruth originally belonged to a different people has been as irrelevant to the Jewish people as the color of her hair.

The rabbis of the Talmud likewise delighted in tracing the ancestry of some of their most illustrious teachers to non-Jews. They claimed, for example, that Rabbi Akiva, one of the greatest figures of the Talmud and the most famous martyr in Jewish history, was a descendant of converts, and that one of his ancestors was Sisera, the great military enemy of the Jews (as described in Judges, chap. 4).

Almost every nation sees itself as special in some sense—from the Chinese, whose word for China is "center of the earth," to the Americans and the belief, which we share, in being a "bright, shining light." Many Christians believe that only Christians go to heaven, and Muslims see themselves as God's messengers. Yet of all the world's peoples, the Jews, with their doctrine of chosenness, elicit the sharpest attacks. This is yet another unique aspect of the unique phenomenon known as Jew-hatred.

FOUR

The Higher Quality of Jewish Life as a Cause of Antisemitism

I N NEARLY EVERY SOCIETY in which the Jews have lived for the past
two thousand years, they have been better educated, more sober,
more charitable with one another, committed far fewer violent
crimes, and have had a more stable family life than their non-Jewish
neighbors. *These characteristics of Jewish life have been independent of Jews'
affluence or poverty.* As the noted black economist Thomas Sowell has
concluded: "Even when the Jews lived in slums, they were slums with
a difference—lower alcoholism, homicide, accidental death rates than
other slums, or even the city as a whole. Their children had lower tru-
ancy rates, lower juvenile delinquency rates, and (by the 1930s) higher
IQs than other children. . . . There was also more voting for congressmen by low income Jews than even by higher income Protestants or
Catholics. . . . Despite a voluminous literature claiming that slums shape
people's values, the Jews had their own values, and they took those values into and out of the slums."[1]

Of course, it is impossible to measure precisely to what extent the
higher quality of Jews' lives has been a major cause of antisemitism.
Few antisemites list the Jews' good qualities as reasons for attacking

them. But it is human nature for individuals and groups perceived as living better lives, however that may be understood, to elicit jealousy and resentment.

There are, as we shall see, specific reasons for believing that Jews generally have led higher-quality lives (quite aside from questions of economic status), and that Judaism is responsible for that higher level. In exploring that claim, we shall also see the role of certain Jewish beliefs and laws in causing antisemitism.

JEWISH EDUCATIONAL AND PROFESSIONAL SUCCESS

The high level of Jewish intellectual and professional achievement in the Western world is the most obvious example of Jews successfully applying to the secular world a value they acquired from Judaism. Since its inception, Judaism has made study a *religious obligation* for its adherents. Unlike Christianity, for example, which, until the Protestant Reformation, required only its clergy to study, among the Jews, study was not only a commandment but, along with charity, the supreme commandment.[2] The biblical injunction "you shall teach your children" (Deuteronomy 6:7) was translated two thousand years ago into a system of universal education.[3]

The Talmud legislated that every city was required to have schools and that no teacher could be assigned more than twenty-five students. The poor were to be taught free of charge. Parents were forbidden to live in a city without a school system, and if they spent time in such a place, the father bore full responsibility for his children's education.

The purpose of all this education was not to achieve professional and financial success (though in the contemporary world it has brought Jews such rewards), but to understand what God required of human beings. Thus, study was obligatory even when it was financially disadvantageous. In his code of Jewish law, Moses Maimonides ruled: "Every Jew is under an obligation to study Torah, whether he is poor or rich, in sound health or ailing, in the vigor of youth or very old and feeble. *Even a man so poor that he is maintained by charity or goes begging from door to door*, as also a man with a wife and children to support, are *under the obligation to set aside a definite period during the day and night for the study of the Torah.* . . . Until what period in life ought one to study Torah? Until the day of one's death."[4] At a time when nearly all Christian and Muslim men, and certainly women, were illiterate, a very high percentage of Jewish men and women could read and write, and many of them achieved high levels of knowledge. A twelfth-century monk, a student of the great Catholic theologian Abelard, reported, "A Jew, however poor, if he has ten sons, would put them all to letters, not for gain, as the Christians do, but for the understanding of God's Law, and not only his sons but his daughters."[5]

A letter written by a Jewish woman on her deathbed in the same century in Egypt exemplifies Abelard's description: "I tell you my sister . . . that I have fallen into a grievous disease and there is little possibility of recovering from it. . . . If the Lord on High should decree my death, my greatest wish is that you should take care of my little daughter and make an effort for her to study. Indeed I know that I am imposing a heavy burden on you. For we do not have the wherewithal for her upkeep, let alone the cost of tuition. But we have an example from our mother and teacher, the servant of the Lord."[6] The historian of medieval Jewry Haim Hillel Ben-Sasson commented on this letter: "Here is an instance of a Jewish family that was certainly not well-to-do in which the women of two generations were educated and saw to the education of their daughters."[7]

Because they believed that study was sacred, Jews made every effort to prolong their children's education. While many of their poor non-Jewish neighbors put young children to work, Jewish parents, even those who were poor, strove to keep their children in school at least until Bar Mitzvah, at age thirteen. And once the children started working, no matter what the nature of their work, their education was expected to continue.

The Jewish theologian Abraham Joshua Heschel quotes a Christian scholar who visited Warsaw during World War I: "Once I noticed a great many coaches on a parking place but with no drivers in sight. In my own country I would have known where to look for them. A young

Jewish boy showed me the way; in a courtyard on the second floor was the *shtiebl* [combination of synagogue and study hall] of the Jewish drivers. It consisted of two rooms, one filled with Talmud volumes, the other a room for prayer. All the drivers were engaged in fervent study and religious discussions. . . . It was then that I found out . . . that all professions, the bakers, the butchers, the shoemakers, etc., have their own *shtiebl* in the Jewish district; and every free moment which can be taken off from work is given to the study of Torah."[8]

An old book saved from the millions of Jewish books burned by the Nazis, and now at the YIVO library in New York, bears the stamp THE SOCIETY OF WOODCHOPPERS FOR THE STUDY OF MISHNAH [the earliest part of the Talmud] IN BERDICHEV. That the men who chopped wood, an arduous job with low social status, met regularly to study Jewish law demonstrates the pervasiveness of study in the Jewish community.

In the modern world, in which general education has become widely available and the key to professional advancement, Jews are in a very advantageous position, thanks to Judaism's tradition of intellectual achievement. The secularization of this commitment to study among American Jews has produced remarkable results. It is not surprising that the American grandchildren of Jews such as the woodchoppers of Berdichev, though numbering just over 2 percent of the population, have won almost a third of the Nobel Prizes awarded American scientists, are overrepresented in medicine, law, and mathematics by more than three times their proportion to the general population, in psychiatry by more than five times, and in dentistry by four times.[9] The two most significant studies of American Jews, the 1990 Combined Jewish Federation National Jewish Population Survey and the 2001 American Jewish Identity Survey, documented that American Jewish males are twice as likely as non-Jewish males to have completed a college or graduate degree, and American Jewish women are three times as likely as their non-Jewish counterparts to have done so. American Jews are twice as likely as non-Jews to graduate college,[10] and are represented among Ivy League students more than five times their percentage in the population.[11] This Jewish passion for study in turn helps to explain why Jews have the highest income of any ethnic group in the United States.[12]

This unique intellectual achievement is not due, as is sometimes alleged, to some innately superior intelligence among Jews, but solely and directly to Judaism. Though many Jews have ceased to keep the laws of Judaism, the belief in the need for education has remained a significant value for almost all Jews.

JEWS AND ALCOHOLISM

That Jews have a low rate of alcoholism has long been a part of both Jewish and non-Jewish folk wisdom. An old Yiddish folk song bears the title "A Drunkard Is a Non-Jew."

Is this perception of Jews and sobriety based on fact? At least until the relatively recent past, yes. In 1925, separate studies were conducted in Warsaw and New York, comparing alcoholism among Jews and non-Jews. The Warsaw study revealed that non-Jews were 68.6 times as likely as Jews to be alcoholics, and in New York non-Jews were 59 times more likely than Jews to be admitted to hospitals for treatment of alcoholism.[13] Even more remarkably, the Jews achieved this much higher level of sobriety even though 87 percent of Jews drink liquor, whereas a 1950s study documented that only 79 percent of Catholics and 59 percent of Protestants drink.[14]

How is this low level of alcoholism among Jews to be explained? The evidence again points to their religion. Judaism made drinking a mitzvah (religious obligation) and sanctified it (the kiddush), while drunkenness was deemed a sin. Thus, Jewish law encouraged, and even commanded, moderate drinking. The Psalmist's praise "Wine makes glad the heart of man" (104:15), along with the Talmudic dictum "There is no [meal of] joy except with wine," became popular adages in Jewish life. The Sabbath meals commence with the kiddush prayer over wine, in which even children participate. At the Passover Seder, it is a mitzvah for each participant to drink four cups of wine.

On the other hand, in the words of the third-century Rabbi Yochanan, "A Jew should never have a passion for wine" (Genesis Rabbah 36:4). The Hebrew Bible and other classical Jewish texts repeatedly warn against drunkenness. The story of Noah's drunkenness and its tragic results (Genesis 9:18–28) is part of the Torah reading one Sabbath a year in synagogues. The prophets Hosea and Isaiah condemned drunkenness, and the biblical book of Proverbs cataloged a variety of results from drunkenness,[15] "including foolishness, poverty, woes, ravings, wounds, confusion and in the case of kings and princes perversions of justice."[16] Later the Talmud ruled: "A drunken person is forbidden to say the prayers. One who recites the prayers while drunk is like one who serves idols" (Berakhot 31b).

Anthropologist Raphael Patai has concluded: "Since until the Enlightenment the Bible and Talmud were by far the most potent formative influences upon Jewish thinking, attitudes and values, one need not wonder that these sources acted as effective deterrents against inebriety. . . . Thus . . . deterrents on the negative side combined with traditional approval of moderate drinking, and the frequent ritual use of wine on the positive side, made wine a regular part of the God centered life of the traditional Jew and effectively removed it from the realm of dangerous excess or frenzy. One may say that the ritual use of wine immunized the Jews against drinking to the point of intoxication and thus against alcoholism."

That Jews' sobriety is a function of Judaism is attested to further by the enormous rise in alcoholism among Jews that has accompanied the corresponding decline in Jews' religiosity in recent generations. Patai summarizes the various studies with the observation, "the traditional Jewish resistance to alcoholism is weakened to the extent to which Jews become assimilated to their Gentile environment." A comprehensive study of drinking patterns among students in New Haven, Connecticut, showed that as Jewish religious observance went from religious to secular and unaffiliated, the pattern of drunkenness went from very low to a percentage that was identical to the Protestant students.[17] Patai reports that, in March 1976, Commissioner Jerome Hornblass of the New York City Addiction Services Agency called attention to data which showed that Jews with a strong commitment to Judaism or to Jewish national causes had very low rates of alcoholism. However, among assimilated Jews rates of alcoholism had become virtually the same as among non-Jews.

When Jews drop the kiddush, they apparently drop their model for moderate drinking.

JEWS AND CHARITY

Jews give a higher percentage of their income to charities and public causes, both Jewish and non-Jewish, than do non-Jews with comparable earnings.[18] Although Jews in the United States constitute only a little over 2 percent of the population, the United Jewish Communities (formerly the UJA) alone annually raises over $1 billion (as of 2002), making it one of the largest American charities. This is remarkable considering that many charities appeal to a constituency almost fifty times larger than does the UJC.

This disproportionate Jewish philanthropy is unique neither to American Jewry nor to the present time. Jewish communities have always been extraordinarily charitable. This is why Jews have always been less likely than non-Jews to be in need of food or clothing. For example, for the few thousand Jews living in seventeenth-century Rome, seven charitable societies provided clothes, shoes, linens, and beds for the poor. Two other societies provided trousseaus for poor brides, another aided families struck by a sudden death, and yet another was responsible for visiting the sick. One special society collected charity for Jews in the land of Israel, and another eleven groups raised money for Jewish educational and religious institutions.[19] Another striking, though not atypical, example of Jewish charitableness was in London in the early 1800s, where about half of the Jewish community was supported by contributions from the other half.[20]

This Jewish giving has not always made a favorable impression on non-Jews. While some have seen Jewish philanthropy as a model to emulate, some non-Jews have concluded that Jews must all have money, since extreme Jewish poverty is rarely encountered. In a seventeenth-century account of the Jews of North Africa, Christian observer Lancelot Addison warned against the erroneous belief that "Jews had no beggars." He attributed this misconception to the "regular and commendable way" in which the Jews supplied the needs of their poor and thus "concealed their poverty."[21]

The Talmudic declaration that "Charity is as important as all the other commandments together" (Bava Bathra 9a) indicates the importance of charity in Jewish life. *Tzedaka*, the Hebrew word for "charity," actually means "justice." *Tzedaka* is, therefore, a duty, an act of justice, and withholding *tzedaka* is not simply uncharitable, it is also unjust.

Jewish tradition mandated that the poor be given a minimum of 10 percent of one's net income, and in general it seems that Jews came close to observing this law. By the second century C.E. every Jewish community had a charity campaign supervised by three trustees. Two respected members of the community went door to door each week to collect 10 percent of each family's income. Those whom the Jewish court determined were not giving a sufficient amount were compelled to pay. In addition to cash, food and clothing were collected and distributed by special committees.[22]

Tzedaka laws also helped to reduce the number of Jews needing public funds. First, they obligated Jews to accept *tzedaka* only as a last resort—"Better [to earn money by] skinning an animal's carcass [a particularly unprestigious job] than by taking charity" was the Talmudic admonition (based on Pesachim 113a). Second, the highest form of *tzedaka* was to start a poor person in a business or profession so that he never again would need *tzedaka*. Finally, most Jewish communities have had a *gemilut hesed* society to provide interest-free loans to the needy, a device intended to help people avoid poverty and the need for *tzedaka*.

The relative absence of poor Jews has led many non-Jews to believe all Jews have money. But Jews have simply aided their needy more than other groups have aided theirs. This pattern continues. To cite one large-scale example, between 1948 and 1952, Israel more than doubled its population by absorbing more than 700,000, largely penniless, Jewish refugees who had fled the Arab world, along with Holocaust survivors brought in from Displaced Persons camps. The 650,000 Jews of Israel, with help from Jews elsewhere, housed, clothed, fed, educated, and provided a livelihood for these Jews. In contrast, at the very same time, an equal number of Palestinian refugees were left in great poverty by all the Arab states, and this never changed, despite the enormous growth of Arab oil wealth. It was *non-Arabs* who have provided the large majority of the Arab refugees' aid.

Jews' aid to other Jews has led to the anti-Jewish canard that "Jews only care for their own." Aside from this being untrue, that is not the point. Those who make this charge are not so much complaining that "Jews only care for their own" as that "only Jews care for their own."

THE JEWISH FAMILY

Judaism's insistence on the sanctity of the nuclear family differentiated Jews from non-Jews more in ancient times than today. Even the Greeks, who had a more advanced culture than other ancient peoples, differed markedly in this regard from the Jews. Plato, in his *Republic* (Book V) and his *Laws* (Book V), on the basis of the Greek proverb "Friends have all things in common," advocated that everyone be friends without the need for creating nuclear families as we know them today. Lycurgus, credited as being the formulator of Sparta's constitution, decreed that Spartans should give "their wives to those whom they should think fit, so that they might have children by them," and thereby produce strong soldiers for Sparta.[23] Similar ideas were offered by two other leading Greek philosophers—Zeno (late fourth and early third century B.C.E.), who founded the Stoic school in Athens, and Diogenes the Cynic.[24]

The first-century writings of the leading scholars of Rome, Seneca, Juvenal, and Tacitus portray a society filled with heterosexual and homosexual promiscuity. The Reform Jewish leader Rabbi Abba Hillel Silver noted that examination of Greek and Roman writings on the family "helps us to realize the violent contrast between the standards of [their] society and the Jewish standards of sexual decency, the sanctity of marriage and of family life."[25]

While Christianity profoundly and positively helped alter the ancient world's negativism toward the family, it, too, idealized non-family life, but in a very different way. Paul saw marriage as a concession to human weakness: "It is well for a man not to touch a woman. But because of the temptation to immorality, each man should have his own wife and each woman her own husband. . . . I say this by way of concession, not of command. I wish that all were as I myself am [unmarried]."[26] Two hundred years later, Origen, one of Christianity's most influential theologians, wrote that three sacrifices are pleasing to God: a martyr's death, voluntary celibacy, and abstinence from sexual intercourse by married persons.[27]

At about the same time, the rabbis of the Talmud were formulating an entirely different set of values for Jews. According to the Talmud, "Did you fulfill your duty with regard to establishing a family?" is among the first questions a Jew will be asked on his Day of Judgment. Basing themselves on the verse "Be fruitful and multiply" (Genesis 1:28), the rabbis declared that it was a male's obligation to have at least two children (Jewish women were not obligated to bear children because it, so often, was a life-threatening procedure). A man could not be a high priest unless he was married, nor a member of the Jewish high court unless he had children, it being the Jewish sages' belief that raising children humbled, humanized, and increased a judge's wisdom.[28] Even among Jewish mystics sexual asceticism was never a value (as it was among Christian and Eastern mystics). The foremost scholar of Jewish mysticism, Gershom Scholem, has concluded: "At no time was sexual asceticism accorded the dignity of a religious value, and the mystics made no exception."[29]

The family also was strengthened by other Jewish laws as well. The Jewish Sabbath, for example, is observed more at home than in the synagogue. Many of its religious rituals are fulfilled in the house: the Sabbath candles, the parental blessing of the children, the kiddush over the wine, the festive meal and concluding Grace After Meals, and the custom that a husband and wife have sexual relations on Friday night.[30]

Judaism's effects on the stability and well-being of the Jewish family have been powerful. Sociologists long have noted that fewer observant Jewish families break up than do secular Jewish and non-Jewish ones,[31] and that among families that stay intact, the members of Jewish families generally remain closer than do members of non-Jewish families.[32]

That Judaism has been the source of Jewish family values has been reconfirmed of late by the rates of divorce and spouse desertion among secular Jews, which are approximately the same as for the non-Jewish society.[33]

CONCLUSION

The higher quality of Jewish life is objectively verifiable. That it has provoked anti-Jewish sentiments especially, though not only, when accompanied by the Jews' commitments to God, law, nationhood, and chosenness is more difficult to prove. People rarely admit to envy as the cause of their resentment. Nevertheless, the link here is undeniable. Had the Jews been committed to being different and been social failures, few people would have bothered to hate them. It has been the Jews' very success that has made their being Jewish so challenging. To put it another way, the Jews' belief in Jewish chosenness has provoked hostility precisely because the quality of Jewish life has made Jews seem as if they really were chosen.

Besides provoking hostility, the higher quality of Jewish life has made otherwise irrational charges against Jews sound plausible. It has rendered credible antisemitic accusations that Jews dominate the intellectual, economic, and political life of nations where they make up less than 5 percent of the population (usually much less—in pre-1933 Germany, for example, Jews constituted 1 percent of the population). In 1975, the highest-ranking military figure in the United States, General George Brown, chairman of the Joint Chiefs of Staff, accused Jews of dominating American society through owning or controlling the banking industry and the press. Brown's statements were factually false, but the nature of the accusation he made was very revealing. Had Brown wanted to attack any other ethnic group, it is inconceivable that he would have leveled a similar charge, or that it would have been taken seriously. Yet such a charge when made against Jews, though false, is not obviously so. Jews, after all, have the highest earnings of any ethnic group in the United States, and they are significantly overrepresented in the most prestigious and well-paying professions (so prominent are Jews in the United States that polls routinely show that many Americans assume that they make up between 15 and 20 percent of the population).

Perhaps the best way to understand the admiration and resentment elicited by the quality of Jewish life is to compare the reactions of the world to America's quality of life. No other country has so many people seeking to move there. At the same time, no country, *with the exception of Israel*, is the target of so many hateful and false attacks.

The United States, because of its success and its ideals, challenges many people throughout the world. How did America, a nation composed largely of those rejected by other societies ("The wretched refuse of your teeming shore" declare the words at the base of the Statue of Liberty), become the most affluent, freest, most powerful, and most influential society in the world? Americans generally attribute this success to the values of America's founding generations (such as individual liberty, religious tolerance, Judeo-Christian morality, and secular government), to a work ethic, and to the subsequent waves of immigrants who embraced these values. Enemies of America attribute it to the country's natural resources, just as many people attribute Jewish success to their natural resource, alleged greater innate intelligence. Others claim that through capitalist exploitation, America cheated poorer countries, paralleling charges that Jewish success has been attained through economic "bloodsucking." Still others develop an imperialist version of America's past and present, similar to the anti-Jewish charge of a world Jewish conspiracy.

But the United States is hardly the only society with great natural resources, and it has been the least imperialistic of the world's powers. America's values, not unfair resource distribution or world exploitation, have made the United States better, just as Judaism and its values, not genetic advantage or economic conspiracies, account for the quality of life led by Jews. The two people's quality of life has provoked similar reactions—many admire them, and many resent them.

FIVE

Non-Jewish Jews and Antisemitism

THROUGHOUT JEWISH HISTORY, Jews have identified with one or more of Judaism's components or converted to another religion. Beginning in the nineteenth century and through the present day, however, an entirely new group of Jews emerged. These people do not feel rooted in anything Jewish, religious or national; their Jewish identity consists of little more than having been born Jews, and they affirm none of Judaism's components. They remain Jews by virtue of having not converted to another religion. We refer to these people as non-Jewish Jews.[1]

Among non-Jewish Jews there have been some who, in addition to their alienation from Jewish roots, have not felt rooted in the non-Jewish society in which they lived. During the last century, some of these Jews have contributed to intense Jew-hatred. These are radical and revolutionary Jews. The reasons for the antisemitism they engender are unique. First, their challenges to non-Jews do not come from within Judaism. Second, they not only challenge the non-Jews' *values*, but the non-Jews' national and religious *identity* as well. Third, they are as opposed to Jews' values and identity as to non-Jews'. Nevertheless, and unfortunately for other Jews, the behavior of these radical non-Jewish Jews is identified as Jewish.

The association of Jews with revolutionary doctrines and social upheaval has not, unfortunately, been the product of antisemites' imaginations. Marx, Trotsky, Kamenev, Zinoviev, Rosa Luxemburg, Béla Kun, Mark Rudd, Abbie Hoffman, Jerry Rubin, William Kunstler, Norman G. Finkelstein, and Noam Chomsky are among the better known.[2] The phenomenon of the highly disproportionate role played by Jews in radical causes often has been commented upon. As the social psychologist Ernest van den Haag noted, "although very few Jews are radicals, very many radicals are Jews: out of one hundred Jews five may be radicals, but out of ten radicals five are likely to be Jewish. Thus it is incorrect to say that a very great number of Jews are radicals but quite correct to say that a disproportionate number of radicals are Jews. This was so in the past, and it has not changed."[3]

How are these Jewish radicals made and why do they cause antisemitism?

The making of a Jewish radical is a complex social and psychological process but its essential elements can be discerned. First, these individuals have inherited a tradition of thousands of years of Jews challenging others' values—though of course in the name of Judaism and ethical monotheism rather than radical secular ideologies. Non-Jewish Jews do not base their radical doctrines on the Jewish tradition; indeed, they usually denigrate it, but the tradition's impact could not be avoided, only transformed.[4]

Second, radical non-Jewish Jews are rootless in that they do not feel rooted in either the Gentiles' or the Jews' religion or nation. They may very well have become revolutionaries precisely to overcome this rootlessness or alienation. Because they refuse to become like the non-Jews by identifying with the non-Jews' religious or national identities, they seek to have non-Jews (and Jews) become like them, alienated from all religious or national identities. Only then, these revolutionaries believe, will they cease to feel alienated.* These reflections on why non-Jewish

---

*There is a related problem of Jews who do feel Jewish but who are rootless in terms of religion. These secular Jews, like non-Jewish Jews, feel much more secure, much more rooted, when non-Jews become like them, secular. This is one major reason (the

Jews have flocked to the radical Left have been made before. For example, one of the leading sociologists in the United States, Stanford's Seymour Martin Lipset, writing in the late 1960s (when a disproportionate number of those active in the New Left were Jews—60 percent of the leadership of the Students for a Democratic Society, for example),[5] noted that "participation in the Socialist and Communist world meant for many Jews a way of escaping their Judaism, of assimilating into a universalistic non-Jewish world."[6]

The historian Peter Pulzer likewise has noted the need for European Jews who had abandoned their Jewish roots to adopt the universalist, nonnationally rooted idea of socialism. Pulzer writes that it is mainly "those Jews who attempted to cut themselves most completely from their Jewish environment who became the Socialist leaders, such as Adler and Bauer in Austria, Singer and Kurt Eisner in Germany, Rosa Luxemburg in Poland and Germany, and Trotsky and Zinoviev in Russia."[7]

As rootless individuals, many non-Jewish Jews have felt it necessary to turn radical and work to tear down traditional and national values and institutions in the name of socialism, communism, and other universalist ideologies. Feeling no kinship, hence no responsibility, to any nation (only to "mankind"), they have not felt concerned with the consequences of such destructiveness. Neither the demoralization of the non-Jewish nation nor the resultant non-Jewish antipathy to Jews concerns these people. They feel part of neither community, only the "community of man."[8] For example, Leon Trotsky, when asked whether he considered himself a Russian or a Jew, responded, "No, you are mistaken. I am a social-democrat. That's all."[9] Fifty years later, Jerry Rubin referred to himself and other American Jewish radicals as "ex-Amerikan [*sic*] ex-jews."[10]

These alienated radical Jews have been active in societies as diverse as despotic and antisemitic czarist Russia, the democratic Weimar Ger-

---

other is traditional Jewish fear of Christianity) why secular Jews have been disproportionately involved in contemporary movements to secularize America. Religious Jews, on the other hand, have less fear of American Christians and support more religious expression in the United States.

many, and the United States. In Russia, non-Jewish Jews were so disproportionately represented in the less radical Menshevik wing of the Communist Party that the Bolshevik Stalin is reported to have said that, with one large pogrom, there would no longer be a Menshevik movement. Among the Bolsheviks there were fewer Jews than among the Mensheviks, though by 1922 they constituted 15 percent to 20 percent of the Bolshevik leadership.[11] After Lenin's death in 1924, the struggle to succeed him took place among five men: Stalin, Bukharin, Trotsky, Kamenev, and Zinoviev. The latter three were non-Jewish Jews.

Certainly, much of the Russian populace identified Marxism with Jews. Since a vast number of Russians and Ukrainians did not support communism, popular identification of Jews with communism exacerbated already deep antisemitism among those two peoples. During the 1918–20 civil war that followed the Bolshevik Revolution, the anti-Communist Ukrainian fighters (the "Whites" who fought the Red Army) murdered fifty thousand Ukrainian Jews. Their anti-Jewish passions were raised by General Simon Petlura, who constantly referred to the Bolshevik armies under the leadership of "the Jew Trotsky."

Russian and Ukrainian Jews found themselves in the oft-repeated modern Jewish horror story of being hated by both the far Left and the far Right. Had the Whites won the civil war, the Jews would have suffered as a result of age-old Ukrainian and Russian antisemitism, as well as the new popular association of communism with Jews. The Communists emerged victorious, and under their rule, the Jews suffered terribly since, in addition to traditional Russian (and Ukrainian, and Lithuanian, and other) antisemitism, it was a basic tenet of Marxism and Leninism that the Jews should disappear through assimilation (see Chapter 11). Thus, the Russian Jewish radicals helped increase antisemitism both among Communists and among anti-Communists: among Communists by advocating the persecution of religious and Zionist Jews, and among anti-Communists by the Jew-hatred that the Jewish Communists aroused. The only Jews who did not suffer from antisemitism, at least not immediately, were the Jewish Bolsheviks. As Moscow's chief rabbi, Jacob Mazeh is reported to have said to Trotsky in 1920, after the latter refused to help Jews suffering from the civil war pogroms:

"The Trotskys make the revolutions, and the Bronsteins pay the price" (Trotsky's original name was Bronstein).

A related, though almost forgotten, chapter of Jewish radical activity is the Soviet-inspired Hungarian revolution of 1919. Béla Kun, a Jew, established the short-lived Hungarian Soviet Republic in March of that year. Of the 48 people's commissars in his government, 30 were Jews, as were 161 of its 202 highest officials.[12]

In Germany, until 1933 when Hitler came to power, the predominance of Jews on the radical Left was as pronounced as in Russia. Unlike the radicals in Russia, however, in Germany the Left did not attain power. But there is much to be learned from studying the German Jews of the Left prior to 1933, for while Nazi and German antisemitism was caused by factors far older and deeper than German Jewish radicalism, the radical non-Jewish Jews of the Weimar Republic greatly exacerbated German antisemitism. Along with radical non-Jews, they helped to undermine the Weimar democracy.

These Jewish radicals wielded a major influence over the cultural and intellectual life of Weimar Germany, an influence utterly disproportionate to their numbers. Among them were brilliant and successful satirists, writers, playwrights, artists, and orators, whose influence was seen by many Germans as destructive of traditional German values (both good and bad), and this perception was a major component of Weimar German antisemitism. The great majority of German Jews voted for center parties in the Weimar Republic, but these Jews were not in the political and cultural limelight; the non-Jewish Jews of the Left were, and to many Germans they therefore stood out as destroyers of everything German.

Foremost among those radicals who wielded such immense power over the intellectual and cultural life of Weimar Germany were those who convened around and published in the Berlin weekly *Die Weltbühne*. Of the magazine's sixty-eight writers whose religious origins could be established, forty-two were Jews. They were of course non-Jewish Jews, so non-Jewish that "only a few of the *Weltbühne* circle openly acknowledged that they were Jews."[13] A sample of *Die Weltbühne's* statements about Germany illustrates the nihilism of the German radicals and why the Jews among them helped to increase German antisemitism. The magazine utilized its prestige and the abundant talent of its writers to *indiscriminately* attack German culture and national life. They did not advocate reform so much as attack the very *idea* of the German nation itself.[14] The following was written by its longtime editor and best-known writer, Kurt Tucholsky, a Jew:

> This country which I am allegedly betraying is not my country; this state is not my state; this legal system is not my legal system. Its different banners are to me as meaningless as are its provincial ideals. . . . We are traitors. But we betray a state that we disavow in favor of a land that we love, for peace and for our true fatherland: Europe.[15]

Concerning Tucholsky, the Columbia University historian Istvan Deak wrote: "Tucholsky abominated the majority of his fellow citizens. Princes, barons, Junkers, officers, policemen, judges, officials, clergymen, academicians, teachers, capitalists, *Bürger*, university students, peasants and all Bavarians he condemned collectively."[16] According to Tucholsky, the only thing in Germany worth loving was the countryside.

While some of the left-wing intellectuals' criticisms were specific, pointing to genuine weaknesses of German society, their overall attacks were perceived by the overwhelming majority of Germans, including anti-Nazis, as purely destructive. Today, when one reads excerpts from *Die Weltbühne*, it is difficult not to share that view. "The left-wing intellectuals opposed the Weimar Republic all along the line," writes George Mosse, one of the foremost historians of modern Germany, "without providing what might prove to be a viable alternative method of change. Thus they tended to become critics rather than builders and in that process alienated, almost masochistically, large parts of the intellectual community from a state which, for all its injustices, provided an almost unprecedented freedom of expression and political action."[17]

Possibly the only nationalism that these non-Jewish Jews hated as much as the Germans' was the Jews'. Only a year before the Nazis came to power, in 1932, *Die Weltbühne* published an article titled "Hitler in Jerusalem," which likened Zionism to Nazism.[18] As Mosse explains, these non-Jewish Jews "wanted to be not Jews, but part of the progressive brotherhood of all humanity . . . [this] made them impassioned enemies of Zionism."[19]

After the Nazis assumed power, Tucholsky fled to Sweden, where, during World War II, he committed suicide. But his ideological heirs live on in the United States, where, again, non-Jewish Jews have played a disproportionate role in vilifying America and Israel.

Since the 1930s, a highly visible proportion of those perceived as the America-hating Left have been Jewish. While the overwhelming majority of American Jews are not radical, a significant number of American radicals are as identified with destructive attacks on America as were radical Jews in Weimar with such attacks on Germany. And like their German and Russian predecessors, they have generally been non-Jewish Jews, equally hostile to Jewish and American values and identity.*

In the 1930s and 1940s, non-Jewish Jews were among the leading pro-Soviet and anti-American agitators. During these two decades Jews constituted half of the membership of the American Communist Party.† Two alienated Jews, Julius and Ethel Rosenberg, were convicted in the early 1950s of helping to smuggle America's atom bomb technology to Stalin. A study by Professor Joseph Adelson in the early 1960s of the relationship between political orientation and personal background among undergraduates at the University of Michigan revealed that 90 percent of radical students came from Jewish backgrounds.[20] A

---

*A 1982 study of radical students revealed that among Jewish radicals, 92 percent termed themselves either hostile or indifferent toward Judaism. See Stanley Rothman and S. Robert Lichter, *Roots of Radicalism: Jews, Christians and the New Left*, p. 410.

†Nathan Glazer, *The Social Basis of American Communism*, chap. 4. Glazer and Daniel Patrick Moynihan also point out, however, that the Jews were the dominant group among the Socialists who opposed and led the opposition to the Communists. "When the Cold War broke out, they inevitably supplied a good number of the experts—who else had spent their college (and even high school) years fighting the Stalinists?" (*Beyond the Melting Pot*, p. lx.)

national survey sponsored by the American Council of Education in 1966–67 revealed that the "best single predictor of campus protest was the presence of a substantial number of students from Jewish families." In 1970, a Harris study showed that 23 percent of Jewish college students termed themselves "far Left" versus 4 percent of Protestants and 2 percent of Catholics.

American radical Jews' similarity to the non-Jewish Jews who attacked Weimar Germany is remarkable. For example, just as the only thing about democratic Germany that Kurt Tucholsky could admit to liking was its scenery, so, too, the leftist philosopher Herbert Marcuse (who declared the United States to be Fascist) could find only one beautiful thing about America: its scenery. The *New York Times Book Review* reported: "When Professor Marcuse, who had insisted that he loved and understood America, was pressed to specify which aspects of American life he found attractive, he fumbled for an answer, said he loved the hippies, with their long hair, and after some more fumbling, mentioned the beautiful American scenery, threatened by pollution. Despite an obvious effort, he could think of no other items."[21]

A reader of Noam Chomsky's political writings would conclude that the world's most evil nations are the United States and Israel. They are the target of nearly all his invective. For example, he has denied that Israel is a democracy or that it could even become one.[22] Typical of his statements about the evil nature of America was his comment during the war in Vietnam that the U.S. Defense Department is "the most hideous institution on earth."[23] As regards the Jews and Zionism, Chomsky is so hate-filled that in 1980 he defended the publication of a book written by a French neo-Nazi who claimed that the Holocaust was a fiction made up by Zionists. Chomsky's defense was subsequently published as the introduction to the book. He claims that he was merely defending the French professor's academic freedom. But when Herbert Mitgang of the *New York Times* asked Chomsky to comment on the professor's views, Chomsky noted that he had no views he wished to state. As Martin Peretz, editor of the *New Republic*, has noted: "On the question, that is, as to whether or not six million Jews were murdered, Noam Chomsky apparently is an agnostic"[24] (for a further analysis of

Chomsky, and the phenomenon of Jewish antisemitism, see this chapter's epilogue, on pages 52–55).

During the 1960s and early 1970s, the *New York Review of Books* could have been labeled an American *Die Weltbühne*. It was edited by Robert B. Silvers and Barbara Epstein, many of its political writers were Jews, and its tone, in the words of the late Irving Howe, a Democratic Socialist and identifying Jew, was a "snappish crude anti-Americanism."[25]

For example, in describing America, Jason Epstein of the *Review*'s governing board echoed *Die Weltbühne*'s view of the Weimar Republic. Epstein found America a sick civilization. Each morning on his way to work he was oppressed by the sight, as he put it, of "so much dead culture . . . where, in the deepest winter . . . lines of New Jerseyites and others—thousands of them—stand in rows, uncomfortable, patient, grinning."[26] So worthless is American life in Epstein's view that he sympathetically portrayed the mind-set of the terrorist Weathermen. Epstein wrote that the Weathermen have been suppressed by an American "culture that has perverted and collectivized their energies and converted them to purposes of mass killing, leaving its individual members psychologically feeble and thus unable to confront their brutal culture with sufficient force."[27]

The journalist Richard Rovere summarized the *Review*'s attitude toward America: "their American politics are Stone's and Chomsky's."[28]

The Stone mentioned in Rovere's assessment was the late I. F. Stone (Isidor Feinstein Stone), then a contributing editor of the *New York Review of Books*, and for half a century a major American journalist. Stone devoted his influential career to attacking American policies, and, after 1967, Zionism and Israel. Stone's negative view of America was evidenced by the overwhelming proportion of his essays that attacked American policies, by the few that ever defended or praised anything American, and by the few that criticized America's adversaries.

In Stone's book *The Hidden History of the Korean War*, he accused the United States of bearing equal responsibility with China for starting that war. As regards Israel, after 1967 Stone announced that "I feel honor-bound to report the Arab side, especially since the U.S. press is so overwhelmingly pro-Zionist."[29] Martin Peretz wrote in response: "One would think that a writer's compulsion would be to tell the truth, regardless of whether it has been aired or not."[30] Moreover, as the Arab position increasingly became the only one heard on the Left, Stone did not feel any consummate obligation to report the Israeli side. Rather, during the last two decades of his life, he increased his anti-Israel rhetoric.

A similar if not quite as extreme view of American culture is noted by Ben Stein among many of those who write and produce American television programs: "A distinct majority [of the producers and writers] is Jewish. . . . TV writers and producers do not hold criminals responsible for crimes but rather place the blame on [American] society. . . . Middle-class people appear generally as either heavies or fools." Furthermore, these producers and writers hold that "religion is trivial and unimportant" and when depicted as significant "we see religion as sinister." And echoing Tucholsky's descriptions of Weimar's respected groups, Stein observes that "the sum of it is that groups that have leadership or power roles—businessmen, bankers, government leaders, military men, religious figures—are treated as bad or irrelevant."[31]

No hater of Weimar Germany described that society in more destructive terms than those used by Norman Mailer to describe America: "We kill the spirit here [in America]. . . . We use psychic bullets and kill each other cell by cell. . . . We have a tyranny here. . . . We have been fighting with sick dead hearts against the cold insidious cancer of the power that governs us . . . our police, our secret police, our corporations, our empty politicians, our clergymen, our editors and cold frightened bullies who govern a machine made out of people they no longer understand."[32]

There are innumerable other examples of radical non-Jewish Jews in America, particularly among journalists, writers, and professors whose basic attitude toward American society is one of hostility.*

*Two Jewish political scientists, Stanley Rothman of Smith College and S. Robert Lichter of George Washington University, who published a major study of American radicalism, *Roots of Radicalism: Jews, Christians and the New Left*, wrote: "The basic thrust [of a radical] is to undermine all aspects of the *culture* which contribute to his or her marginality. Thus Jews in the United States and Europe have been in the forefront of not only political radicalism but also various forms of cultural 'sub-

We are surely not the first observers to comment on the problem of the small but destructive number of non-Jewish Jews undermining the national and religious identities of Jews and non-Jews. This phenomenon was most clearly described by the prominent modern historian Walter Laqueur in an essay entitled "The Tucholsky Complaint."[33] It has also been commented upon by the distinguished political scientist Leonard Schapiro: "Why were there so many Jews among the intellectuals searching for utopia in Russia, China, or Cuba, *and motivated in their search by hatred of the United States?* Perhaps simply because the proportion of Jews among all intellectuals is generally high? Or is there some more profound reason?"[34]

The problem of radical non-Jewish Jews is painful to committed Jews. So painful that most of the writings about their harmful roles come from other Jews—Walter Laqueur, Leonard Schapiro, Nathan Glazer, Ben Stein, Stanley Rothman, and S. Robert Lichter, to cite only those people quoted in this chapter. There is, however, one other group concerned with the writings of radical non-Jewish Jews—antisemites, who attribute the destructive words and actions of these Jews to all Jews.

EPILOGUE: SELF-HATING JEWS: EXPLAINING JEWISH ANTISEMITISM

How is one to explain Jews who devote their lives to hurting Jews—such as Professors Noam Chomsky, Norman Finkelstein, and other radical Jews? The question demands an answer. Among no group in the world

---

version.' The *Weltbühne* circle played this role in the Weimar Republic. In America there was a tradition of literary criticism. Nevertheless, in the 1960s deracinated Jewish authors such as E. L. Doctorow, Joseph Heller, and Norman Mailer were disproportionately represented among those whose critical efforts, even when not overtly political, were designed to demonstrate the 'sickness' of the society. . . . Often such subversion involves an attack upon genuine inequities or irrationalities. Since all societies abound in both, there is never an absence of targets. However, the attack is generally not directed at the particular inequity or irrationality per se. Rather such inequities or irrationalities are used as a means for achieving a larger purpose: the general weakening of the social order itself" (p. 130).

are there so many individuals who so single-mindedly attempt to damage the group into which they were born.

For example, we cannot think of a single black who devoted himself to defending racists or who wrote a preface to a book defending black slavery. As far as we know, such a person does not exist, and, if he did, he would be deemed a lunatic, not haled by many as a major intellect.

Yet, as noted (see page 49), it is writings of MIT professor Noam Chomsky that serve as a foreword to a book that denies the Holocaust occurred, and Chomsky has devoted much of his life to defending those who wish to destroy Israel. The 1995 catalog of the Noontide Press, the publishing wing of the Holocaust-denying *Institute for Historical Research*, offers books by Hitler and Joseph Goebbels, *The Protocols of the Elders of Zion*, and five items by Noam Chomsky. The catalog comments that Chomsky "enlightens as no other writer on Israel, Zionism, and American complicity." As for hatred of Israel, in his book on the Middle East, *The Fateful Triangle: The United States, Israel and the Palestinians*, Chomsky makes twelve references to Hitler: "In each case," notes the sociologist Werner Cohn, "some Jewish action is said to be like Hitler's or some attribute of the State of Israel or the Zionist movement reminds Chomsky of Hitler."[35]

DePaul University (Chicago) professor Norman Finkelstein lectures throughout Germany as two Holocaust survivors' son, calling Israel a Nazi state, and comparing Israeli actions toward the Palestinians to what the Nazis did to his parents.

There are thousands of Jews who share in these anti-Jewish hostilities. There are Jewish professors who led the campaign at the University of California campuses to have the university divest from investment in any company that does business with Israel. Companies that do business with Iraq, or Iran, or China, or any of the other major violators of human rights are fine with these people. Only companies that do business with the Jewish state are targeted by these Jews.

How does one explain all these radical Jews—a group that in terms of self-loathing may be unique in the world?

These Jews themselves have an answer—they are morally enlightened, while the bulk of Jewry is morally benighted. They see Israel as Nazi-like because they have the moral clarity that the rest of us lack.

That Israel is one of the most decent democracies on earth, with one of the most elevated records on civil rights and liberties; that it offered those who opposed its existence a state of their own; that it is a tiny state engulfed in a massive sea of hatred; that its enemies have among the worst human rights records in the world—all this is ignored by radicals who loathe Israel.

Moreover, virtually everything these radicals *claim* to care about the most—women's equality, tolerance, pluralism, gay rights, rights of the accused, freedom of speech—is honored in Israel and is essentially non-existent among its Arab enemies. Obviously, then, morality does not move radical Jews (or non-Jews) to support Israel's enemies. What does?

We believe that there are two primary answers.

One is that radical Jews, like other radicals, have no roots. By and large, they have no national or religious identity, and they disdain Jews (and Americans) who do. The *Übermensch*, which is how they see them-selves, rises above such parochial identities.

While that explanation applies to radicals in general, there is another that is specific to the Jews who work to hurt Israel and Jewry. They likely believe (even if only subconsciously) that if they side with those who hate Jews, they will not be hated by them.

To understand the Chomskys and the Finkelsteins, one has to appreciate how much Jews have been hurt by antisemites. The Jews have humanity's longest history of being tortured and murdered, and this history has pathologically affected more than a few Jews. Finkel-stein is a poignant example. As the child of two Holocaust survivors, he has almost surely been adversely affected psychologically by his parents' experiences—just as most children of Holocaust survivors have been. In that sense, for survivors and their children, the Holocaust is far from over.

But most children of Holocaust survivors do not act out in public whatever psychological problems they have inherited or developed—and certainly do not want the Jewish people harmed. Finkelstein apparently does. How else to explain an individual who goes to the land where

Nazism and the Holocaust were born to tell audiences there, as a Jew and as the child of survivors, that there is Nazism today, and it is Jews who are practicing it?

Jews alienated from Judaism, and Jews aiding enemies of the Jews, is not a new development. The primary witnesses against Jews in the Spanish Inquisition were conversos, Jews who had converted to Catholicism. They acted either out of malice against a particular Jew or, more frequently, believed (with reason) that they were buying themselves life insurance by aiding the Jews' enemies.

The Jewish people have suffered terribly at the hands of non-Jewish antisemites. As this book makes clear, because antisemitism is ultimately a hatred of Jewish values, beliefs, and chosenness, it is no wonder that more than a few Jews are antisemites as well.

SIX

Other Theories of Antisemitism

OR NEARLY ALL OF JEWISH HISTORY people recognized that antisemitism was a reaction to the Jews and Judaism. But today, Jew-hatred is generally attributed to factors having little to do with Jews and Judaism; rather, its causes are generally held to be economic, political (the use of the Jews as scapegoats), ethnic prejudice, and the psychopathology of hate—all of which dejudaize antisemitism.

Among those most committed to these dejudaizing interpretations are secular and non-Jewish Jews committed to the notion that the Jews are a people like all other peoples. Accordingly, they want to believe that antisemitism is but another form of bigotry, and that in the secular world it will die out. These individuals believe that there are no rational reasons for Jew-hatred and/or that antisemitism is a kind of societal sickness. Another reason why many modern Jews believe in these explanations for Jew-hatred, rather than in the one held by Jews for thousands of years, is simply that these explanations are more or less the only ones offered. Modern scholars tend to promote secular and universalist explanations for nearly all human problems, including, of course, antisemitism. In contrast, the traditional Jewish understanding of antisemitism has been the opposite—religious and particularist.

Among modern scholars there are a large number of Jews whose universalist worldviews make them particularly averse to the Jewish explanation of antisemitism. Indeed, they oppose any thesis, about anything, not only antisemitism, which depicts the Jews as distinctive, let alone unique. Accordingly, they have expended great efforts to prove that the Jews are not different from anyone else.[1]

The dejudaization of antisemitism reached its nadir in the 1955 theatrical adaptation of the most famous document of the Holocaust, *The Diary of Anne Frank*. As an adolescent in Amsterdam, Anne Frank and her family spent more than two years hiding before being captured by the Nazis. During this time Anne Frank kept a diary that was found and published after the war.

Though raised in a secular and assimilated home, Anne came to feel during her years in hiding that there were specific Jewish reasons for the suffering she and other Jews were undergoing. On April 11, 1944, she wrote: "Who has inflicted this upon us? Who has made us Jews different from all other people? Who has allowed us to suffer so terribly up till now? It is God who has made us as we are, but it will be God, too, who will raise us up again. If we bear all this suffering and if there are still Jews left, when it is over, then Jews, instead of being doomed, will be held up as an example. Who knows, it might even be our religion from which the world and all peoples learn good, and for that reason and that reason only do we now suffer. We can never become just Netherlanders, or just English, or representatives of any country for that matter. We will always remain Jews, but we want to, too."

But Anne Frank's beliefs that Judaism was at the root of Jew-hatred and that the Jews were different were eliminated in the Broadway version of *The Diary of Anne Frank*. The authors, Alfred and Frances Hackett, with the advice of the Jewish playwright and political radical Lillian Hellman, simply deleted the above passage, which had been central to Anne's thinking as well as to writer Meyer Levin's original version of the play. Instead, the Hacketts' put into her mouth words she had never said but that reflected their own universalist views: "We are not the only people that have had to suffer . . . sometimes one race sometimes another."

The Hacketts thus presented their dejudaized interpretation of antisemitism in place of the Jewish interpretation offered by Anne Frank, that the Jews are hated precisely because of the Jews' unique role in the world.

JEWS AS SCAPEGOATS

Perhaps the most widely held interpretation of antisemitism, the scapegoat theory, thoroughly dejudaizes antisemitism. It posits that Jews are merely convenient targets for a society in trouble, and that antisemitism is orchestrated by the society's leaders in order to direct popular discontent away from themselves. For example, the pogroms against Jews in late-nineteenth- and early-twentieth-century Russia are seen as being fomented by the czar and his ministers to divert poor and otherwise oppressed Russians' resentment away from them. The Nazis too are believed by many to have primarily used Jew-hatred as a tactical device to achieve power.

The major fallacy of the scapegoat theory is not that Jews have not been used as scapegoats. They have. The problem with the scapegoat thesis is that it does not explain antisemitism. It only explains why, when, or how people *use* antisemitism—not why they are antisemitic. It does not even purport to answer the question, why, to begin with, do people hate Jews? What is it about this small group that enables so many people to believe the most horrible accusations leveled against them?[2]

The authors have asked many Jews how they understand Nazi antisemitism and the Holocaust. Very commonly, they answer that the Nazis blamed Germany's problems on the Jews and used antisemitism to gain power. But the widespread belief in the scapegoat theory as an explanation of Nazi antisemitism and the Holocaust is wrong. Nazi Jew-hatred was an end, not a means. Hitler was so preoccupied with Jews that he withdrew troops and vehicles from the war fronts so that the killing of European Jewry would not slacken. The killing of millions of Jews itself proves that Hitler did not view the Jews as scapegoats. If the Jews had been only scapegoats, then why murder them? Why not, let us say, compel them to do forced labor? The Nazis ordered the overwhelming majority of Jews to be immediately murdered, and those who were used as slave labor were treated so abominably that most died within a few months. Antisemitism was not a vehicle for the Nazis; Nazism was a vehicle for antisemitism.

The real question to be asked remains, why the Jews? And this question is unanswered by the scapegoat thesis.

ECONOMIC EXPLANATIONS

Various theories of antisemitism suggest economic explanations. Jew-hatred in medieval Europe, for example, is said to have been a reaction to the Jews having been usurious moneylenders. Elsewhere Jews evoked Jew-hatred because they collected taxes from poor peasants on behalf of corrupt landowners. The Jews' identification with the emergence of capitalism in Europe is cited as another economic cause of antisemitism. And in the modern period, the Jews' disproportionate wealth and concentration in business and in the professions is said to provoke anti-Jewish hostility.

Undeniably, economic factors can and often do exacerbate antisemitism, and often create crises in which antisemites may flourish. After all, such factors impinge on virtually all aspects of society, and when an economic crisis occurs, the resultant social upheaval may unleash many of the worst aspects of a society, among them Jew-hatred. But economic factors do not cause Jew-hatred; *they only provide opportunities for it to be expressed.*

For one thing, there is little if any correlation between Jews' wealth and antisemitism. Jews have often suffered the worst antisemitism when they were poor, as was true of the overwhelming majority of Jews in nineteenth- and twentieth-century Poland and Russia, and have encountered the least amount of antisemitism when affluent, as in the United States and Canada today.

As regards attributing medieval antisemitism to the Jews' role as moneylenders, this puts the cart before the horse. Because of Christian European antisemitism during the Middle Ages, Jews were often denied the right to practice professions other than moneylending. *Jews were not hated because they lent money; they lent money because they were hated.* Obviously, once Jews became moneylenders, Jew-hatred was exacerbated.

Nor was that the only time when the Jews' economic status exacerbated antisemitism. In many societies Jews, because of antisemitism, have played economic roles that sometimes intensified hostility toward them. But Jew-hatred preceded these economic factors and is much deeper than any economic factors. Thus, antisemites have equally hated poor Jews and rich Jews, and they ceased hating rich Jews not when they became poor Jews, but when they became rich members of the antisemites' religion or cause.

Regarding the Marxist notions that antisemitism is caused by capitalism and that socialism will eliminate antisemitism, suffice it to say that both socialist theory and socialist countries often have fostered terrible Jew-hatred, while capitalist societies have been the least antisemitic societies in history.

In our research we could find no major instance of a society's antisemitism created by economic factors. In each case—pagan, Christian, Muslim, Enlightenment, Nazi, Communist, and contemporary anti-Zionist antisemitism—factors unrelated to economics have been at the root of Jew-hatred. In every instance, two groups would have found absurd the attribution of antisemitism to economics: the antisemites and their Jewish victims.[3]

HANNAH ARENDT'S ECONOMIC AND SOCIOLOGICAL EXPLANATION

In the 1950s the political scientist and philosopher Hannah Arendt offered a novel economic and sociological interpretation of modern antisemitism. In her classic work *The Origins of Totalitarianism*, she argued that modern antisemitism was something new, basically unrelated to pre-nineteenth-century Jew-hatred. As Europe's nation-states developed in the nineteenth century, national leaders found that they could dispense with the court Jews and wealthy Jewish bankers who had been so important until then. In the modern era, the Jews no longer filled their previous economic functions and became superfluous.

In Arendt's words: "Wealth without visible function is much more intolerable because nobody can understand why it should be tolerated. Antisemitism reached its peak when Jews had similarly lost their public functions and their influence and were left with nothing but their wealth."[4] Thus the Jews and their functionless wealth bred the antisemitism that culminated in the Holocaust.

Even if Arendt were entirely correct, her analysis applies only to nineteenth- and early-twentieth-century antisemitism in Europe. It in no way explains 2,000 years of Jew-hatred throughout the world. As the Columbia University historian Arthur Hertzberg writes, "Hannah Arendt was eager to avoid the notion of an eternal anti-Semitism."[5] And was Auschwitz really the result of Jewish wealth without a visible social role? Or, as Hertzberg puts it, "is it conceivable that the enormous power of this hatred was bred in a few short years and decades? Did the new antisemitism of the nineteenth century really arise essentially out of the contemporary historical situation?"[6]

PSYCHOLOGICAL EXPLANATIONS

Psychological explanations of antisemitism have become very popular. Given the widespread belief that psychology can ultimately account for nearly all human behavior, this is to be expected. But there are additional reasons why psychological explanations of antisemitism are so attractive, especially to Jews. Most important, they offer grounds for optimism. By describing Jew-hatred as a psychological abnormality and labeling antisemites sick, psychology renders antisemitism curable. If antisemites are sick people, then Jews have nothing to fear from the normal men and women among whom they live. An additional comfort to many is that psychological explanations universalize and thus dejudaize Jew-hatred, thus placing it under the general heading "prejudice." Such psychological explanations make the abnormality of the antisemites rather than the Jewishness of the Jews the cause of Jew-hatred.

The most widely acclaimed psychological explanation of antisemitism is in a multivolume work on prejudice commissioned by the American Jewish Committee (AJC). The preface to the study's major volume,

The Authoritarian Personality,[7] summarizes its thesis: "The central theme of the work is a relatively new concept—the rise of an 'anthropological' species we call the authoritarian type of man. . . . He seems to combine the ideas and skills . . . of a highly industrialized society with irrational or anti-rational beliefs. . . . This book approaches the problem with the means of socio-psychological research."[8]

The entire study revolves around this theme, that prejudiced people are disturbed and irrational, and that antisemitism is merely one more form of prejudice, though perhaps a more virulent one than others. That orientation also is reflected in the title of and contents of another volume in this work, *Anti-Semites and Emotional Disorders*. A third volume, *Dynamics of Prejudice* by Bettelheim and Janowitz, analyzes the connection between personality traits and prejudice. A fourth volume, *Prophets of Deceit*, attempts to "expose the psychological tricks" used by demagogues to attain power.

Four years after the publication of the American Jewish Committee's study of prejudice, one of the most widely acclaimed books ever written on that subject was published, *The Nature of Prejudice*, by the Harvard psychologist Gordon Allport. The essential thesis of this work, which includes substantial discussions of antisemitism, is that prejudiced people are psychologically abnormal. In his preface, Allport refers to the long and tragic history of group hatreds, but he concludes: "Yet the situation is not without its hopeful features. Chief among them is the simple fact that human nature seems, on the whole, to prefer the sight of kindness and friendliness to the sight of cruelty. Normal men everywhere reject, in principle and by preference, the path of war and destruction. They like to live in peace and friendship with their neighbors."[9]

Thus, ten years after the Holocaust, Jew-haters were pronounced sick by a preeminent organization of American Jewry and a preeminent psychologist of Harvard University.

This explanation of Jew-hatred generally and of the Holocaust specifically must have come as welcome news to Jewry after Auschwitz. The Nazis were sick, as are all deeply prejudiced people. That was the lesson to be learned. There was one other lesson for American Jews that the authors of *The Authoritarian Personality* noted: "The major concern [is] with the potentially fascistic individual."[10] Antisemitism is a function of Fascism, and the danger to Jews is on the Right. Hitler was a Fascist, therefore the Right is the threat to Jews. But this single-minded concern with Fascist individuals is wrongheaded. Why not an equal concern with Communist antisemites? The lesson that these authors, like so many contemporary Jews, have drawn from the Holocaust is that six million Jews were murdered because their murderers were sick and Fascist—not because the six million were Jews.

While there is little doubt that Adolf Hitler and many of his associates were psychologically disturbed, this fact did not cause antisemitism, let alone the Holocaust. Were the tens of millions of Germans and other Europeans who supported Nazi antisemitism also sick? Did tens of millions of Christians in medieval Europe hate Jews because they were sick? Was Soviet antisemitism a function of some psychosis? Are all Muslims and Arabs who want Israel destroyed psychopaths?

We do not believe that antisemites are models of psychological health. But until we recognize that it is possible to be psychologically unhealthy and not be an antisemite, and that to be antisemitic does not necessarily imply psychopathology, we will never be able to combat antisemitism. Antisemitism is evil, and evil is not necessarily sick. Unfortunately.

SARTRE'S EXPLANATION

All the attempts to dejudaize Jew-hatred are embodied in what may be the most widely read modern explanation of antisemitism, Jean-Paul Sartre's *Anti-Semite and Jew*.[11] In this work, the Nobel Prize–winning French philosopher offers all the major dejudaizing explanations for antisemitism we have cited: the use of Jews as scapegoats, general ethnic prejudice, economic (especially capitalist) reasons, and the psychological problems of antisemites. "The Jew," he writes, "only serves [the antisemite] as a pretext; elsewhere his counterpart will make use of the Negro or the man of yellow skin."[12] Sartre also labels antisemitism a capitalist problem: "What is there to say except that the socialist revolution is necessary and *sufficient* for the suppression of the anti-Semite?" (our emphasis). But he goes further than all others in dejudaizing Jew-hatred. Not only does Sartre hold that the Jews are not the *cause* of Jew-hatred, he holds that they are not even the real *object* of Jew-hatred. As he writes: "the anti-Semite . . . is a man who [is] afraid. Not of the Jews to be sure, but of himself, of his own consciousness, of his liberty . . . of everything except the Jews."[13]

Sartre then takes his complete dejudaization of Jew-hatred to its logical conclusion: the dejudaization of the Jew. Jews, being neither the cause nor even the object of Jew-hatred, do not really exist. They are made to feel as Jews by Jew-haters (who, of course, do not hate Jews but themselves). "The Jew," writes Sartre, "is one whom other men consider a Jew. . . . It is the anti-Semite who makes the Jew. . . . It is neither their past, their religion, nor their soil, that unites the sons of Israel. . . . The sole tie that binds them is the hostility and disdain of the societies which surround them."[14]

With Sartre's thesis, then, modern interpretations of antisemitism, all of which seek to deny anything specifically Jewish to Jew-hatred, reach their incredible conclusion: Jews do not cause antisemitism, Jews are not hated by antisemites, Jews do not actually have their own existence; Jew-haters have invented them.

For well over two thousand years, people have hated a group that does not really exist outside of the haters' minds. "We [non-Jews] have created this variety of men who have no meaning [except as scapegoats)."[15] Thus concludes Jean-Paul Sartre, one of the most esteemed minds of the twentieth century.

When you ask the wrong questions, you get the wrong answers. That is what happens when you ask for an explanation of Jew-hatred that starts with the belief that it is not a response to Jews and Judaism.

THE HISTORICAL EVIDENCE

Part Two documents the thesis—the traditional Jewish view—that Judaism, with its distinctiveness and moral challenge, is at the root of Jew-hatred. It is not intended to imply that all Christians, Muslims, pagans, men of the Enlightenment, or Leftists (as opposed to Nazis or contemporary "anti-Zionists") were enemies of the Jews, but only to explain the antisemitism of those who were.

SEVEN

Antisemitism in the Ancient World

P HILOSTRATUS, A THIRD-CENTURY TEACHER AND RESIDENT of Athens and Rome, summarized the pagan world's perception of the Jews: "For the Jews have long been in revolt not only against the Romans, but against humanity; and a race that has made its own life apart and irreconcilable, that cannot share with the rest of mankind in the pleasures of the table nor join in their libations or prayers or sacrifices, are separated from ourselves by a greater gulf than divides us from Sura or Bactra of the more distant Indies."[1]

In the pagan world, the Jews' God and laws were clearly the causes of Jew-hatred. Pagans generally tolerated different peoples and different gods, but the Jews and "their" God did not merely differ, they also were threatening. The Jews' God alone was God, and He was the God everywhere—which meant, of course, that all gods of the pagans were false. Understandably, this infuriated the Jews' neighbors. No nation or religion had ever made such audacious claims. As the historian of the classical world Yitzhak Heinemann has described it: "no other nation at that time denied the gods of its neighbors. . . . None of the peoples refrained from partaking of the sacrifices offered to the gods, except the

Jews. None of the peoples refused to send gifts to its neighbors' temples, except the Jews."[2] As the first-century Greek writer Apion protested: "Why, if they [the Jews] are citizens, do they not worship the same gods?"[3]

The Jews' laws, too, angered their neighbors. For example, the Jewish dietary laws restricted what and where Jews ate, and many non-Jews interpreted the Jewish refusal to eat with them as motivated by hostility. So, too, they interpreted Judaism's ban on intermarriage as hostile.

The Jews of the pre-Christian world were hated because they were Jews, not because they were rich, or successful, or for any other reason not directly related to their Judaism. If a Jew ceased practicing Judaism and adopted the majority culture's religion, he was not persecuted. A Jew willing to give up Judaism to worship and respect his neighbor's gods, to eat his neighbor's food, to marry his neighbor's child, and, in short, to cease challenging the non-Jews' values was accepted by the surrounding pagan society. Jews were rejected and characterized as haters of humankind because they practiced Judaism.

THE HELLENIC WORLD

The first non-Jewish record of antisemitism dates from Alexandria, Egypt, where in the third-century B.C.E., many Greeks and Jews had migrated as a result of Alexander's conquest of Egypt.

Given the human propensity to resent strangers, it is not surprising that the indigenous Egyptian population came to resent the Jewish immigrants. What is noteworthy, however, is that the Egyptians bore much greater animosity toward the Jews than toward the other large group of foreigners, the Greeks. Apparently, the Egyptians' dislike of the Jews was deeper than their usual hostility toward foreigners.

The Egyptians found the Jews' religious culture and traditions offensive. One prominent example was the Egyptian priest Manetho, who, annoyed by the Jews' liturgy and Bible (which had just been translated into Greek) with its depictions of the Jews' exodus from Egypt, decided to rewrite that event. According to Manetho, the Jews did not flee Egypt, but were expelled because they were lepers.*

In succeeding generations, the Alexandrians developed other anti-semitic themes. In addition to allegedly having spread leprosy, the Jews were accused of hating all other people, a charge that became one of the most often repeated in Jewish history. The Jews were also accused of being atheists because they worshiped a God that no one, themselves included, had ever seen, while dismissing all visible gods as false.

Lysimachus, an Egyptian historian of the second or first century B.C.E., summarized the perceptions held about the Jews. "Moses exhorted them to show kindliness to no one, to follow only the worst advice, and overthrow all the sanctuaries and altars of the gods they might come upon."[4]

In 167 B.C.E., the first recorded antisemitic persecution in the post-biblical period took place. The Hellenic ruler of Syria and Palestine, Antiochus Epiphanes, incited in part by a number of assimilated Jews, attempted to destroy Judaism, which he correctly perceived as the basis of the Jewish opposition to his leadership. Antiochus understood that it was because of their religious beliefs that the Jews rejected his claim to being "god manifest" ("Epiphanes" in Greek). Consequently, Antiochus sent an emissary to Judea "in order to force the Jews to transgress the laws of their fathers and not to live according to God's commandments" (Maccabees II 6:11). He renamed the Holy Temple in Jerusalem after Zeus Olympus, prohibited the observance of the Sabbath and the rite of circumcision, and forced the Jews to participate in the festival procession in honor of Dionysus.[5]

Antiochus's action was virtually without precedent for a Hellenic

---

*The absence of any historical basis for Manetho's statements did not deter later anti-Jewish writers from repeating this accusation. In the first century, the leading historian of Rome, Tacitus, recorded that the Jews had apparently been expelled from Egypt as lepers (*The Histories*, 5:3). Two thousand years after Manetho, the eighteenth-century leader of the Enlightenment, Voltaire, repeated the same slander. A century later, the libel was repeated in a letter of Karl Marx (see p. 124).

ruler, because the Greeks, and the Hellenic rulers influenced by them
in other societies, rarely attempted to suppress a religion or philosophy.
Only when it was deemed a serious challenge to the legitimacy of the
Greek gods, and capable of undermining the state, was a religion suppressed or a philosopher put to death. The most famous challenger was
Socrates, who was charged with bringing new gods into Athens and
corrupting the youth.[6]

But Judaism was far more dangerous than any other ideology to the
Hellenic leaders. *Jews constituted the one instance when an entire nation,
not one or two philosophers, held values in opposition to Hellenic society.*

Hellenic antisemitism increased accordingly. Even the accusation of ritual murder, associated almost exclusively with Christian
antisemitism (and today with Islamic antisemitism), was first made
by a Greek. Apion, the noted Homeric scholar, charged the Jews with
slaughtering and eating non-Jews in religious rituals. In his *History of
Egypt,* Apion wrote that when Antiochus invaded the Jewish Temple
he found a Greek prisoner inside who recounted to Antiochus "the
unutterable law of the Jews. . . . They would kidnap a Greek foreigner,
fatten him up for a year, and then convey him to a wood, where they
slew him, sacrificed his body with their customary ritual, partook of
his flesh, and, while immolating the Greek, swore an oath of hostility
to the Greeks."[7]

ROME

By the time the Romans assumed control over Judea in 63 B.C.E.,
antisemitism was already deeply rooted in the classical world. Though
the Roman rulers recognized Judaism as a licit religion, they soon found
reason to water those anti-Jewish roots. The Jews' insistence on denying Roman gods, living by different values and rules, and leading their
own national life through the maintenance of religious/political institutions such as the Sanhedrin was regarded by the Romans, particularly
the intellectuals, as proof of the Jews' hatred for others. In the words of
the greatest Roman historian, the first-century Tacitus, the Jews "reveal

a stubborn attachment to one another . . . which contrasts with their implacable hatred for the rest of mankind."[8]

Tacitus regarded the Jews' attachment to their own God, laws, and peoplehood as a challenge to Rome's highest values: "The Jews regard as profane all that which we hold sacred: on the other hand, they permit all that we abhor." Another of Tacitus's attacks on the Jews demonstrates how central the conflict of moral values was to Roman antisemitism: "The Jews," he wrote, "regard it as a crime to kill any newborn infant." In contrast, the Romans, like the Greeks before them, killed mentally and physically handicapped infants. To the Roman and Greek mind keeping such children alive was pointless and unaesthetic.

That the Jews' refusal to acknowledge the divinity of the Roman gods and emperors caused Roman antisemitism is well illustrated by the meeting in 39 c.e. between a Jewish delegation and the emperor Caligula (see p. 15). The emperor was furious over the Jews' refusal to place his statue in their Temple. Only his sudden death saved the Jews of Palestine from a massacre.[9]

While the attitude toward Judaism was almost uniformly negative among Rome's politicians and intellectuals, many other Romans, disenchanted with Roman paganism's immorality and vacuity, and repulsed by such horrors as the gladiator fights, were attracted to the ethical monotheism and spirituality of the Jews. By the middle of the first century, between 7 and 10 percent of the people living in the Roman Empire, as many as seven million out of seventy million, were Jews, many of them converts.[10] To the leadership of Rome this was distressing, for as Seneca, the first-century Stoic philosopher and adviser to Emperor Nero, complained, "the conquered have given their laws to the conquerors."[11]

Throughout the first century the Jews found themselves under continuous attack from Romans of all ranks. For example, Josephus, the first-century Jewish historian, reported that Roman soldiers in Jerusalem publicly demonstrated their contempt for Judaism, one going so far as to expose his backside in the Temple court during Passover, while another destroyed a Torah scroll before the eyes of the Jews.[12]

As a result of Roman provocations, the Jews of Palestine rebelled twice, each time failing to overthrow Roman rule. With the second failure in 135 c.e., the Jews lost for over eighteen hundred years whatever sovereignty they had managed to maintain in their homeland.

CONCLUSION

There was one basic reason for pagan antisemitism, hostility to Judaism, which the pagan world found threatening to many of its most cherished values. Pagan antisemitism was therefore directed only against Jews who upheld Judaism. Jews willing to disavow Judaism were accepted into pagan society. For example, one of the Roman-appointed procurators in Judea, Tiberius Alexander, was a convert from Judaism. Only those Jews who insisted on observing Judaism with its monotheistic rejection of pagan gods and its general opposition to the pagan way of life were subjected to literary and physical attacks.

Consequently, and perhaps inevitably, the recurring theme of pagan antisemitism was that the Jews are haters of humankind. To pagans, the Jews' hostility, or at least indifference, to the values and lifestyle of the non-Jews could only be attributed to a Jewish sense of superiority and contempt for humanity (exacerbated by the Jewish belief in chosenness—see pages 25–29). As Tacitus wrote: "toward every other people they feel only hate and enmity, they sit apart at meals and they sleep apart, and although as a race they are prone to lust, they abstain from intercourse with foreign women."[13]

That the Jews regarded their values as so important that they were willing to die for them only reinforced the conviction that they must hate their neighbors, for they preferred to die than to live like them.

Though antisemitism reached a new and far more intense phase when Rome became Christian, hatred of the Jews preceded Christianity. Salo Baron, the great Jewish historian, noted that "almost every note in the cacophony of medieval and modern antisemitism was sounded by the chorus of ancient writers."[14] And this antipathy, as Catholic historian Rosemary Ruether has shown,[15] was "a reaction caused by the special social consequences of Jewish religious law. . . . This reaction was not racial, since it would disappear as soon as a Jew gave up . . . Jewish law."[16]

Nearly all the causes and themes of subsequent antisemitism were present in the pagan world. But the rise of Judaism's first daughter religion, Christianity, gave birth to new and more frightening expressions of Jew-hatred.

EIGHT

Christian Antisemitism

I N THE FOURTH CENTURY, the Roman Empire substituted a mono-theistic faith for paganism. That faith should logically have been Judaism. It was Judaism that introduced God to the Roman world, it was Judaism alone that had opposed paganism for over a thousand years, and it was Judaism that by the first century of the Common Era counted approximately one out of every ten citizens of the Roman Empire as an adherent.

Yet the new, Roman-sanctioned faith was Christianity (the creation of a handful of Jews), and not Judaism, the religion from which Christianity took its God, its Bible, its Messiah, its apostles, and its founders. Why?

Christianity was in many ways more accessible to the pagan world. Christianity offered pagans not only the incorporeal God of the Jews, but also a god in human form who died and was resurrected. In addition, it announced the good news that the Messiah had come, whereas the Jews were still waiting for him.

Christianity also dropped Jewish law, which had been a major obstacle to many prospective converts. The church adopted Paul's position, as articulated in Romans 3:28, that now that Christ had come all God demanded was proper faith, and this faith ensured eternal salvation. Judaism, on the other hand, continued to demand adherence to its laws, and it focused much more on this world than on salvation.

Christianity was also easier to convert to. Whereas conversion to Judaism meant not only adoption of the Jewish religion but also membership in the Jewish nation, conversion to Christianity implied no breaking of, or adding to, previous national ties. Moreover, Christianity made the process of conversion for males physically painless by dropping the requirement of circumcision.

The Jews rejected the messianic, and far more important, the divine claims Christianity made for Jesus, along with the deemphasis on law and elimination of peoplehood. But church leaders could not ignore the Jews' denial of the validity of Christianity. The Jews were not merely another group of non-Christian pagans; if it were not for the Jews, there would be no Christianity. Jesus was an observant Jew.[1] All his apostles were Jews. The Jewish Bible was the entire basis for the messianic claims made for Jesus. The Jews were God's chosen people, and the people to whom Jesus addressed his words "I am sent only to the lost sheep of the house of Israel" (Matthew 15:24).

Yet it was the Jews who rejected Jesus' claims. The people to whom Jesus belonged and addressed his message, and therefore the people most able to validate his message, rejected the Christian claims made on his behalf.

The founders of Christianity felt that they were confronted with a terrible fact—the Jews, *merely by continuing to be Jews*, threatened the very legitimacy of the church. If Judaism remained valid, they believed, then Christianity was invalid. Therein lie the origins of Christian antisemitism, the longest-lasting Jew-hatred in history.

The church fathers had to deal with this Jewish challenge, and they did so in a most logical manner. Since the existence of the Jews and Judaism challenged the legitimacy of the church, the church had to deny the legitimacy of the Jews and Judaism. The church would now be Israel; and the other Israel would be discredited.

To that end the early church promulgated a number of doctrines that theologically invalidated the Jews' continuing existence. These doctrines were given the greatest possible significance, divine authentication, by being placed in the Christian Bible and by often being attributed to Jesus himself. In this way, for Christian antisemites, the New Testament canonized antisemitism.

The New Testament did not depict the Crucifixion as the Roman execution it was, nor did it merely discredit the Jews' theological arguments against the divine claims made for Jesus. Rather, the Jews (of the time, as most Christians today understand it; the Jews *always* for Christian antisemites), not just their arguments, were discredited. Thus, it is Jews who are depicted as having had Jesus killed. And Jews forever are to bear responsibility for that crime: "Let his blood be on our heads and the heads of our children," the Jews are reported to have announced (Matthew 27:25).

Now, it is critical to note that many Christians, especially American Christians for centuries and modern Christians elsewhere today, have shown that a believing Christian need not read various passages in the New Testament in an antisemitic way. For example, many Christians regard the Jews who are negatively depicted in the New Testament as symbolizing all of sinning humanity. Nevertheless, for most of Christian history, various New Testament portrayals of the Jews did lead to great Jew-hatred.

The portrayal of the Jews' eternal responsibility for the Crucifixion gave rise to the most oft-repeated Christian accusation against Jews and the greatest source of Christian Jew-hatred: every Jew in every age is a "Christ-killer." This charge gave legitimacy to the brutalizing of Jews for more than 1,500 years in Christian Europe.

And the charge of deicide, as destructive as it was, gave birth to other, equally antisemitic, libels.

For example, only one explanation could account for the Jews' rejection and killing of God's son. The Jews were incarnations of the Devil, for who else would have the desire or power to murder God?

For the Christian antisemite, this identification of the Jews with the Devil had New Testament origins. In the Gospel of John, the Jews' persecution of Jesus is ascribed to the Jews being of the Devil—a charge depicted as made by Jesus himself (the three other Gospels, each written in closer proximity to Jesus' life, attribute no such statement to him). In chapter 8:43–44, 47, John reports that Jesus said to the Jews: "Why do you not understand what I say? It is because you cannot bear to hear my word. You are of your father, the Devil, and your will is to do your father's desire. . . . The reason why you do not hear [the words of God revealed in Jesus] is because you are not of God."[2]

With these charges of deicide and collusion with the Devil, the early church put the Jews on the theological, not to mention moral and ultimately physical, defensive. It established the logic of the oft-repeated Christian doctrine that merely by being Jews, Jews in effect murder Jesus anew in every generation.

THE CHURCH FATHERS

The antisemitic themes were expanded and spread throughout the Roman Empire by the early church leaders. Among these were John Chrysostom and Bishop Ambrose, both of whom were later declared saints. Living during the formative century when the Roman Empire became Christian, these men were able to permanently influence Christian attitudes and policies toward the Jews.

St. John Chrysostom of Antioch, Archbishop of Constantinople

Among the most admired and beloved figures in church history is St. John Chrysostom, whose Greek name translates as St. John the Golden Mouthed. The nineteenth-century Protestant cleric R. S. Storrs called him "one of the most eloquent preachers who ever since apostolic times have brought to men the divine tidings of truth and love." Storrs's contemporary, the great Catholic theologian John Henry Cardinal Newman, described Chrysostom as a "bright, cheerful, gentle soul, a sensitive heart . . . all this elevated, refined, transformed by the touch of heaven—such was St. John Chrysostom."[3]

Chrysostom's warmth did not extend to the Jews: "They know only one thing," he said, "to satisfy their stomachs, to get drunk, to kill."[4]

"The synagogue," according to Chrysostom, "is worse than a brothel. . . . It is the den of scoundrels and the repair of wild beasts . . . a criminal assembly of Jews . . . a place of meetings for the assassins of Christ . . . the refuge of devils." When some Christians argued that synagogues were entitled to a degree of respect if only because they contain the writings of Moses and the Prophets, Chrysostom objected. The fact that synagogues contain holy books is yet another reason to despise the Jews; they recognize the holy books as holy, but obstinately refuse to accept or understand their true Christian meaning. Clearly, then, they are of the Devil as the Gospel of John declares.

When Chrysostom learned that some Christians in Antioch were continuing to maintain cordial relations with Jews, he denounced them: "The Jews have assassinated the Son of God! How dare you . . . associate with this nation of assassins and hangmen!"

Perhaps Chrysostom's most significant contribution to antisemitism was his theological justification for violence against Jews. He argued that when Christians beat and murder Jews, it is divinely sanctioned: "It was men, say the Jews, who brought these misfortunes upon us, not God. On the contrary, it was in fact God who brought them about. If you attribute them to men, reflect again that, even supposing men had dared, they would not have had the power to accomplish them, unless it had been God's will." Concerning such justifications of Jewish suffering, the Catholic historian Malcolm Hay has noted that "such logic would justify the German race murderers. St. John Chrysostom could have preached a powerful sermon beside the mass [Jewish] grave at Dubno [Poland]. He could have explained that a revengeful God had chastised the little Jewish boy who had tried to keep back his tears so that the Germans would not see that he was afraid; and the little baby, and the Jewish family who all went down into the pit. . . . [Chrysostom's thinking] would have been useful to the defense at Nuremberg."[5]

St. Ambrose of Milan

At about the time St. John Chrysostom was reviling the Jews of Antioch, St. Ambrose, to this day revered as among the greatest of the church fathers, was bishop of Milan. During his term as bishop, a bishop in Mesopotamia (in 388) instigated the burning of a synagogue. The Roman emperor, Theodosius the Great (379–95), ordered the bishop to pay for the rebuilding of the synagogue. Upon learning of this, St. Ambrose wrote a letter of protest to Theodosius, which the emperor ignored.

A short time later, the emperor attended a church service officiated by Ambrose. The bishop refused to perform the Mass unless the emperor assured him that the order to rebuild the synagogue would be rescinded. "There is no adequate cause for such a commotion," Ambrose told Theodosius, "that the people should be so severely punished for the burning of a building; and much less since it is the burning of a synagogue, a home of unbelief, a house of impiety, a receptacle of folly, which God Himself has condemned."[6] This time, Ambrose's protest was successful, and a precedent sought by this fourth-century church father was established: if Christians destroy a synagogue, the Jews are to pay for its rebuilding.

THE CRUSADES

By the eleventh century, the church had converted virtually all the inhabitants of Europe, except the Jews. Until then, the situation of the Jews was tenuous but tolerable. With the First Crusade in 1096, however, the status and security of European Jewry declined precipitously.

In 1095, at the Council of Clermont-Ferrand, Pope Urban II called for a Crusade to regain the Holy Land from the Muslims, and tens of thousands of Christians obeyed his call. But the Muslims were not the crusaders' only enemies. As the historian Leon Poliakov noted, the crusaders "were God's avengers, appointed to punish all infidels, whoever they might be . . . What could be more natural than to take revenge along the way upon the various infidels living in Christian territories?"[7]

A contemporary chronicler, Guibert de Nogent, quoted the crusaders of Rouen: "We desire to go and fight God's enemies in the East;
but we have before our eyes certain Jews, a race more inimical to God
than any other."

Wherever crusaders found Jews they offered them the choice of
Christianity or death. The experience of the Jews of Worms, Germany,
is typical of what happened to French and German Jews during this crusade. In May 1096, upon learning of the crusaders' murder of the Jews of
Speyer, the Jews of Worms sought assistance. Some hoped to find refuge in the palace of Bishop Adalbert (and some bishops did try to hide
Jews), while other Jews, having been promised help by the local bur-
ghers, remained in their homes. The latter were immediately murdered,
while those in the palace, after refusing Bishop Adalbert's offer to save
them from the Christian mobs only if they converted, were murdered.

In all, eight hundred Jews were killed in two days. A Christian
chronicler, Albert of Aix, wrote: "Only a small number of Jews escaped
this cruel massacre, and a few accepted baptism, much more out of the
fear of death than from love of the Christian faith."[8]

In many places, bishops and counts tried to protect the Jews from
the Christian masses and offered the Jews the choice of baptism or death
only when pressured by the Christian mobs. But once danger passed,
the Jews, who were saved through conversion, were to be gravely disap-
pointed by the church hierarchy. When the few Jews who chose baptism over death wished to return to Judaism after the crusaders passed
their city, they were prohibited from doing so. This prohibition was
formalized in a bull issued by Pope Innocent III in September 1201:
"he who is led to Christianity by violence, by fear and by torture, and
who received the sacrament of baptism to avoid harm (even as he who
comes falsely to baptism) receives indeed the stamp of Christianity. . . .
They [the forced converts] themselves having been anointed with the
holy oil and having participated in the body of the Lord, must be duty
constrained to abide by the faith they had accepted by force." The only
option, according to the pope, was for a person to "object expressly" to
baptism, and to refuse to undergo the ceremony. As Poliakov notes,
"Since those who 'objected expressly' to a forced baptism were gener-

ally executed on the spot, all cases of baptism became valid in practical terms."[9]

The Second Crusade, begun in 1147, accelerated the decline of the Jews' status among Christians. Some clerics stirred the Christian masses to an anti-Jewish frenzy. In France, the Abbé Pierre of Cluny challenged his parishioners: "What is the good of going to the end of the world, at great loss of men and money, to fight the Saracens, when we permit among us other infidels a thousand times more guilty towards Christ than the Mohammedans?"[10]

During the decades following the Crusades new anti-Jewish libels helped lead to the murders of hundreds of thousands of other Jews.

THREE MEDIEVAL LIBELS

Throughout the Middle Ages, Christians repeated the accusation that the Jews are the Devil's children. Millions of Christians came to believe that the Jews were not actually human beings, but creatures of the Devil, allies of Satan, and personifications of the Antichrist.

This dehumanization of the Jews rendered plausible every accusation against them. Three anti-Jewish libels were widely circulated by the medieval clergy and believed by the large majority of Christians: Jews murder Christians and drink their blood for ritual purposes; Jews poison Christians; and Jews kidnap the wafer that is transubstantiated into the body of Jesus and stick needles into it, thus torturing Jesus.

Each of these three charges was made and believed despite the non-existence of *any* supporting evidence except for confessions extracted under torture.[11] But the absence of any evidence fooled few Christians; agents of the Devil are notoriously tricky.[12]

Ritual Murder

The first accusation of ritual murder was made in 1144 in England. According to a contemporary Christian document: "The Jews of Norwich brought a child before Easter, and tortured him with all the tortures wherewith our Lord was tortured, and on Long Friday hanged him on a rod in hatred of our Lord, and afterwards buried him." A

Christian convert from Judaism, Theobold of Cambridge, testified that Jews were required to sacrifice a Christian child annually, the choice of place being made at an annual conference of rabbis.[13]

This first accusation of ritual murder had no immediate consequences. Because no evidence was ever produced that a murder had been committed, let alone a Jewish ritual murder, no Jew was tried for the alleged crime.

But the long-term effects of this accusation were devastating. Between the twelfth and the twentieth centuries, on over 150 occasions, Jews, and often entire Jewish communities, were put on trial for engaging in ritual murder. In almost every instance, Jews were tortured and put to death.

The case of Hugh of Lincoln provides a typical example. In 1255, a large number of Jews visited Lincoln, England, to attend the wedding of a prominent Jew's daughter. The day after the wedding, the body of a Christian boy, Hugh of Lincoln, missing for over three weeks, was found in a cesspool into which he had accidentally fallen.

Matthew Paris, a contemporary Christian chronicler, wrote what he and other Christians believed to have really occurred: "The child was first fattened for ten days with white bread and milk, and then . . . almost all the Jews of England were invited to the crucifixion."[14] Subsequently, a Jew named Copin was arrested, and under torture confessed "that the Jews had crucified the boy in the manner that the Jews had once crucified Jesus." One hundred Jews were arrested, and nineteen, including Copin, were hanged without trial.

The case of Hugh of Lincoln had a profound impact on the popular image of Jews in England and throughout the Western world. A century later Geoffrey Chaucer wrote of the Jews' murder of Hugh in "The Prioress's Tale" in *The Canterbury Tales*. In the nineteenth century, one of the leading essayists in England, Charles Lamb, wrote: "I confess that I have not the nerve to enter their synagogues. Old prejudices cling about me. I cannot shake off the story of Hugh of Lincoln."[15]

Dozens of ballads were inspired by Hugh's death. The two authors, on a visit to the Ozark Mountains of Arkansas, purchased a book of

Ozark Mountain folk songs, printed in 1973, which included a ballad inspired by the "Jewish ritual murder" of Hugh of Lincoln.[16] In it, a Jewish woman is described as inviting a young Christian boy into her house, whereupon:

> *She pinned a napkin o'er his face*
> *And pinned it with gold pin*
> *Then called for a vessel of gold*
> *To catch his heart blood in,*
> *In, in,*
> *To catch his heart blood in.*

The Jews' allegiance to their understanding of God, with its denial of the Christian trinity, was always at the heart of the ritual murder charge. A sixteenth-century document explains that the murder of Christian children and the distribution of their blood among Jews is "a token of their eternal enmity towards Christendom," for "if they had Christ today they would crucify Him as their fathers did, but since they do not have Christ, they martyr in His stead an innocent Christian child."

By the fourteenth century the ritual murder charge had become associated with the Jewish holiday of Passover, attesting to the antisemitism that the Jews' beliefs aroused among Christians. Christians accused Jews of using Christian blood in their unleavened bread (matzo) and in their wine. In Savoy in 1329, Christians claimed that the Jews "compound out of the entrails of murdered Christian children a salve of food called aharance [haroseth], which they eat every Passover in place of a sacrifice; they prepare this food at least every sixth year because they believe they are saved thereby."[17]

The accusations of ritual murder followed the Jews throughout Europe. The historian Haim Hillel Ben-Sasson wrote, "Generation after generation of Jews in Europe was tortured and Jewish communities were massacred or dispersed and broken up because of this libel."[18] The blood libel has, in fact, persisted into contemporary times. The Protestant historian James Parkes reported, "In Central Eastern Europe, among both Roman Catholics and Eastern Orthodox Christians . . . there are almost more examples of the accusation in the years between 1880 and 1945 than in the whole of the Middle Ages."[19]

In the 1930s the Nazis often promulgated the libel. The entire May 1, 1934, issue of the newspaper *Der Stürmer* was devoted to Jewish ritual murder, and the regular weekly edition of the paper routinely carried illustrations of rabbis sucking the blood of German children.

In the 1960s and the 1970s the blood libel was spread by the then leading financial figure in the Arab world, King Faisal of Saudi Arabia. On a number of occasions, Faisal informed newspaper interviewers that the Jews annually celebrated Passover by murdering a non-Jew and consuming his blood.[20] Since then, the blood libel has been a staple feature of contemporary Arab/Islamic antisemitism, and today might well be believed in by more people than at any other time in history (see pages 108–110).

In response to this heinous libel, two ironic points are worthy of note. First, the blood libel was directed against the first nation in history to outlaw human sacrifice (Genesis 22, Deuteronomy 18:10) and the only nation in the ancient Near East to prohibit the consumption of blood (Leviticus 3:17; 7:26; 17:10–14; Deuteronomy 12:15–16; 12:23–25).[21]

Second, the libel actually strengthened Jewish identity in a most unexpected manner. The early Zionist thinker Ahad Ha-Am contended that the blood libel was actually of some psychological benefit to the Jews in that it enabled them to resist internalizing the world's negative portrayal of them. "This accusation is the solitary case in which the general acceptance of an idea about ourselves does not make us doubt whether all the world can be wrong, and we right, because it is based on an absolute lie. Every Jew who has been brought up among Jews knows as an indisputable fact that throughout the length and breadth of Jewry there is not a single individual who drinks human blood for religious purposes. . . . 'But,' you ask, 'is it possible that everybody can be wrong, and the Jews right?' Yes, it is possible: the blood accusation proves it possible."[22]

Plots to Poison Christians

"If a king had a Jewish physician," notes James Parkes, "and did not actually perish on the battlefield, cloven in two by the battle-axe of the enemy, there is nothing surprising in his unfortunate doctor being accused of poisoning him."[23] Parkes cites several instances of Jewish royal physicians being executed after a king's death.

In actuality almost every medieval Jewish doctor in Europe (and other Jews as well) was endangered. In 1161, in Bohemia, eighty-six Jews were burned as punishment for an alleged plot of Jewish physicians to poison the populace.[24] Such accusations were endorsed by leading intellectual circles in European society. In 1610, the medical faculty of the University of Vienna declared that Jewish physicians were bound by Jewish law to kill every tenth Christian through the use of drugs.[25]

Martin Luther said that "if they [the Jews] could kill us all, they would gladly do so, aye, and often do it, especially those who profess to be physicians. They know all that is known about medicine in Germany; they can give poison to a man of which he will die in an hour, or in ten or twenty years; they thoroughly understand this art."[26]

The libel that the Jews were continually plotting to poison the Christian world had particularly tragic results during the Black Death of 1348–49. This plague, which killed about one-third of Europe's population, was blamed on the Jews despite the fact that the plague also killed Jews.

A Christian physician, Konrad of Regensburg, in his *Buch der Natur*, was one of the few Christians to recognize the irrationality of blaming the Jews: "But I know that there were more Jews in Vienna than in any other German city familiar to me, and so many of them died of the plague that they were obliged to enlarge their cemetery. To have brought this on themselves would have been folly on their part." But the doctor's reasoning had no impact.

Jews were first tortured to confess to spreading the Black Death in Switzerland in September 1348. According to the "confession," a rabbi had instructed the Jews: "See, I give you a little package, which contains a preparation of poison and venom. . . . This you are to distribute among the wells, the cisterns and the springs . . . to poison the people who use the water." A month later, the verdict against the Jews was announced: "all Jews from the age of seven cannot excuse themselves from this crime, since all of them in their totality were cognizant and are guilty of the above actions. Jewish children under the age of seven were then baptized and reared as Christians after their families were murdered."[27]

Antisemitic libels die hard. In 1953, Joseph Stalin accused a group of doctors, most of them Jews, of a plot to poison the Communist leadership of the Soviet Union. Stalin died three days before the doctors' trial was to begin, but we now know that Stalin intended to use the "Doctors' Plot" to arouse the Soviet public against the Jews, and in the ensuing crisis, exile the USSR's Jews to Siberia.

In a 1988 address to Louis Farrakhan's Nation of Islam, Steve Cokely, an aide to Chicago Mayor Eugene Sawyer, charged, "The AIDS epidemic is a result of doctors, especially Jewish ones, who inject AIDS into blacks." Mayor Sawyer hesitated almost a week before firing Cokely, and only three of Chicago's eighteen black aldermen called for his dismissal. A similar accusation was directed against the Jews of Israel by Ambassador Nabil Ramlawi, the Permanent Observer of Palestine to the UN Commission on Human Rights, who testified in 1997 to the United Nations in Geneva that "The Israeli authorities have infected by injection 300 Palestinian children with the HIV virus."

Desecration of the Host

In 1215, the Fourth Lateran Council accepted the doctrine of transubstantiation as official church dogma. This dogma asserted that the wafer used at the Mass was miraculously transformed into the body of Jesus; the wafer was to be regarded not as a symbolic representation of Jesus, but as his actual body. Just how literally Christians accepted this teaching is exemplified in the writings of a leading preacher of the thirteenth century, Berthold of Regensburg. He explained that Christ, though present in the wafer, does not allow himself to be seen in it, for "who would like to bite off the little head, or the little hands, or the little feet of a little child?"[28]

Antisemitic usage of the doctrine of transubstantiation soon led to the torture and murder of thousands of Jews. Since Jesus becomes present through the wafer, the reasoning went, would not the Jews who had once crucified him wish to torture and kill him again? In 1243, only twenty-eight years after the Fourth Lateran Council, the first accusation of "host desecration" occurred in Berlitz, near Berlin. The city's entire Jewish community was burned alive for allegedly torturing a wafer.

Charges of "host desecration" spread throughout Europe. In Prague, in 1389, the Jewish community was collectively accused of attacking a monk carrying a wafer. Large mobs of Christians surrounded the Jewish neighborhood and offered the Jews the choice of baptism or death. Refusing to be baptized, three thousand Jews were murdered. In Berlin, in 1510, twenty-six Jews were burned and two beheaded for reportedly "desecrating the host." A charge of host desecration was reported as late as 1836 in Romania.

The "host desecration" libel is among the clearest examples of the Christian perception of the Jews as devils. Clearly, no one, not even a Jew, tortures wafers. If a person does "torture" one, it could mean only one thing: he, too, recognizes that the wafer is the body of Jesus, and wishes to make him suffer. Who but the people of the Devil recognize the divinity of Jesus but wish to destroy him?

CHRISTIAN ROOTS OF THE HOLOCAUST

Sixteen hundred years of such hatred of Jews culminated in the Holocaust. Christianity did not create the Holocaust—indeed, Nazism was anti-Christian—but it made it possible. Without Christian antisemitism, the Holocaust would have been inconceivable.

Nazi antisemitism differed from Christian antisemitism, however, in at least two important ways. Nazis did not allow the Jews the choice of conversion or death, as medieval Christian antisemites had, but only death. And it called for the murder of all Jews, rather than, as the medieval Christian world had called for, the suffering of all Jews. In virtually every other way, Nazism depended upon Christian antisemitic ideas, libels, policies, and legislation.

Hitler and the Nazis found in medieval Catholic anti-Jewish legislation a model for their own, and they read and reprinted Martin Luther's virulently antisemitic writings. It is instructive that the Holocaust was unleashed by the only major country in Europe that had an approximately equal number of Catholics and Protestants.

CATHOLICISM

When the church was Europe's most powerful force, from the fourth until the eighteenth century, its laws, many of which were directed against Jews, were Europe's laws. Concerning church anti-Jewish legislation the Holocaust historian Raul Hilberg has noted: "in reviewing the documentary record of the destruction of the Jews, one is almost immediately impressed with the fact that the German administration knew what it was doing. . . . The German bureaucracy could draw upon . . . precedents and follow . . . a guide, for the German bureaucrats could dip into a vast reservoir of administrative experience, a reservoir which church and state had filled in fifteen hundred years of destructive activity."[29] In *The Destruction of the European Jews,* Hilberg presented a chart substantiating his thesis.[30]

More obvious than the Nazi copying of medieval Christian antisemitic legislation was the Nazi use of centuries-old Christian antisemitic libels. Almost all of the negative images created by Catholics in

CHURCH LAW	NAZI LAW
Jews not allowed to hold public office, Synod of Clermont, 535.	Law for the Re-establishment of office, the Professional Civil Service, April 7, 1933.
Jews not allowed to show themselves in the street during Passion Week, Third Synod of Orleans, 538.	Decree authorizing local authorities to bar Jews from the street on certain Nazi holidays, Dec. 3, 1938.
Burning of the Talmud and other Jewish books, 12th Synod of Toledo, 681.	Book burnings in Nazi Germany.

Christians not permitted to patronize Jewish doctors, Trulanic Synod, 692.	Decree of July 25, 1938.
Jews obliged to pay taxes for the support of the church to the same extent as Christians, Synod of Gerona, 1078.	The "Sozialaugleichsabgabe," which provided that Jews pay a special income tax in lieu of donation for party purposes imposed on Nazis, Dec. 24, 1940.
The marking of Jewish clothes with a badge, Fourth Lateran Council, Canon 68 (copied from Islamic legislation that had decreed that Christians wear blue belts and Jews, yellow belts).	Decree of Sept. 1, 1941, authorizing that Jews are required to wear yellow star.
Christians not permitted to attend Jewish ceremonies, Synod of Vienna, 1267.	Friendly relations with Jews prohibited, Oct. 24, 1941.
Compulsory ghettos, Synod of Breslau, 1267.	Order by Reinhard Heydrich for ghettoization of Jews, Sept. 21, 1939.
Christians not permitted to sell or rent real estate to Jews, Synod of Ofen, 1279.	Decree providing for compulsory sale of Jewish real estate, Dec. 3, 1938.
Jews not permitted to obtain academic degrees, Council of Basel, Sessio XIX.	Law against Overcrowding of German Schools and Universities, April 25, 1933.

the early and late Middle Ages were echoed by the Nazis. Though anti-Christian (in large part because of Christianity's Jewish roots and values), the Nazis filled their speeches and journals with stories of Jews murdering non-Jews to drink their blood, and of Jews poisoning Ger-

many's water systems. Julius Streicher, the chief Nazi antisemitic ideol-
ogist, who was hanged at Nuremberg for his war crimes, often appealed
to the Christian instincts of his fellow Germans by describing the Jews
as the "people of whom Christ said its father was the devil."[31]

PROTESTANTISM

The centuries-old Catholic antisemitism in Germany was more than
matched by the virulence of Protestant antisemitism.

Martin Luther (1483–1546), who was one of history's most vehe-
ment Jew-haters, was both the founder of Protestantism and a father
of German nationalism. Accordingly, his antisemitic statements profoundly influenced the attitudes of nearly all Germans, not only Protestants.

In his early days, Luther was critical of church anti-Jewish policies
because he believed that such policies prevented the Jews from converting to Christianity. When Luther later realized that his kinder approach
did not prompt Jews to cease being Jews, he turned furiously against
them. His later writings against the Jews were so venomous that the
Nazis often cited them. Indeed, Julius Streicher argued in his defense
at the Nuremberg trials that he had never said anything about the Jews
that Martin Luther had not said four hundred years earlier.[32]

Streicher was largely correct. There was a genuine similarity of
themes between Luther and the Nazis, and Hitler was quite familiar with
and admired Luther's writings. In *Mein Kampf*, Hitler called Luther one
of the three great figures of Germany, along with Frederick the Great
and Richard Wagner.[33] In conversations as early as 1918, Hitler said:
"Luther was a great man, a giant. With one blow he heralded the new
dawn. . . . He saw the Jew as we are only beginning to see him today."
When, on November 9–10, 1938, the Nazis carried out a large-scale
pogrom throughout the country (*Kristallnacht*) in which they destroyed
almost all of Germany's synagogues and murdered thirty-five Jews, they
announced that the pogrom was in honor of the anniversary of Martin
Luther's birthday.[34]

Just as Catholic legislation anticipated virtually every Nazi anti-Jewish decree with the exception of genocide, so too did Martin Luther's words anticipate most Nazi actions against the Jews. In a pamphlet published toward the end of his life, *Concerning the Jews and Their Lies*, Luther outlined eight actions to be taken against the Jews:

> Burn all synagogues.
> Destroy Jewish dwellings.
> Confiscate the Jews' holy books.
> Forbid rabbis to teach.
> Forbid Jews to travel.
> Forbid Jews to charge interest on loans to non-Jews and confiscate Jewish property.
> Force Jews to do physical labor.
> Expel the Jews from provinces where Christians live.[35]

It is fair to say that insofar as Luther's anti-Jewish writings are concerned, the Nazis saw themselves as his followers. The Nazi depiction of the Jews as vermin to be exterminated echoed Luther's depiction of the Jews as "a plague, pestilence, pure misfortune in our country."[36] Owing to the towering role he played in German national and religious thought, Luther constituted an important ally for the Nazis in the carrying out of the "Final Solution."

CONCLUSION

For nearly two thousand years, Christian antisemitism was a reaction to Judaism. The mere act of remaining a Jew constituted, in the eyes of millions of Christians, a living repudiation of Christ. Consequently, the Christian world dehumanized the Jew, ultimately helping lay the groundwork for the Holocaust, the ultimate consequence of this dehumanization. While it is true that many Nazis were anti-Christian (and that Nazism itself was anti-Christian), they were, as the late Jewish philosopher Eliezer Berkovits pointed out, the children of Christians,[37] who had been raised to believe antisemitic hate.

While the Holocaust took place in Christian Europe, Jews' assessments of the Christian world must adapt to the contemporary reality. While never forgetting the past, Jews must recognize that major changes have taken place within all major branches of Christianity, and that American Christianity has no such history of antisemitism. While there are still Jew-haters in all branches of Christianity, particularly among the extreme Right and extreme Left in Europe and South America, there are now also many Christian philo-semites. Jews must also recognize that in the contemporary world Christians, particularly in the United States, are often an ally, sometimes the most loyal ally, of Jews. Over the past century, Nazism, the Left, and Islam have replaced Christianity as the world's foremost purveyors of antisemitism. Moreover, the ideals of both religions demand that Jews and Christians forge an alliance to "repair the world under the rule of God."

Of course, such an alliance will not develop easily. Many Jews, knowledgeable of Christianity's past, are reluctant to believe that Christians have really changed. But the time has come for Jews to recognize that there have been major changes in Christianity, that there are forces, particularly in the United States and Western Europe, that are very open to the Jews. In the United States today, religious Christians are among those most supportive of Israel's attempts to defend itself against those bent on its destruction (see page xvii).

Christians, for their part, must acknowledge the horrors of Christian antisemitism and the latent—and blatant—antisemitic elements that still live on in Christendom. They must also understand that the Jews retain their place in God's scheme despite their rejection of Christian claims for Jesus. One Christian who did was Pope John XXIII. Shortly before his death, he composed this prayer: "We realize now that many, many centuries of blindness have dimmed our eyes, so that we no longer see the beauty of Thy Chosen People and no longer recognize in their faces the features of our firstborn brother. We realize that our brows are branded with the mark of Cain. Centuries long has Abel lain in blood and tears, because we had forgotten Thy love. Forgive us the curse which we unjustly laid on the name of the Jews. Forgive us that, with our curse, we crucified Thee a second time."[38]

When Judaism and Christianity work in tandem, something marvelous happens—the making of a Judeo-Christian society. Which is what uniquely defines America and what has made it great—for Christians, for Jews, and for the world.

NINE

Islamic Antisemitism

I SLAM WAS THE SECOND RELIGION to emanate from Judaism, but as its founder was not a Jew and as it was not originally a Jewish sect, Islam's encounter with Judaism was significantly less bitter than Christianity's. As Salo Baron notes: "It was, therefore, from the beginning, a struggle between strangers, rather than an internecine strife among brethren."[1] Largely because of this factor, Jews in the Islamic world were rarely persecuted as violently as their brethren in the Christian world. S. D. Goitein, perhaps the twentieth century's leading historian of Jewish life in the Arab world, concludes: "when the known facts are weighed, I believe it correct to say that as a whole the position of the non-Muslims [Christians and Jews under medieval Islamic rule] was far better than that of the Jews in medieval Christian Europe."[2]

Goitein's assessment is valid, but it tells us much more about the Jews' condition under Christians than about their treatment by Muslims. For while the Jews of the Muslim world may have rarely experienced the tortures, pogroms, and expulsions that typified Jewish life under medieval Christian rule, their life under Islam was usually a life of degradation and insecurity. At the whim of a Muslim leader, a synagogue would be destroyed, Jewish orphans would be forcibly converted to Islam, or Jews would be forced to pay even more excessive taxes than usual.

MUHAMMAD AND THE JEWS

Like Christianity's, Islam's anti-Judaism is deeply rooted. Islam too was born from the womb of Judaism; it too was rejected by the Jews whose validation was sought; and it too suffered an identity crisis vis-à-vis Judaism.

When Islam was born in the seventh century, there was a substantial Jewish population in Medina, where the first Muslim community arose. The Jews of pre-Islamic Arabia were active advocates of their religion, to such an extent that several kings of Himyar, now Yemen, converted to Judaism. Contemporary inscriptions described Dhu Nuwas As'ar, the last Jewish king of Himyar, as a believer in one deity whom the king called Rahman, the Merciful One, as God was called in Judaism and later in Islam.

During his early years, Muhammad related well to the Jews of Arabia, and their religious practices and ideas deeply influenced him. As Goitein noted: "The intrinsic values of the belief in one God, the creator of the world, the God of justice and mercy, before whom everyone high and low bears personal responsibility came to Muhammad, as he never ceased to emphasize, from Israel."[3]

The profound influence of the Jews, their Bible, and their laws on Muhammad is clearly expressed in the Koran, the Muslim bible, and in Muhammad's early religious legislation. Indeed, Muhammad saw himself as another Moses. In the Koran, he writes of his message (Sura 46, verse 12), "Before it the Book of Moses was revealed. . . . This Book confirms it. It is revealed in the Arabic tongue."[4] Moses is a dominant figure in the Koran, in which he is mentioned over one hundred times.

The Jewish doctrine that most deeply influenced Muhammad was monotheism: "There is no God but God." Muhammad's monotheism was so attuned to the uncompromising nature of Judaism's monotheism that though he had also been influenced by Christian teachers, he rejected the Christian trinity and the divinity of Jesus as not monotheistic: "Unbelievers are those that say: 'Allah is the Messiah, the son of Mary' . . . Unbelievers are those that say, 'Allah is one of three.' There is but one God. If they do not desist from so saying, those of them that disbelieve shall be sternly punished" (5:71–73).

Jewish law also deeply influenced Muhammad. In the early days of Islam, Muslims prayed in the direction of the Jews' holy city, Jerusalem, and observed the most solemn Jewish holiday, Yom Kippur, the Day of Atonement. Only later, when Muhammad reluctantly concluded that the Jews would not embrace him as their prophet and convert to Islam, did he substitute Mecca for Jerusalem, and the fast of Ramadan for Yom Kippur. Similarly, Muhammad based Muslim dietary laws upon Judaism's laws of Kashrut: "You are forbidden carrion, blood, and the flesh of swine; also any flesh . . . of animals sacrificed to idols" (5:3). The five daily prayers of Islam are likewise modeled on the three daily services of the Jews.

Second in importance only to his adoption of the Jews' God was Muhammad's adoption of the Jews' founding father, Abraham, as Islam's founder. In Sura 2, verse 125, Muhammad writes how Abraham and his son Ishmael converted the Kaaba, the holy rock of Arabian paganism, into the holy shrine of Islam.

Believing himself to be the final and greatest prophet of Mosaic monotheism, and having adopted so much of Jewish thought and practice, Muhammad appealed to the Jews of Arabia to recognize his role and to adopt Islam as the culmination of Judaism. "Even Luther," the late renowned philosopher Walter Kaufmann wrote, "expected the Jews to be converted by his version of Christianity, although he placed faith in Christ at the center of his teaching and firmly believed in the trinity. If even Luther . . . could expect that, how much more Muhammad, whose early revelations were so much closer to Judaism?"[5] Muhammad's deep desire for Jewish recognition reflected the similar needs of Jesus and his followers. No group could validate Muhammad's religious claims as could the Jews, nor could any so seriously threaten to undermine them.

The Jews rejected Muhammad's claims as they had Jesus', holding in both cases that what was true in their messages was not new, and that what was new was not true. Islam may have served as a religious advance for Arabian pagans, but for the Jews it was merely another offshoot of Judaism.

One major factor that rendered Muhammad's prophetic claims untenable to Jews was his ignorance of the Bible. In large part because Muhammad never read the Bible, but only heard Bible stories, his references to the Jews' holy text were often erroneous. In Sura 28:38, for instance, he had Pharaoh (from Exodus) ask Haman (of the book of Esther) to erect the Tower of Babel (which appears at the beginning of Genesis).

Another obstacle to Jewish acceptance of Muhammad was the moral quality of some of his teachings. They did not strike the Jews, or the Arabian Christians, as equaling, let alone superseding, the prophetic teachings of Judaism and Christianity. In 33:50, for example, Muhammad exempts himself from his own law limiting a man to four wives, and in 4:34 he instructs men to beat disobedient wives. Walter Kaufmann notes that "there is much more like this, especially in the 33rd Sura," and that "it must have struck the Jews as being a far cry from Amos and Jeremiah, and the Christians as rendering absurd the prophet's claim that he was superseding Jesus."[6]

Finally, Muhammad's suspension of many Torah laws invalidated him in the Jews' eyes.

For these and other reasons, the Jews rejected Muhammad's prophetic claims and refused to become Muslims. This alone infuriated Muhammad. But it was even more infuriating that the Jews publicly noted the errors in Muhammad's biblical teachings and may have even ridiculed his claims to prophecy. Goitein concludes, "it is only natural that Muhammad could not tolerate as a neighbor a large monotheistic community which categorically denied his claim as a prophet, and probably also ridiculed his inevitable blunders."[7]

As a result Muhammad turned against the Jews and their religion, and never forgave them for not becoming his followers. And just as early Christian hostility to the Jews was canonized in the New Testament, so

Muhammad's angry reactions to the Jews were recorded in the Koran. These writings gave Muslims throughout history a seemingly divinely-sanctioned antipathy to the Jews.

In the Koran, Muhammad attacked the Jews and attempted to invalidate Judaism in several ways. First, and most significantly, he changed Abraham from a Jew to a Muslim: "Abraham was neither Jew nor Christian. [He] surrendered himself to Allah. . . . Surely the men who are nearest to Abraham are those who follow him, this Prophet" (3:67–68).

Second, he condemned the Jews and delegitimized their law by advancing a thesis similar to Paul's, that the many Torah laws had been given to the Jews as punishment for their sins: "Because of their iniquity we forbade the Jews good things which were formerly allowed them" (4:160).

Third, Muhammad charged the Jews with falsifying their Bible by deliberately omitting prophecies of his coming.[8] For example, in the Koran (2:129), Muhammad has Abraham mouth a prophecy of his (Muhammad's) coming. Muhammad charged that the Jews "extinguish the light of Allah" (9:32) by having removed such prophecies from their Bible.

Fourth, Muhammad asserted that Jews, like Christians, were not true monotheists, a charge he substantiated by claiming that the Jews believed the prophet Ezra to be the Son of God. "And the Jews say: Ezra is the son of Allah . . . Allah fights against them. How perverse are they." (9:30).

These anti-Jewish fabrications, articulated by Muhammad as reactions to the Jews' rejection of him, have ever since been regarded by Muslims as God's word. Though originally directed against specific Jews of a specific time, these statements often have been understood by succeeding generations as referring to all Jews at all times, and thus form the basis of Islamic antisemitism.

One common example is 2:61: "And humiliation and wretchedness were stamped upon them and they were visited with wrath from Allah. That was because they disbelieved in Allah's revelations and slew the prophets wrongfully. That was for their disobedience and transgression." This Koranic description of the Jews of seventh-century Arabia has often been cited by Muslims to describe Jews to this day.*

Muhammad and the Koran thus laid the basis for subsequent antisemitism just as the early Christians had—and for basically the same reason: Jews remaining Jewish constituted a living refutation of Islamic beliefs. Thus, under Islam, just as under Christianity, Jew-hatred was ultimately Judaism-hatred. Any Jew who converted to Islam was accepted as an equal.

Christians under Muslim rule fared little better. Muslims and their laws generally dealt harshly with both Christians and Jews.

As long as Christian communities survived in the Muslim world, discriminatory legislation also applied to them as well. However, whereas Jewish communities often flourished as vibrant Jewish communities, Christian communities for the most part did not survive the intense Muslim hostility. Under the yoke of Muslim laws against Jews and Christians, hundreds of thousands of people in some of the oldest and strongest Christian communities in the world converted to Islam.

No fact better underscores the intensity of Muslim persecution of *dhimmis* (non-Muslim monotheists) than this disappearance of so many Christian communities under Islam. The fact that under similar conditions many Jewish communities flourished bears witness to the Jews' tenacious commitment to Judaism, not to Muslim benevolence toward them. This is often lost sight of when favorably comparing Muslim antisemitism with Christian antisemitism. Yet the conversion to Islam of nearly every pre-Islamic Christian community in the Muslim world

*In a speech before his army officers on April 25, 1972, the late Egyptian President Anwar as-Sadat cited this Koranic verse, and then added: "The most splendid thing our prophet Muhammad, God's peace and blessing on him, did was to evict them [the Jews] from the entire Arabian peninsula . . . I pledge to you that we will celebrate on the next anniversary, God willing and in this place with God's help, not only the liberation of our land but also the defeat of the Israeli conceit and arrogance so that they must once again return to the condition decreed in our holy book: 'humiliation and wretchedness were stamped upon them' . . . We will not renounce this."

(the Copts of Egypt constituting the most notable exception) eloquently
testifies to what Jews had to endure in their long sojourn through the
Muslim world.

ATTITUDES AND ACTIONS OF ISLAM'S LEADERS TOWARD THE JEWS FROM MUHAMMAD'S DEATH UNTIL THE MODERN PERIOD

The two guiding principles of Islam's treatment of Jews and Christians are that Islam dominates and is not dominated, and that Jews and
Christians are to be subservient and degraded.[9] Nonmonotheists were
usually given the choice of conversion to Islam or death.

The Muslim legal code that prescribed the treatment of Jews and
Christians, or *dhimmis* as they both are referred to in Islam, was the Pact
of Umar, attributed to Muhammad's second successor, but assumed to
date from about 720.[10] Its key characteristic was the requirement that
dhimmis always acknowledge their subservient position to Muslims.
Jews and Christians had to pledge, for example, "We shall not manifest
our religion publicly nor convert anyone to it. We shall not prevent any
of our kin from entering Islam if they wish it." The subservience that
dhimmis were required to show publicly to Muslims is analogous to the
behavior once expected of blacks in the Jim Crow American South:
"We shall show respect . . . and we shall rise from our seats when they
[Muslims] wish to sit." They also had to pledge "not to mount saddles,"
since riding a horse, or, according to some Muslims, any animal, was
considered incompatible with the low status of a *dhimmi*.[11] The *dhimmis* also had to vow, "We shall not display our crosses or our books in
the roads or markets of the Muslims nor shall we raise our voices when
following our dead."[12]

Anti-*dhimmi* legislation did not end with the Pact of Umar. In the
Koran, Muhammad had urged Muslims, "Fight against such of those
who have been given the Scripture . . . and follow not the religion of
truth, until they pay the tribute readily, being brought low" (9:29).
Accordingly, Muslim officials often insisted that when paying tribute,
dhimmis must be "brought low," that is, humiliated.

An early Muslim regulation precisely prescribed how to humiliate

Jews and Christians when they pay tribute: "The *dhimmi*, Christian or Jew, goes on a fixed day in person to the emir, appointed to receive the poll tax, who occupies a high throne-like seat. The *dhimmi* stands before him, offering the poll tax on his open palm. The emir takes it so that his hand is on top and the *dhimmi*'s underneath. Then the emir gives him a blow on the neck, and a guard, standing upright before the emir, drives him roughly away. The same procedure is followed with the second, third and the following taxpayers. The public is admitted to enjoy this show." The public was not merely "admitted" to this humiliating spectacle, but as Baron observes, "Public participation was, indeed, essential for the purpose of demonstrating, according to the Shafi'ite school, the political superiority of Islam."[13]

In the course of time Muslim rulers developed additional ways to humiliate *dhimmis*. Baron describes one of them: "Equally vexatious was the tax receipt, which in accordance with an old Babylonian custom, was sometimes stamped upon the neck of the 'unbelieving' taxpayer. This ancient mark of slavery . . . expressly prohibited in the Talmud under the sanction of the slave's forcible emancipation, occasionally reappeared here as a degrading stamp of 'infidelity.'"[14]

These humiliating and painful procedures had a terrible effect on the Jews: "An Arab poet rightly spoke of entering the door with bent heads 'as if we were Jews.'"[15]

Another law designed to humiliate *dhimmis* required them to wear different clothing. The purposes of this law were to enable Muslims to recognize Jews and Christians at all times, and to make them appear foolish. In 807, the Abbasid Caliph Haroun al-Raschid, legislated that Jews must wear a yellow belt and a tall conical cap.[16] This Muslim decree provided the model for the yellow badge associated with the degradation of Jews in Christian Europe and most recently imposed by the Nazis.[17]

A Jew living in Baghdad in the days of Al-Muqtadir (1075–96) described additional measures passed by the vizier, Abu Shuja, to humiliate Jews: "each Jew had to have a stamp of lead . . . hang from his neck, on which the word *dhimmi* was inscribed. On women he likewise imposed two distinguishing marks: the shoes worn by each woman had to be one red and one black. She also had to carry on her neck or attached to her shoe a small brass bell. . . . And the Gentiles used to ridicule Jews, the mob and children often assaulting Jews in all the streets of Baghdad."[18]

During the same century in Egypt, the Fatimid Caliph Hakim ordered Christians to wear a cross with arms two feet long, while Jews were ordered to wear around their necks balls weighing five pounds, to commemorate the calf's head that their ancestors had once worshiped.[19]

These clothing regulations were not only enforced in the Middle Ages. Until their departure from Yemen in 1948, all Jews, men and women alike, were compelled to dress like beggars.* In fact, Yemen offers us a unique opportunity to understand Muslim attitudes toward the Jews. For it was the one Muslim country with a non-Muslim minority (Jews) that was never ruled by a European power. It was therefore able to treat its Jews in the "purest" Muslim manner, uninfluenced by non-Muslim domination.

---

*In addition to living under these humiliating laws, Jews constantly lived with the fear that some new interpretation of Muslim sources would lead to greater oppression. The worst instance took place under the Almohades, a Berber Muslim dynasty that ruled Morocco and Spain in the twelfth and thirteenth centuries. "At the beginning of the twelfth century, a Muslim jurist in Cordova [Spain] claimed to have found . . . a tradition, soon widely accepted in Morocco and Spain, that Muhammad's original decree of toleration of Jews had been limited to a period of five hundred years from the hegira [Muhammad's flight from Mecca]. If by that time the expected Jewish Messiah were not to arrive, the Jews were supposed to give up their religion and join the ranks of Islam. The time limit expired, of course, in 1107" (Salo Baron, *A Social and Religious History of the Jews*, 3:124). On the basis of this new doctrine, in 1146, Abd al-Mu'min, the builder of the Almohade Empire in North Africa and Spain, gave the Jews the choice of Islam or death. When nearly all of them refused to convert, nearly every Jew in Fez, the capital of Morocco, was murdered. As for those who converted, the Almohades put them under constant surveillance, and those whose conversions seemed insincere were executed, had their property confiscated, and their wives given to Muslims. Goitein notes: "All the horrors of the Spanish Inquisition were anticipated under Almohade rule" (Goitein, *Jews and Arabs: Their Contact Through the Ages*, 3d ed., p. 80).

In 1679, Jews in most of Yemen were expelled from their cities and villages. When allowed to come back a year later, they were not allowed to return to their homes, but were forced to settle in Jewish settlements outside of the cities. During their expulsion the synagogue of San'a, the capital, was converted into a mosque, which still exists under the name Masjid al-Jala (the Mosque of the Expulsion).

Among the many indignities to which the Jews of Yemen were constantly subjected was the throwing of stones at them by Muslim children, a practice that was religiously sanctioned. When Turkish officials (the Turks occupied Yemen in 1872) asked an assembly of Muslim leaders to see that this practice be stopped, an elderly Muslim scholar responded that throwing rocks at Jews was an *Ada,* an old religious custom, and thus it was unlawful to forbid it.

The greatest recurrent suffering that Yemenite Jews experienced was the forced conversion to Islam of Jewish children whose fathers had died. This was practiced until the Jews fled Yemen in 1948, and was also based upon Islamic doctrine. Muhammad was believed to have said, "Everyone is born in a state of natural religion [Islam]. It is only his parents who make a Jew or Christian out of him." Accordingly, a person should grow up in "the natural religion" of Islam.

When a Jewish father died, there was often a "race" between Jewish communal leaders who sought to place the man's children with Jewish parents and the Muslim authorities who wanted to convert the children to Islam and place them in Muslim homes (in the Yemenite Islamic culture it would appear that the surviving mother was regarded as irrelevant). The Jews often lost. Goitein reports that "many families arrived in Israel with one or more of their children lost to them, and I have heard of some widows who have been bereaved in this way of all their offspring."

Yet, as persecuted as the Yemenite Jews were, they were also denied the right to leave the country.[20]

THE MODERN ERA

By the nineteenth century, the Jews' situation under Islam went from degradation to being recurrent victims of violence—as these examples from Jewish life in Egypt, Syria, and Palestine illustrate.

Egypt

In his authoritative book, *An Account of the Manners and Customs of the Modern Egyptians*, Edward Lane wrote that, at the time of his study (1833–35), the Jews were living "under a less oppressive government in Egypt than in any other country of the Turkish Empire." He added, however, that the Jews "are held in the utmost contempt and abhorrence by the Muslims in general." Lane explained: "Not long ago, they used often to be jostled in the streets of Cairo, and sometimes beaten merely for passing on the right hand of a Muslim. At present, they are less oppressed; but still they scarcely ever dare to utter a word of abuse when reviled or beaten unjustly by the meanest Arab or Turk; for many a Jew has been put to death upon a false and malicious accusation of uttering disrespectful words against the Kuran [*sic*] or the Prophet. It is common to hear an Arab abuse his jaded ass, and after applying to him various opprobrious epithets, end by calling the beast a Jew."[21]

That this was the Jewish situation in Egypt, "a less oppressive government" than elsewhere in the Muslim Arab world, tells us a great deal about Muslim antisemitism in the nineteenth century—prior to the Zionist movement.

Syria

In 1840, some French Catholics introduced the blood libel into the Arab world. After a Capuchin monk in Damascus vanished, Ratti-Menton, the local French consul, told police authorities that the Jews probably had murdered him to procure his blood for a religious ritual. Several Damascus Jews were then arrested, and under torture, one of them "confessed" that leaders of the Jewish community had planned the monk's murder. Many other Jews were then arrested, and under torture more such confessions were obtained. French officials pressured Syria's ruler, Muhammad Ali, to try the arrested men, and it was only after an international protest organized by Jewish communities throughout the world that the Jews who survived their tortures were released.[22]

The blood libel immediately became popular among Muslims, who attacked Jews as drinkers of Muslim blood in Aleppo, Syria, in 1853, Damascus again, in 1848 and 1890, Cairo in 1844 and 1901–2, and Alexandria in 1870 and 1881.[23]

The blood libel played a decisive role in unsettling the lives of nineteenth-century Syrian Jews, and since then it has been repeatedly utilized in Arab anti-Jewish writings (see pages 109–110).

Palestine

Jews have lived continuously as a community in Palestine since approximately 1200 B.C.E. The only independent states ever to exist in Palestine have been Jewish. After the destruction of the second Jewish state in 70 C.E. and the suppression of the Bar Kochba revolt in 135 C.E., Jews always maintained a presence in Palestine, awaiting the reestablishment of the Jewish state. But these Jews often had to live under degrading conditions.

In nineteenth-century Palestine, which was under Ottoman Muslim rule, Jews had to walk past Muslims on their left, as the left is identified with Satan, and they always had to yield the right of way to a Muslim, by "stepping into the street and letting him pass." Failure to abide by these degrading customs often provoked a violent response.

In Palestine as elsewhere, Jews had to avoid anything that could remind Arabs of Judaism: therefore, synagogues could be located only in hidden, remote areas, and Jews could pray only in muted voices. In addition, despite the widespread poverty among Palestinian Jews, they had to pay a host of special protection taxes (in actuality, a form of extortion). For example, Jews paid one hundred pounds a year to the Muslim villagers of Siloam (just outside Jerusalem) not to disturb the graves at the Jewish cemetery on the Mount of Olives, and fifty pounds a year to the Ta'amra Arabs not to deface the Tomb of Rachel on the road to Bethlehem. They also had to pay ten pounds annually to Sheik Abu Gosh not to molest Jewish travelers on the road to Jerusalem, even though the Turkish authorities were already paying him to maintain order on that road.[24]

These anti-Jewish laws, taxes, and practices had a rather intimidating effect on the Jews. The British consul James Finn, who lived in Jerusalem in the 1850s, described in his book *Stirring Times* how "Arab merchants would dump their unsold wares on their Jewish neighbors and bill them, safe in the knowledge that the Jews so feared them that they would not dare return the items or deny their purchase."[25]

THE TWENTIETH CENTURY

Muslim antisemitism continued to be brutally expressed through the twentieth century. Albert Memmi, the noted French-Jewish novelist, who grew up in North Africa, cites a few examples:

> In Morocco in 1907, a huge massacre of Jews took place in Casablanca, along with the usual embellishments—rape, women carried away into the mountains, hundreds of homes and shops burned, etc. . . . In 1912 a big massacre in Fez. . . . In Algeria in 1934, massacre in Constantine, twenty-four people killed, dozens and dozens of others seriously wounded. . . . In Aden in 1946 . . . over one hundred people dead and seventy-six wounded, and two-thirds of the stores sacked and burned. . . . In June, 1941, in Iraq, six hundred people killed, one thousand seriously wounded, looting, rapes, arson, one thousand houses destroyed, six hundred stores looted. . . . [In Libya]: November 4th and 5th, 1945, massacre in Tripoli; November 6th and 7th in Zanzour, Zaouia, Foussaber, Ziltain, etc. girls and women raped in front of their families, the stomachs of pregnant women slashed open, the infants ripped out of them, children smashed with crowbars. . . . All this can be found in the newspapers of the time, including the local Arab papers.[26]

Memmi summarizes the Jewish status under Islam in the twentieth century: "Roughly speaking and in the best of cases, the Jew is protected like a dog which is part of man's property, but if he raises his head or acts like a man, then he must be beaten so that he will always remember his status."[27]

MUSLIM HATRED OF ISRAEL

It is the Jews' refusal to accept an unequal, inferior status that lies at the heart of the Arab-Muslim hatred for Israel.* As Yehoshafat Harkabi, a leading scholar of the Arab world's attitude toward Israel, put it: "The existence of the Jews was not a provocation to Islam . . . as long as Jews were subordinate or degraded. But a Jewish state is incompatible with the view of Jews as humiliated or wretched."[28]

This hatred of Jewish nationalism was so intense that during World War II, most Arab leaders were pro-Nazi. Among them was the head of the Muslims in Palestine, the mufti Haj Amin el-Husseini (who in 1929 had helped organize the large-scale murders of the ultra-Orthodox, *non-Zionist* Jews of Hebron).

An ardent supporter of Hitler, the mufti spent much of the war in Nazi Germany; on November 2, 1943, at a time when the Nazis were murdering thousands of Jews daily, the mufti declared in a speech: "The overwhelming egoism which lies in the character of Jews, their unworthy belief that they are God's chosen nation and their assertion that all was created for them and that other peoples are animals . . . [makes them] incapable of being trusted. They cannot mix with any other nation but live as parasites among the nations, suck out their blood, embezzle their property, corrupt their morals. . . . The divine anger and curse that the Holy Koran mentions with reference to the Jews is because of this unique character of the Jews."[29]

Though many Arab nations formally declared war against Germany in 1945, when German defeat was imminent, in order to be eligible for entry into the United Nations, extensive Arab sympathy with

---

*It is this, not the Palestinian refugee issue, that has been the basis of Muslim anti-Zionism. Without minimizing the personal difficulties of the Palestinians, Memmi notes that, for a large percentage of the Palestinian Arabs, their misfortune is having been moved about thirty miles within one vast Arab nation." *Jews and Arabs*, p. 35.

the Nazis continued even after Germany's surrender. The Egyptians and Syrians long welcomed Nazis to their countries, offering them the opportunity to further implement the "Final Solution," by assisting in their efforts to destroy Israel and wipe out the Jewish community living there.[30]

Among many Arabs the Holocaust has come to be regarded with nostalgia. On August 17, 1956, the French newspaper *Le Monde* quoted the government-controlled Damascus daily *Al-Manar* as observing, "One should not forget that, in contrast to Europe, Hitler occupied an honored place in the Arab world. . . . [Journalists] are mistaken if they think that by calling Nasser Hitler, they are hurting us. On the contrary, his name makes us proud. Long live Hitler, the Nazi who struck at the heart of our enemies. Long live the Hitler [i.e., Nasser] of the Arab world."[31]

On June 9, 1960, after Israeli agents captured Adolf Eichmann, the Nazi official who had supervised the murder of six million Jews, the Beirut daily *Al-Anwar* carried a cartoon depicting Eichmann speaking with Israeli Prime Minister David Ben-Gurion. Said Ben-Gurion: "You deserve the death penalty because you killed six million Jews." Responded Eichmann: "There are many who say I deserve the death penalty because I didn't manage to kill the rest."

On April 24, 1961, the Jordanian English-language daily *Jerusalem Times* published an "Open Letter to Eichmann," which concluded: "But be brave, Eichmann, find solace in the fact that this trial will one day culminate in the liquidation of the remaining six million to avenge your blood."[32] At the UN-sponsored "Conference Against Racism" in September 2001, an Arab pamphlet displayed at the Durban Exhibition Center featured a picture of Adolf Hitler with the caption, "If I had won the war there would be no . . . Palestinian blood lost."

Arab Jew-hatred also has brought about the resurrection of the blood libel. In 1962, the Egyptian Ministry of Education reissued *Talmudic Sacrifices* by Habib Faris, a book originally published in Cairo in 1890. The editor notes in his introduction that the book constitutes "an explicit documentation of indictment, based upon clear-cut evidence that the Jewish people permitted the shedding of blood as religious duty enjoined in the Talmud."[33]

On April 24, 1970, Fatah radio, under the leadership of Yasir Arafat, broadcast, "Reports from the captured homeland tell that the Zionist enemy has begun to kidnap small children from the streets. Afterwards the occupying forces take the blood of the children and throw away their empty bodies. The inhabitants of Gaza have seen this with their own eyes."[34]

Even more disturbing, the blood libel accusations have been made by the most prominent figures within the Arab world. In November 1973, the late King Faisal of Saudi Arabia said that it was necessary to understand the Jewish religious obligation to obtain non-Jewish blood in order to comprehend the crimes of Zionism.[35] A decade later, in 1984, the Saudi Arabian delegate to the UN Human Rights Commission Conference on religious tolerance, Marouf al-Dawalibi, told the commission, "The Talmud says that if a Jew does not drink every year the blood of a non-Jewish man, he will be damned for eternity." In *The Matzah of Zion*, a book that has remained in print since its publication in 1983, Mustafa Tlas, the Syrian Defense Minister since 1972, wrote, "The Jew can kill you and take your blood in order to make his Zionist bread." A 2000 article about Tlas's book in *Al-Ahram*, Egypt's largest, and government-controlled, newspaper, reported, "The bestial drive to knead Passover matzahs with the blood of non-Jews is [confirmed] in the records of the Palestinian police where there are many recorded cases of the bodies of Arab children who had disappeared without being found, torn to pieces, without a single drop of blood. The most reasonable explanation is that the blood was taken to be used in matzahs to be devoured during Passover." As one American journalist commented: "If this is 'the most reasonable explanation,' can you imagine an unreasonable one?"[36] The *Al-Ahram* article went on to report that an Egyptian movie company is planning to shoot a multimillion-dollar film version of *The Matzah of Zion*, which will retell, *as truth*, the story of the Damascus blood libel (see pages 104–105).

And still the blood libel goes on. A 2001 cartoon in the Jordanian newspaper *Al-Dustour* depicts an Israeli soldier presenting his mother with a Mother's Day gift of a bottle containing the blood of a Palestinian child. At about the same time (November 2001), Abu Dhabi Television depicted a caricature of Israeli Prime Minister Ariel Sharon preparing to drink a cup of blood taken from a Palestinian. A March 10, 2002, article in Saudi Arabia's *Al-Riyadh*, the government-controlled newspaper, by Dr. Umayma Ahmad Al-Jalahma of King Faisal University, creates a new twist to this ancient libel, claiming that Jews use blood for Purim pastry and not just for Passover matzo: "Let us now examine how the victims' blood is spilled. For this, a needle-studded barrel is used; this is a kind of barrel, about the size of the human body, with extremely sharp needles set in it on all sides. [These needles] pierce the victim's body, from the moment he is placed in the barrel. These needles do the job, and the victim's blood drips from him very slowly. Thus, the victim suffers dreadful torment—torment that affords the Jewish vampires great delight as they carefully monitor every detail of the blood-shedding with pleasure and love that are difficult to comprehend."[37]

Arab Muslims have also reached back to classical themes of Islamic antisemitism to attack the Jews and Israel. Many Arab speakers and publications echo Muhammad's charge in the Koran (5:82) that the Jews are the greatest enemies of humankind. For example, an Egyptian textbook, published in 1966 for use in teachers' seminars, taught that Jews (not only Israelis) are the "monsters of mankind [and] a nation of beasts."[38]

Perhaps the favorite antisemitic publication in the Arab world for over fifty years has been *The Protocols of the Elders of Zion*. In an interview with the editor of the Indian magazine *Blitz*, on October 4, 1958, President Gamal Abdel Nasser of Egypt praised the *Protocols:* "I wonder if you have read a book called 'Protocols of the Learned Elders of Zion.' It is very important that you should read it. I will give you an English copy. It proves clearly, to quote from the Protocols, that 'three hundred Zionists, each of whom knows all the others, govern the fate of the European continents and they elect their successors from their entourage."[39]

The late King Faisal of Saudi Arabia gave copies of the *Protocols* to the guests of his regime. When he presented the *Protocols*, along with an anthology of antisemitic writings, to French journalists who accompanied French Foreign Minister Michel Jobert on his visit to Saudi Arabia in January 1974, "Saudi officials noted that these were the king's favorite books."[40]

Article 32 of the 1988 Palestinian Hamas (the Islamic Resistance Movement) Covenant claims that the Zionist "scheme" for takeover of the Arab world "has been laid out in *The Protocols of the Elders of Zion*, and their present [conduct] is the best proof of what is said there." Hamas literature repeatedly accuses Jews of controlling the world's wealth and its most important media, and using them to promote Jewish and Zionist interests, even of having established the League of Nations in the 1920s "in order to rule the world."[41]

It is perhaps no surprise that, as of 2002, over sixty editions of the *Protocols* are being sold throughout the Arab world, and this libelous "warrant for genocide" is probably more widely distributed today than at any other time in its history. In 2002, the *New York Times*, in a front-page story, reported that a major Egyptian television station was about to launch a forty-one-episode TV series based on the *Protocols* (complete with Jewish villains dressed in black hats, side curls, and beards) to run before and during the Muslim holy month of Ramadan (October 26, 2002).

The Islamic world today, particularly the powerful regime in Iran, and the powerful movement of Islamists, have combined antisemitic motifs from Nazism and medieval Christendom, as well as from its own tradition. This potent combination has made the Arabs the major source of antisemitic publications in the world today. And as in other forms of antisemitism, in the words of Yehoshafat Harkabi, "the evil in the Jews is ascribed not to race or blood, but to their spiritual character and religion."[43] Thus, when Pakistani Islamic terrorists kidnapped *Wall Street Journal* reporter Daniel Pearl in January 2002, they forced Pearl to say, "I am a Jew" (and videotaped him doing so) before slitting his throat.

CONCLUSION

Only through an understanding of the deep theological roots of Muslim antisemitism and an awareness of its continuous history can present-day Muslim hatred of Israel be understood. Only then does one recognize how false are the claims of Israel's enemies that prior to Zionism, Jews and Muslims lived in harmony and that neither Islam nor Muslims have ever harbored Jew-hatred. The creation of the Jewish state in no way created Muslim Jew-hatred; it merely intensified it and gave it a new focus.

So long as the Jews acknowledged their inferior status among Muslims, they were humiliated but allowed to exist. But once the Jews decided to reject their inferior status, to become sovereign after centuries of servitude, and worst of all, to now govern some Muslims in a land where the Jews had so long been governed, their existence was no longer tolerable. Hence the passionate Arab Muslim hatred of Israel and Zionism, a hatred that entirely transcends political antagonisms. Hence the widespread Muslim call within Iran and among Islamists not merely for a military defeat of Israel, but for its annihilation.

Those Muslims and Arabs who claim that the issue is anti-Zionism rather than antisemitism really mean that so long as the Jews adhere to their *dhimmi* status in Arab Muslim nations, their existence as individuals is acceptable. But for a Jew to aspire to equality among Muslims, for a Jew to aspire to a status higher than "humiliation and wretchedness," is to aspire too high.

TEN

Secular Antisemitism: The Enlightenment

OWARD THE END OF THE EIGHTEENTH CENTURY, Christianity's domination of European life and thought was increasingly challenged. Its chief opponents, the men of the Enlightenment, challenged both biblical beliefs and Christian political power.

Not surprisingly, many Jews welcomed the Enlightenment with open arms. Having so long suffered antisemitism from religious groups, many Jews expected the secularization of Europe to lead to a dramatic improvement in their status. The calls for greater human rights and fraternity so eloquently made by leaders of the Enlightenment were welcomed by no one more than the Jews.

The Jews' hopes were far from fully realized, however, for this equality was offered to them as individuals rather than as Jews. Their emancipation usually was made conditional upon their ceasing to identify as a distinct people. The Jews quickly learned that the Enlightenment did not end Jew-hatred; it only changed its target from the God and law (religious) components of Judaism to its peoplehood component.

Most Jews to this day have found Enlightenment (and other secular expressions of) antisemitism most incomprehensible. Most modern Jews, themselves secular, have believed that the demise of religion would

113

lead to the end of antisemitism. Yet the twentieth century, the most secular century in history, was the most antisemitic. A dispassionate look into modern antisemites show as many to be secular as religious, with hatred of the Jews having been planted in large part by the leaders of the Enlightenment.

FRANCE

From the Enlightenment on, in the most universalist hearts there has often been a hostile spot for the Jews. Fittingly it began with Voltaire, the father of the Enlightenment. This man, whose thinking had such a profound impact on eighteenth- and nineteenth-century Europe that the eighteenth century came to be known as the "century of Voltaire," was an antisemite.

Though the Jews numbered fewer than 1 percent of France's population in the second half of the eighteenth century, Voltaire was obsessed with them. In his most important work, *Dictionnaire Philosophique,* 30 of his 118 articles dealt with the Jews, and described them in consistently deprecating ways.[1] As examples, in an article on Abraham, he describes the Jews as "our masters and our enemies . . . whom we detest," and under the entry "Anthrouphagi," Voltaire defines Jews as "the most abominable people in the world." The article "Jew," the longest in the *Dictionnaire,* contains this characteristic assessment: "In short they are a totally ignorant nation who, for many years, have combined contemptible miserliness and the most revolting superstition with a violent hatred of all those nations that have tolerated them. Nevertheless, they should not be burned at the stake."[2] In 1770 Voltaire appended to his entry on Jews that the Jews engage in ritual murder: "your priests have always sacrificed human victims with their sacred hands."

During the German occupation of France in World War II, an antisemitic history teacher at the Sorbonne, Henri Labroue, compiled a 250-page book of Voltaire's anti-Jewish writings.[3]

Contemporary scholars, heirs to many Enlightenment values, have been perplexed by Voltaire's extraordinary hatred of the Jews. How could the rational and tolerant Voltaire be so irrational and illiberal when it came to the Jews? The best-known authority on the Enlightenment, Peter Gay, himself a Jew, while not denying Voltaire's hostility toward the Jews, offered two mitigating explanations for it.[4] First, Voltaire's attacks on the Bible and the Jews were really only a way to attack Christianity: "Voltaire struck at the Jews to strike at Christianity."[5] Second, Voltaire's antisemitism derived from some negative personal experiences with Jews.

Gay's attempts to explain Voltaire's antisemitism do not, however, hold up before the facts.

The first explanation is demonstrably untrue. Its validity rests entirely upon the proposition that for whatever reasons, such as censorship or fear of persecution, Voltaire found it impossible to attack Christianity directly, and therefore attacked Judaism. Although it is true that fears of the censor often caused Voltaire to disguise his anti-Christian critiques by attributing them to others, he nonetheless made his negative attitudes toward Christianity very clear. Evidence for this is amply supplied in Gay's own work, which cites numerous anti-Christian themes developed by Voltaire in the *Dictionnaire:*

The Church has consistently been the implacable enemy of progress, decency, humanity, and rationality.

It has been in the interests of Church officials everywhere to keep people as ignorant and submissive as children.

It is in the interest of Church officials to burn heretics, and to stamp out rational dissent.

It is in the clergy's interest to quibble about meaningless philosophical constructions and waste the time of educated men on ridiculous theological controversies (for example, in "Catechisme du Japonaise" Voltaire ridicules the theological controversies among Christian denominations by portraying schools of cooks disputing over recipes).

For the first time in history, a happy society, based on power over nature, was within human grasp, but Christians were exerting all their efforts to obstruct its realization.[6]

If despite censorship, Voltaire could express such strongly anti-Christian sentiments, why would he need to rely on attacks on Judaism to attack Christianity? One might respond that Voltaire aimed to disprove Christianity by disproving Judaism, since Christianity is based on Judaism. But as true as this may be, it is irrelevant to the issue of Voltaire's antisemitism, since Voltaire did not confine his anti-Jewish attacks to those aspects of Judaism upon which Christianity was based. He repeatedly made it clear that he despised *Jews*.

That attempts to minimize Voltaire's antisemitism are in error is further evidenced by the fact that Voltaire's contemporaries understood his anti-Jewish writings strictly as attacks on Jews. As Arthur Hertzberg, the leading scholar on Voltaire and the Jews, has noted, Voltaire was known by his contemporaries to be an enemy of the Jews, and antisemitic pamphleteers based their arguments against Jewish emancipation on Voltaire's antisemitic ideas.[7]

Gay's second explanation of Voltaire's anti-Jewish writings refers to the oft-commented-upon fact that Voltaire had suffered some severe financial reversals in dealings with Jewish bankers, which constituted in Gay's words, "experiences to which he did not bring his usual keen enlightened spirit."[8]

Here Gay dismissed Voltaire's statements as atypically irrational sentiments. Since the father of the Enlightenment could not possibly be deeply antisemitic, his vitriolic statements about Jews must be considered, at least when it is inconceivable to dismiss them as disguised attacks on Christianity, as atypically emotional and irrational sentiments. It was the Jews' bad luck that Voltaire did not fare well in his financial dealings with some of them. Presumably, had Voltaire had good experiences with Jewish bankers, or equally poor ones with Christians, he would have had more positive opinions about Jews.

Unfortunately for Gay, however, this thesis was specifically denied by Voltaire himself. He insisted that his antisemitism had nothing to do with his financial dealings with some Jews: "I have forgotten about much larger bankruptcies through Christians."[9]

The attempt to deny Voltaire's antisemitism is an exercise in the wishful thinking of fellow enlightened secularists. Voltaire despised the Jews and their religion. In his view, the Jews possessed a vile nature, caused by Judaism and its laws, which in turn reflected the hatred that Jews feel for other people. In fact, Voltaire's antisemitism was so strong that he attacked Judaism even when he agreed with it. His writings on torture in the *Dictionnaire* illustrate this point. Throughout his life Voltaire vigorously opposed institutional torture, such as the church's torture of suspected heretics. Among Jews, torture had always been illegal and unknown. Jewish law not only forbade torture, it rendered it pointless since it did not accept confessions in capital cases, whether voluntary or forced ones. As this had been Jewish law for thousands of years, one would have expected Voltaire to laud the Jewish prohibition of torture, or at the very least omit mention of it. Instead, he used the Jews' opposition to torture as an occasion to mock the Jews' concept of chosenness: "What is very odd is that there is never any mention of torture in the Jewish books. It is truly a pity that so gentle, so honest, so compassionate a nation did not know this means of finding out the truth. The reason for this, in my opinion, is that they did not need it. God always made it known to them as his cherished people. . . . thus torture cannot be in use with them. This was the only thing lacking in the customs of the holy people."[10]

Fundamental to the worldviews of Voltaire and the men of the Enlightenment was admiration for pagan culture. As Voltaire immersed himself in Greco-pagan literature, he became familiar with its anti-Jewish writings and often used them in place of Christian antisemitic arguments. He especially cited pagan claims, with his own embellishments, that the Jews were deadly to the human race, and resurrected the pagan contempt for Judaism's lack of emphasis on physical beauty.[11] Voltaire thus reintroduced the pre-Christian reasons to hate Jews, as well as introducing new Enlightenment ones.

Voltaire's anti-Jewish writings had profoundly negative effects. Hertzberg has documented how Voltaire served as the major link in Western intellectual history between the antisemitism of classical paganism and of the modern age. Voltaire saw himself as Cicero reborn, and "he ruled the Jew to be outside society and to be hopelessly alien even to the future age of enlightened man."[12] Voltaire played a major role in helping develop the idea that the admission ticket for a Jew into Western society was his willingness to stop being a Jew.

Had Voltaire, who has played so preeminent a role in modern intellectual history, been the one Enlightenment figure to have expressed hostility toward the Jew and Judaism, his contribution to modern antisemitism would have been substantial. But he was far from alone. As Hertzberg notes: "Only a few of the men of the Enlightenment were pro-Jewish . . . [the great majority] had their own Enlightenment reasons for regarding Jews as no more within the pale of culture than the ancient Romans regarded slaves to be when they talked of the rights of men in civilized society."[13]

Jean-Baptiste de Mirabaud (1675–1760), the permanent secretary of the Académie Française, the "immortals of France," and a noted writer of antireligious works, contended that the universality of antisemitism proved that the Jews deserve to be hated: "Not only did all the nations despise the Jew; they even hated them and believed that they were as justified in hating as in despising them. They were hated because they were known to hate other men; they were despised because they were seen observing customs which were thought ridiculous."[14]

Paul Henri Dietrich d'Holbach, a German baron in Paris who gave biweekly "philosophical dinners" attended by leading Enlightenment figures, published more than fifty atheist and materialist works between 1760 and 1765.[15] His publications on the Jews were among the most venomous anti-Jewish writings of the eighteenth century. He particularly emphasized the theme of Jews as enemies of humankind: "It must in fact be admitted that even while they perished the Jews were well avenged on the Romans, their conquerors. From the ruins of their country, a fanatic sect emerged which gradually polluted the whole Empire." We here encounter the theme, later expanded by nineteenth- and twentieth-century racists, of Jews as "polluters" of the world.

Because d'Holbach was not a racial antisemite, he attributed the evil of Jews only to Judaism: "If, as cannot be doubted, honest and virtuous people can be found among them, it is because they do not conform to the principles of a law which is obviously calculated to make men unsociable and maleficent, an effect which the Bible and the saints it holds up as models must have produced."

Hertzberg has shown that virtually every major figure of the French Enlightenment was hostile to Judaism. Even those who fought for the

legal emancipation of the individual Jew and battled against antisemitism wished to see the Jews disappear through assimilation. Thus,
Montesquieu in his essay *The Spirit of Laws*, powerfully denounced
Christian antisemitism by condemning the Portuguese Inquisition
through the mouth of a persecuted Jew: "You put us to death, who
believe only what you believe, because we do not believe all that you
believe. We follow a religion, which you yourselves know to have been
formerly dear to God. We think that God loves it still, and you think
that he loves it no more; and because you judge this, you make those
suffer by sword and fire, who hold an error so pardonable as to believe
that God loves what he once loved."[16] In the very same essay, however,
Montesquieu dismissed Judaism as a religion of ignorance, and called
upon the Jews to cease being Jews and become Enlightened men and
philosophers.

GERMANY

In Germany the situation was basically the same as in France. With the
exception of the philo-semite Gotthold Lessing, leaders of the German
Enlightenment were divided between those who favored granting civil
rights to assimilated Jews and those who opposed civil rights for any
Jews.

An example of the latter was Johann Fichte, who pointed to Jewish
values as the source of his antisemitism. "Give them civil rights?" asked
Fichte in a book published in 1793. "I see no other way of doing this
except to cut off all their heads one night and substitute other heads
without a single Jewish thought in them. How shall we defend ourselves against them? I see no alternative but to conquer their promised
land for them and to dispatch them all there. If they were granted civil
rights they would trample on other citizens."[17] Reading Fichte's fears of
the Jews' danger to Germany, one must recall that Jews numbered only
about 1 percent of Germany's population.

But most important is to understand the link between Fichte's
thinking and Hitler's racial antisemitism. Fichte helped paved the intellectual way to Hitler by theorizing that Jews are unchangeable, inassim-

ilable, and incapable of conversion. That is why the only way to solve the "Jewish Problem" is to "cut off all their heads," since those heads hold all those Jewish thoughts. Thus, for Fichte and, as we shall see, for Hitler, it is Jewish thoughts, not Jewish genes, that make the Jews irredeemably Jewish.

Even Immanuel Kant, the most influential German thinker of the eighteenth century, though never advocating the persecution of Jews, called for the end of Judaism and its laws: "The euthanasia of Judaism can only be achieved by means of a pure, moral religion, and the abandonment of all [its] old legal regulations."[18]

ENGLAND

The one major, if partial, exception to the antisemitism of the Enlightenment took place in England. There, as early as 1689, John Locke had written the first of his four *Letters on Toleration*, stating that "Neither pagan nor Mohametan [*sic*] nor Jew ought to be excluded from the civil rights in the commonwealth because of his religion."[19] Well before the French Enlightenment, Locke had formulated a theory of religious tolerance, though no state yet practiced it. Among those who shared Locke's tolerant views was the deist John Toland, who in 1714 published a pamphlet, *Reasons for Naturalizing the Jews in Great Britain and Ireland*.

On the other hand, it would be an error to characterize the men of the English Enlightenment as particularly sympathetic to the Jews or Judaism. The dominant philosophy of the English Enlightenment, deism, held that knowledge of God's existence and belief in an immortal soul were sufficient to prompt moral behavior. Deists rejected religions based on revelation, such as Judaism, and vigorously attacked Judaism for, among other things, introducing this idea to the West. They downplayed the significance of the Bible and particularly the special role it assigned the Jews. The early-seventeenth-century deists Herbert of Cherbury and John Spencer contended that Jewish ideas were copied from the Egyptians. The eighteenth-century writer Anthony Collins argued that Greek wisdom was superior to Jewish wisdom, the Jews being "an illiterate, barbarous and ridiculous people." Matthew Tindal, in a similar vein, contrasted natural religion with Jewish "barbarism." The attacks of English deists on the Bible were important sources for Voltaire's similar attacks.[20]

Since most Jews continued to believe in the Bible and to follow its tenets, they were consequently perceived by many men of the English Enlightenment as acting "barbarously." Thus, in England, as on the Continent, for a Jew to be accepted in enlightened society, he had "to disassociate himself explicitly from the Jews, disavow his despised Jewish past and even condemn it."[21]

CONCLUSION

No violence accompanied Enlightenment antisemitism. As befits enlightened men and women, no violence against the Jew could be tolerated, let alone called for. But Enlightenment opposition to Judaism and its particularism (that is, Jewish peoplehood) helped to lay the philosophic basis for antisemitism in the modern secular world. The Jew as Jew continued to have few friends.

Antisemitism now became even more broadly based, rooted now in Christianity, secular humanism, and nationalism—the new European faith that developed in the eighteenth and nineteenth centuries alongside or instead of Christianity. The manifestation of any of Judaism's components now had religious, secular, and nationalistic opponents. By the twentieth century virtually every popular ideology in Europe wanted the Jews, as a distinctive people that preserved its religion, to disappear.

ELEVEN

Leftist Antisemitism

M ARXISM AND SOCIALISM, LIKE CHRISTIANITY, Islam, nationalism, and the Enlightenment, were born with Jew-hatred.
Their two main ideological sources, Marx and the early French
socialists, developed antisemitic ideas that have characterized much of
the Left to this day.

KARL MARX

The father of Marxist ideologies, Karl Marx, was born in the German
city of Trier in 1818. Though descended on both parents' sides from a
long line of distinguished rabbis, Marx was baptized a Lutheran when he
was six years old. His father, who had converted to Christianity before
Karl's birth in order to continue practicing law (forbidden to Jews by
new Prussian laws), baptized his children so that they would not suffer
from antisemitism. It was into this self-denying, antisemitic world that
Karl Marx was born.[1]

Given this background, it is not surprising that one of Marx's first
major essays was *On the Jewish Question*. He ostensibly wrote the piece
as a response to the philosopher Bruno Bauer's article, "The Jewish

Question," in which Bauer virulently attacked the Jews and Judaism, and argued against emancipation for the Jews until they abandon their "exclusive religion, morality and customs."[2]

Marx, though critical of Bauer's conclusions, not only did not question Bauer's antisemitism, he actually outdid Bauer in antisemitic vituperation. He criticized Bauer for primarily attacking religious Jews, when all who identify as Jews should be attacked: "Not only in the Pentateuch [Torah] and in the Talmud, but also in present-day society we find the essence of the modern Jew."[3] As the historian Robert Wistrich notes, "Marx's hatred was therefore focused not [only] against Bruno Bauer's 'Sabbath-Jew' but rather against contemporary Jewry."[4]

On the Jewish Question is filled with a hatred of Jews and Judaism so extreme that at times it sinks to Nazi-like Jew-hatred: "What is the secular cult of the Jew? *Haggling*. What is his secular god? *Money*. Well then! Emancipation from *haggling* and *money*, from practical, real Judaism would be the self-emancipation of our time."[5] "Money is the jealous God of Israel, beside which no other God may stand."[6]

In the closing passages of *On the Jewish Question*, Marx goes so far as to identify the emancipation of humanity with the abolition of Judaism.[7]

The stark antisemitism of *On the Jewish Question* has always proved an embarrassment to Jewish socialists who retained a Jewish identity. For over a hundred years after its writing, Jewish socialists, who translated almost all of Marx's writings into Yiddish and Hebrew, refrained from translating Marx's only essay devoted exclusively to the Jewish question.

Other Marxists, however, have been only too pleased to translate and learn from Marx's Jew-hating essay. In 1963, for example, the Ukrainian Academy of Sciences, then under Communist rule, published *Judaism Without Embellishment* by Trofim K. Kichko, who liberally quoted from *On the Jewish Question*. The book was so antisemitic that international protests forced the Soviet government to withdraw it from circulation.

Adolf Hitler, too, claimed to have learned from Marx's essay: "It is quite enough that the scientific knowledge of the danger of Judaism is gradually deepened and that every individual on the basis of this knowledge begins to eliminate the Jew within himself, and I am very much afraid that this beautiful thought originates from none other than a Jew."[8]

Nor was the Jew-hatred in *On the Jewish Question* an exception to Marx's views on the Jews. His subsequent writings about Jews, even working-class ones, remained uniformly contemptuous. For example, Marx described the impoverished Jewish refugees from Poland in Germany as "this filthiest of all races, [who] only perhaps by its passion for greedy gain could be related to [the Jewish capitalists of] Frankfort." The April 29, 1849, issue of *Neue Rheinische Zeitung*, which Marx then edited, accused Polish Jews of robbing churches, burning villages, and beating defenseless Poles to death—charges that were "outrageous slanders against a people who lived in daily dread of the very crimes they were accused of."[9]

A contemporary reader of Marx would conclude that wealthy capitalist Jews destroy society and that poorer Jews are too uncivilized to enter it.

Marx even dredged up the ancient libel of Manetho, who had described the Jews' exodus from Egypt as "the expulsion of a 'people of lepers' headed by an Egyptian priest named Moses."[10] And in the 1850s, Marx ridiculed those who fought for the right of Baron Lionel Rothschild to take the seat that he had won in the British House of Commons: "It is doubtful whether the British people will be very much pleased by extending electoral rights to a Jewish usurer."[11]

In keeping with his policy of antagonism toward both rich and poor Jews, Marx ignored the plight of Jewish workers, though they lived near him in London. Likewise, he never commented on the pogroms that swept through Russia in 1881, though he often wrote on behalf of victims of oppression. Throughout his life, Marx identified Jews and Judaism with all that he hated in capitalism.[12]

The historian Edmund Silberner has noted two negative influences of Marx's anti-Jewish writings. They provoked and strengthened anti-Jewish prejudices among Christian Marxists, and they alienated Jewish Marxists from the Jewish people.[13] The latter was evidenced most dramatically in 1891, when Abraham Cahan, later the editor of the Yiddish *Forward* but then a delegate to the Second Socialist International in Brussels, urged that body to condemn Europe's increasing antisemitism. To Cahan's shock, *both the Jewish and non-Jewish delegates opposed a resolution condemning antisemitism.* According to the socialists, the one answer to antisemitism was for all Jews to cease being Jews and to adopt the antisemites' (in this case, a socialist) identity. Thus, the final resolution of the Second International condemned "anti-Semitic and philo-Semitic [i.e., Jewish] outbursts as one of the means by which the capitalist class and reactionary governments seek to divert the socialist movement and divide the workers."[14] The socialists thereby nullified opposition to antisemitism by equating it with Judaism, and by seeing both as enemies of socialism.

THE FRENCH SOCIALISTS

Had socialist antisemitism been promulgated on the Left only by Karl Marx and his followers, it would have caused serious problems for Jews. But the other founders of socialism, the French socialists, were even more anti-Jewish than Marx.

George Lichtheim, one of the foremost twentieth-century historians of socialism, has emphasized the relevance of French socialism to subsequent leftist antisemitism, since France "was the cradle of the socialist movement where socialism developed a full generation before it developed in Germany."[15] Lichtheim documented how from its beginning in the early 1800s, French socialism was hostile to Jews.

Charles Fourier, one of the two founders of French socialism, regarded the Jews as "parasites, merchants, usurers," whose emancipation he termed "the most shameful of all recent vices of society."[16]

Henri de Saint-Simon, the other founder of French socialism, was sympathetic to Jews, acknowledging that the socialist mission was a form of messianism derived from them. Unfortunately, as Lichtheim documents, in the French socialist community the antisemitism of Fourier triumphed over the philo-semitism of Saint-Simon.

In the decades after Fourier and Saint-Simon, strong anti-Jewish

views were expressed by three leading French socialists: Alphonse Toussenel, Pierre Leroux, and Pierre Joseph Proudhon.

In 1845, Toussenel published *Les Juifs, rois de l'époque* (*The Jews:
Kings of the Epoch*), which was favorably reviewed by much of the socialist press. In this essay he developed the theme of "the cosmopolitan
Jew. . . . Europe is subject to the domination of Israel. This universal
domination, of which so many conquerors have dreamed, the Jews have
in their hands."[17] Similar ideas were later expressed by Proudhon. The
belief in Jewish world domination was spread during the twentieth century through *The Protocols of the Elders of Zion*, and used by the Nazis
as a justification for genocide. This mythical worldview was first introduced into the West's consciousness not by racists, Fascists, or Nazis,
but rather by socialists in nineteenth-century France.

Pierre Leroux, creator of the term "socialism," identified the Jews
with the despised capitalism, and regarded them as the incarnation of
mammon, who lived by exploiting others. Leroux, a religious Christian,
saw but one solution to the "Jewish Problem"—the conversion of all
Jews to Christianity.[18]

Pierre Joseph Proudhon, one of the most important theorists of
early socialism, expressed his antisemitism in his public writings in a
"moderate" manner, and in a more extreme form in his journals, which
were published posthumously.

In the journals of this great socialist, we find Nazi-like sentiments
regarding the Jews. In December 1847, he outlined a program for the
disappearance of Jewry: "This race poisons everything by meddling
everywhere without ever joining itself to another people. Demand their
expulsion from France, with the exception of individuals married to
Frenchwomen. Abolish the synagogues: don't admit them to any kind
of employment, pursue finally the abolition of this cult. . . . The Jew is
the enemy of the human race. One must send this race back to Asia or
exterminate it. . . . By fire or fusion or by expulsion, the Jew must disappear. . . . What the peoples of the middle ages hated by instinct I hate
upon reflection, and irrevocably."[19]

It is no wonder that Proudhon's disciples justified the Russian pogroms. As Lichtheim notes: "Four years after [Proudhon's] death, in 1869, his pupil George Duchene . . . [declared]: 'Citizens, when you hear it said that in a notoriously barbarous country [Russia] the population treats the Jews roughly, do not believe one treacherous word. What you have is simply a case of honest people chasing rascals, usurers, and exploiters of labor."[20]

Against this backdrop, the indifference of socialists to the fate of Alfred Dreyfus, the Jewish army officer falsely accused by the French government of having spied for Germany, becomes explicable. One might have expected that French socialists, who were hostile toward the government, church, and military (all three of which led the attack on Dreyfus), would have risen to his defense. But Dreyfus was a Jew. For this reason alone, the French socialist press (January 28, 1898) published a manifesto calling for "non-participation in the Dreyfus Affair on the grounds that while the reaction wishes to exploit the conviction of one Jew to disqualify all Jews, Jewish capitalists would use the rehabilitation of a single Jew to wash out 'all the sins of Israel.'"

Among the manifesto's signatories were the leading socialists of the age, including Alexandre Millerand, Marcel Sembat, Jules Guesde, and Jean Jaurès.[21] When the socialists did subsequently take a stand on the Dreyfus case, they made a point of declaring that the Jewish aspect of the antisemitic affair was irrelevant.

Thus, the French socialists, with the exception of Saint-Simon and a very few others, propounded antisemitism from the beginning. In 1947, the historian Zosa Szajkowski concluded his painstakingly researched article, "The Jewish Saint-Simonians and Socialist Anti-Semitism in France," by noting that try as he might, he could not find a single word on behalf of Jews in the whole of French socialist literature from 1820 to 1920.[22]

COMMUNISM AND THE JEWS IN THE TWENTIETH CENTURY

In the more than one hundred years since Marx and the French socialists, there have been some other socialist responses to the Jews. Social

Democrats, for example, have been among the strongest supporters of Jewish rights in the world. Between 1948 and 1977, Israel itself was governed by the Labor Party, which was founded on socialist principles.

But the further Left one goes, the greater the antisemitism. Wherever Marxists have come to power they have initiated government-supported antisemitism. Before the fall of communism in 1989–91, the Soviet Union and the countries of Eastern Europe expressed antisemitism against native Jews and supported those seeking to destroy Israel. And Third World Marxist countries in which no Jews live (such as China and Vietnam) also have supported groups seeking to destroy Israel and deny Jewish national rights.[23] For example, China voted for the 1975 UN resolution delegitimizing Israel by equating Zionism with racism. Leftists in democratic societies also generally oppose Israel, Zionism, and Jewish nationalism.

Soviet Antisemitism

From its inception in 1917, the Soviet Union was implacably hostile toward Jewish religious and national expressions. As early as 1919 Zionism was designated a counterrevolutionary movement and prohibited.[24]

The Soviet Union's campaign to destroy the Jewish religion in the country was largely successful. Between 1956 and 1965 the number of synagogues in the USSR declined from an already very low 450 to 60. By the 1980s, there were fewer than five rabbis for the more than two million Soviet Jews. In many parts of the Soviet Union it was illegal for a male to pray in a synagogue until he had completed military service, and Soviet Jews were forbidden to take classes in Judaism or even the Hebrew language.

The only permitted books on Judaism were those printed by party-controlled publishers, and they depicted Judaism as a vulgar and immoral anachronism. Characteristic of the material about Judaism legally available in the Soviet Union was this perspective in Trofim Kichko's *Judaism and Zionism* (Kiev, 1968): "The chauvinistic idea of the god-chosenness of the Jewish people . . . the idea of ruling over the peoples of the world. . . . Such ideas of Judaism were inculcated into the Jews first by priests and later by the Rabbis . . . and are inculcated today by Zionists, educating the Jews in the spirit of contempt and hatred towards other people. . . . The ideologists of Judaism, through the 'Holy Scriptures' teach the observant Jew to hate people of another faith and even to destroy them."[25]

While the government published and disseminated such antisemitic material, the Jewish community was forbidden to operate a single Jewish school, let alone publish pro-Jewish books. The government's attempt to annihilate Judaism was almost without precedent in Jewish history. Christian and Muslim antisemites, and for that matter even the Nazis during the 1930s, permitted Jewish schools. Because of the Soviet Communists' prohibition of Jewish education, Soviet Jews became the Judaically most ignorant Jews in history, until the renaissance of Jewish life that began in the former Soviet Union with the fall of communism in 1991.

Having succeeded in stifling the ideological (i.e., God-related) and legal components of Judaism, Soviet antisemitism subsequently focused most of its attacks on Jewish nationalism. The *Great Soviet Encyclopedia* of 1952 defined "Zionism" as "a reactionary movement . . . which denies the class struggle and strives to isolate the Jewish working masses from the general struggle of the proletariat."

The Soviets attempted to destroy the Jewish national identity in a variety of ways. For example, well before neo-Nazi "historical revisionists" arose to deny the Holocaust, Soviet books and films on World War II ignored, virtually to the point of denying, the Holocaust. To cite a typical instance, in a forty-minute Russian-language film shown to Soviet visitors to Auschwitz, Poland, where over a million and a half Jews were murdered, the Jews were not mentioned.[26]

To obliterate Jewish nationalism, Soviet propaganda went one step further and charged that Zionists worked with the Nazis. In 1979, a Soviet art exhibit "featured a grotesque painting of Russian corpses being gloated over by a grinning Nazi soldier and a grinning Jewish prisoner wearing a Star of David. The message: Nazis and Jews were collaborators."[27] Thus, the Soviets not only denied (by omission) the Holocaust, they also used Nazi atrocities to increase antisemitism in the Soviet Union by identifying Zionism with Nazism.

After the Six-Day War in 1967, Soviet media constantly referred to the Jewish state as a Hitlerian state. The tone for this campaign was set by the Soviet president and general secretary of the Communist Party, Leonid Brezhnev, on July 5, 1967: "In their atrocities against the Arabs it seems they [the Israelis] want to copy the crimes of the Hitler invaders."[28]

Two years later, Yuri Ivanov published *Beware Zionism,* which was hailed by *Komsomolskaya Pravda* as "the first scientific and fundamental work on this subject." In this book, Ivanov described Zionism as an ideological offshoot of Nazism.

Both of the authors visited the Soviet Union (Dennis Prager, 1969, 1981, 1990; Joseph Telushkin, 1973) and personally witnessed its antisemitism. When Prager was asked to smuggle out material by Russian Jews detailing governmental antisemitism, he asked one writer, Tina Brodetskaya, "If these letters are published in the West, won't you be sent to prison?" "Where do you think I am now?" she responded.

In 1973, Telushkin danced with Russian Jews in front of the largest Moscow synagogue on Simchat Torah, a joyous Jewish holiday. The dancing was violently stopped by the KGB, the Soviet secret police. A Russian Jew, Dmitri Ramm, who had accompanied Telushkin to the synagogue, was beaten and his leg was fractured.

Both of us met Soviet Jews who had served long prison terms *solely* for seeking to learn about Judaism and/or for desiring to emigrate to Israel. In one noted case, Joseph Begun, a Jewish mathematician who taught an underground Hebrew class, was fired from his job, then convicted for not working and exiled to Siberia. (Begun later emigrated to Israel and, in sweet irony, later taught at a Jewish summer camp outside Moscow, which had formerly been a KGB center. The irony goes deeper: at this camp, KGB officers had plotted the failed putsch against President Mikhail Gorbachev. When Begun told this story in 1999, he noted that one KGB officer was then languishing in the very prison cell Begun had once occupied.)

Government-inspired antisemitism, coupled with renewed Jewish pride after the Six-Day War, led to a large migration of Soviet Jews, many of whom risked their lives to emigrate. Others did not succeed.

In Novosibirsk, Siberia, in 1973, Telushkin met a local Jew, Dr. Isaac Poltinnikov, who had been without work and, along with his wife, Irma, and daughter, Victoria, had been terribly harassed for the three years since he and his family had applied for a visa to Israel. Finally, in 1979, after nine years of refusals, the Poltinnikovs were given permission to emigrate. But Irma Poltinnikov and Victoria, believing it was just a KGB trick, refused to go (on previous occasions the KGB had arrested them, subjected them to long interrogations, and killed their dog). Dr. Poltinnikov did go, and flew to Israel. The Soviets then refused Mrs. Poltinnikov and Victoria permission to join him. Irma soon thereafter died of malnutrition, and Victoria then committed suicide.

In Eastern Europe, Communist antisemitism persisted even though few Jews remained there following the Holocaust. For example, in the early 1950s, thirteen leaders of the Czech Communist Party, ten of them Jews, were accused of being "Zionist agents" and hanged. These trials were ordered as one of a series of antisemitic show trials culminating in 1953 with Stalin's "Doctors' Plot," as mentioned above. Stalin charged a group of physicians, mostly Jews, with plotting to poison the Soviet leadership. He died before the trial, but it was subsequently revealed that he was preparing to use the Doctors' Plot as a pretext to expel over two million Jews to Siberia.

In 1968, Poland's media were dominated by "the unmasking of Zionists in Poland," though *fewer than one out of every fifteen hundred* Poles was Jewish.

Aside from the Soviet Union and Eastern Europe, few Jews lived in Communist-ruled societies. Yet Leftist anti-Jewish hostility remained a worldwide phenomenon. The most serious antisemitic act of the 1970s, the UN General Assembly resolution declaring Zionism to be racism, was the product of an Arab, Muslim, and Communist alliance. Whereas almost the only countries opposing the resolution were democracies, every Communist government in the world (with the exception of Romania, which absented itself from the vote) declared the Jews' national movement racist and therefore illegitimate. The idea for the resolution was originally the Soviets', and among the resolution's sponsors was Cuba.[29]

WESTERN LEFTISTS

The Left in the West is also almost uniformly hostile to Jews and Judaism, and the further Left one is on the political spectrum the more intense is the antisemitism. In the United States, for example, the Socialist Workers Party argued that "the major task confronting American revolutionaries [as regards the Middle East] remains that of educating the radicalizing youth . . . for destruction of the state of Israel."[30] In 1972, the party's paper, *The Militant*, criticized the Palestinian terrorists' murder of eleven Israeli athletes at the Munich Olympics, but only on the grounds that it made "the criminal look like the victim."[31] The Communist Party U.S.A. differed from the Socialist Workers Party in that it conceded Israel's right to exist. But typical of its view of Zionism is this statement in the party's journal by Hyman Lumer, the party's theoretician on the Middle East: "Zionism is . . . in its very essence a racist ideology. It sets the Jewish people apart as a special people, a 'chosen' people—if you will, a superior people. In Israel, the Zionist rulers have created a racist state."[32]

Similar denunciations of Jewish nationalism were made by other Communist parties in the West. Individuals on the revolutionary Left were even more aggressive. Vanessa Redgrave, for example, the Academy Award–winning actress and a member of the Central Committee of the British Workers' Revolutionary Party (a Trotskyite Communist organization) made a propaganda film for the PLO in the late 1970s, at a time when the PLO was officially committed to Israel's destruction. In it, Redgrave performed a sensuous dance with a PLO machine gun. Under the guise of only attacking Zionists and Zionism (the film uses the Arabic word for Jew, *Yahud*, but the English subtitles speak of "Zionists"), the movie utilizes some classic Jew-hating images. In one scene Redgrave asks a young Arab girl, "What would you do if he [a

Jewish soldier] tried to kill you?" Marie Syrkin, in a critique of the film, wrote: "At this point my mind wandered to the prioress of *The Canterbury Tales* who devoutly recounts a medieval tale of a Christian child murdered by the Jews. The killing of children: the hoariest of antisemitic libels."[33]

The non-Communist far Left was similarly single-minded in its attacks on Israel and the Jews who identify with it. For example, during the 1970s the left-wing National Lawyers Guild sent a delegation to only one country in the world to examine human rights—Israel. The delegation met with PLO representatives, heard their story, and returned with a report denouncing Israel. A Jewish lawyer in the group wrote a dissenting report, but the National Lawyers Guild suppressed it.[34]

At the Harvard Law School in 1979, leftist Third World students sponsored a conference on "Human Rights in the Third World." Harvard law professor Alan Dershowitz reported that, "At that time, there were massacres in the Central African Republic, the blood of people killed by Idi Amin was still fresh in people's minds, and the atrocious record of Libya on human rights could well have been discussed. But only one item concerning human rights was placed on the agenda: 'The So-Called Nation of Israel's Terrorism and Genocide.'"[35]

The title of the Harvard leftists' program on Israel exemplifies two characteristics of contemporary left-wing antisemitism: (1) the denial of Jewish nationhood, hence the appellation "the so-called nation of Israel," and (2) the constant accusation of genocide against the Jewish state. The charges are related in an Orwellian manner. The denial of Jewish nationhood legitimates all efforts at annihilating the Jewish state and Zionists, what may truly be called genocide. But this genocidal attempt against Israel is then inverted and projected from the enemies of Israel onto Israel itself.

Thus it is not coincidental that on one issue, the annihilation of Israel, the far Left and neo-Nazis agree. On April 14, 1970, the *New York Times* reported that the radical black power leader Stokely Carmichael declared: "I have never admired a White man, but the greatest of them, to my mind, was Hitler." In Chicago in October 1970, a speech by Israel's foreign minister, Abba Eban, was picketed by the far Left Youth Against War and Fascism and by the American Nazi Party.

Leftist antisemitism has also deeply infected left-wing Christians. Among Protestant groups, the World Council of Churches and affiliates such as the (U.S.) National Council of Churches were among the major advocates of recognizing the Palestine Liberation Organization, even though, at the time, the PLO was committed to the destruction of Israel and was the world's leading supporter of terrorism against Western democracies. Similar support was offered by the American Friends Services Committee, which represents American Quakers.

In 1976, the *Christian Science Monitor* was the only one of the fifty major newspapers in the United States to condemn Israel's raid on Entebbe, Uganda's main airport, where PLO terrorists were preparing to murder Jewish passengers on a hijacked plane.

The same situation holds for the Catholic Church, wherein Leftist theologians, clergy, and lay leaders with Third World orientations have combined traditional church resentment of the "old Israel" with the Left's resentment of the new Israel. One such leader was Archbishop Hilarian Capucci, formerly of Jerusalem. On August 18, 1974, Israeli police caught Capucci smuggling weapons and explosives for terrorists to kill Israeli civilians. Though Israel sentenced him to twelve years in prison, it released him after fewer than three years at the personal request of Pope Paul VI.

Upon his release, Capucci declared: "Jesus Christ was the first *fedayeen* [Arab freedom fighter]. I am just following his example." A short time thereafter, he celebrated a Mass "in protest against the genocide perpetrated against the Arab people." A Catholic journal, *Resumen*, responded to Capucci's activities with a denunciation of his "propaganda pamphlets which revive the myths which make Capucci a Jesus and the Israelis deicidal mercenaries." In January 1979 Archbishop Capucci attended meetings in Damascus of the Palestine National Council, the supreme authority of the PLO, which had earlier made him an honorary member.[36] Twenty-three years later, in 2002, Capucci repeatedly and publicly spoke up in favor of Palestinian suicide bombings directed against Israeli civilians (for more examples of left-wing support for terrorism directed against Israeli civilians, see pages 172–174).

Whereas in the past, Christian attitudes toward Jews were almost uniformly hostile, today such hostility emanates almost exclusively from Christianity's far Right and Left. On the other hand, moderate and conservative Christians in the United States are among the most aggressive supporters of Jewry and Israel's right to exist.

CONCLUSION

The Left has opposed Jews both for their religion and for their nationality. The Jewish fusion of religion and nationality is anathema to both the secularism and the universalism of the Left. This partially explains why the Left, though so hospitable and supportive of the national liberation movements of almost all other peoples, is so antagonistic to the nationalism of the Jews. It was regarding this Leftist hatred of the Jews that Social Democrat Irving Howe wrote, "In the warmest of hearts there is a cold spot for the Jews."

From Marx and the French socialists to the Soviets, the Third World, and Western leftists today, an intense Jew-hatred has prevailed. As the late Senator Daniel Patrick Moynihan said, "Antisemitism has become a unifying global ideology of the totalitarian Left."[37] And many on the nontotalitarian Left have been compromised by their "no enemies on the Left" attitude. Thus a movement founded, established, and supported in large part by Jews has come to constitute, along with the Arab/Muslim world, the Jews' greatest enemy at this time.

TWELVE
Nazi Antisemitism

PERHAPS NO UNDERSTANDING OF AN ANTISEMITIC IDEOLOGY is so widely held and unchallenged as that which ascribes Nazi antisemitism to racism. The Nazis, so the belief goes, were racists and therefore hated Jews and all other "non-Aryans."

History and reason, however, point to a very different understanding of Nazi antisemitism. The Nazis were indeed racists when they claimed the inferiority of "non-Aryan races" (though who was "non-Aryan" had little to do with race, and much to do with politics—they did not, for example, racially denigrate Japanese or Arabs, both Nazi allies). But Nazi antisemitism was not an outgrowth of racist ideology. Racism was fundamentally irrelevant to Nazi antisemitism. Attempts to subsume Nazi antisemitism under the heading of racism is another mistaken endeavor to dejudaize Jew-hatred.

The commonly accepted view of Nazi antisemitism as an expression of racism must be questioned on two scores. First, and most basic, why did the Nazis label the Jews a race? There are Jews of every race, and since anyone of any race can become a Jew, Jews can hardly constitute a race. The entire racial claim, therefore, needs explanation. Why did the Nazis need it? After all, thousands of years of pre-Nazi antisemites needed no racial basis to hate the Jews.

Second, if racism was the basis of the Nazis' worldview, why did their hatred focus on the Jews to the virtual exclusion of all other "races"—including the Gypsies, who though murdered en masse were, quite unlike the Jews, incidental to the Nazi worldview and not the objects of genocide?[1] And if race was the issue, why did the Nazis show such fondness for that other Semitic "race," the Arabs?

In holding the simplistic view that the Nazis hated Jews because of racism, we once again commit the fundamental error (wishful thinking?) of other modern explanations of antisemitism: we dejudaize it. In this instance it seems perfectly logical to do so: the Nazis hated "non-Aryans"; the Jews were "non-Aryans"; therefore, the Nazis hated the Jews. Yet, the Jews were the only "non-Aryans" whom the Nazis attempted to annihilate, and antisemitism, not anti–non-Aryanism, was the essence of Nazism.

It was not because of racism that Nazis hated Jews but rather because of their hatred of Jews that the Nazis utilized racist arguments. The Jew-hatred came first. A racial basis for Jew-hatred was needed to explain the one new belief of Nazi antisemitism. Whereas former antisemites believed that a Jew could change and become like them, Hitler and other Nazis denied this possibility. Once a Jew, always a Jew. As Hitler wrote in *Mein Kampf,* "In his new language [the Jew] will express the old ideas; his inner nature has not changed . . . the Jew . . . can speak a thousand languages and nevertheless remains a Jew. His traits of character have remained the same. . . . It is always the same Jew."[2] According to Hitler, the Jews seek to dominate the non-Jewish world through various instruments: Christianity, Marxism, socialism, capitalism, democracy. All are products of Jews and their values, no matter what their non-Jewish guises are.

Hitler viewed himself as insightful and courageous enough to conclude what previous antisemites had either not realized or shirked from concluding. A Jew cannot become a non-Jew any more than a black man can become white; the Jews' permanent "traits of character" render them a "race." Therefore any campaign directed against Jews must be directed against all of them no matter what non-Jewish religious or national identity they hold. Their non-Jewish identity is irrelevant; they remain Jews because they have fixed characteristics that only members of a race possess. These fixed characteristics are alien Jewish ideas.

Nazi antisemitism was before all else hatred of the Jewish character, not hatred of the Jews' "non-Aryan" blood. It was, like all other forms of antisemitism, hatred of the challenges posed by Jews and Jewish values. This Jewish challenge formed the basis of Nazi beliefs that humankind's ultimate conflict is between the Jews and the Aryans, and that only one of them could survive.

By Hitler's own account in *Mein Kampf,* he was first an antisemite, not a racist. His innovation was to amalgamate the two and develop a new program to solve the "Jewish Problem" once and for all. Only racial antisemitism could correctly understand and deal with the Jewish Problem. All other forms of antisemitism were in error. Prior to racial antisemitism, antisemites had assumed that Jews who abandoned Judaism and adopted the antisemites' values and identity could fully assimilate and become non-Jews. Antisemitic Christians believed that Jews could really become Christians; the secular nationalists expected the Jews to abandon their national identity and identify only with the nation in which they lived; and the Left demanded that Jews give up their particularism and become universalists.

To Hitler, however, all attempts to solve the Jewish Problem through conversion or assimilation were futile. No matter what new identity a Jew might assume, he carries subversive Jewish values with him and merely uses his new guise as a Christian, or Marxist, or German to spread his values. As Hitler put it, "the Jews speak German, but they think Jewish."

Apparently no Nazi ever stopped to question how a race could be defined by something as unbiological as ideas and traits of character.*

---

*Hitler himself is reported as having told his intimate associate, Hermann Rausch-ning: "I know perfectly well that in the scientific sense there is no such thing as a race. As a politician I need a conception which enables the order which has hitherto existed on a historic basis to be abolished and an entirely new order enforced and given

Yet this notion typified Nazi thinking about the Jews. On August 23, 1936, SS-Oberscharführer Schröder, Eichmann's superior at the time, issued a statement typical of Nazi thinking: "Wherever [the Jew] tries to transmit his work, his influence and his world outlook to the non-Jewish world, he discharges it in hostile ideologies, as we find in Liberalism . . . in Marxism, and not least in Christianity. These ideologies then accord with a broader concept of the Jewish mentality."[3]

To cite one other example: *Schwarze Korps*, the official publication of the SS, reported in its May 15, 1935, issue: "The assimilationist minded Jews deny their race, and insist on their loyalty to Germany or claim to be Christians, because they have been baptized, in order to subvert National-Socialist principles."[4]

Hitler and the Nazis had to account for the extraordinary fact that Jews have fixed "traits of character." Only race could explain this phenomenon. Once this was understood, the age-old solution to the Jewish challenge, converting the Jews to the majority identity, became utterly untenable. If you want to rid the world of the Jews' "hostile ideologies," then you must physically rid the world of the Jews. The Nazi conclusion was as rationally thought out as the means they ultimately adopted for implementing it. Every other solution had been tried and had failed; the Nazis would implement the "Final Solution."

Racism is one of two commonly held explanations for Nazi antisemitism that deny its explicitly anti-Jewish character. The second is the scapegoat thesis. According to this explanation, in order to attain power, Hitler and the Nazis needed a scapegoat upon whom to blame the ills of Germany, and the Jews served this purpose most conveniently. The Nazis attacked the Jews not because attacking Jews was central to the Nazi worldview, but because attacking the Jews was the politically wise thing to do.

The historical record unambiguously affirms the *opposite* of the scapegoat thesis. The Nazis did not attack the Jews to achieve power; rather, they wanted power in large measure to attack the Jews.

---

an intellectual basis. And for this purpose the conception of race serves me well." Hermann Rauschning, *Hitler Speaks* (London: T. Butterworth, 1939), p. 229.

This point is hardly a revelation. It was documented by the Holocaust historian, the late Lucy Dawidowicz, in *The War Against the Jews, 1933–1945:* "Serious people, responsible people, thought that Hitler's notions about the Jews were, at best, merely political bait for disgruntled masses, no more than ideological window dressing to cloak a naked drive for power. Yet precisely the reverse was true. Racial imperialism and the fanatic plan to destroy the Jews were the dominant passions behind the drive for power."[5]

To Hitler, the "Final Solution" to the "Jewish Problem" was more important than winning World War II. Late in the war, when the Germans were losing, their trains were taken from the Allied fronts and deployed to murder Jews. In July 1944, when the Germans needed every train to begin their evacuation of Greece, not a single train was diverted from those taking Jews to death camps. When the Germans declared a ban on all nonmilitary rail traffic to free trains for a summer offensive in southern Russia, the only trains exempted were those transporting Jews to death camps.[6]

A second fact that negates the scapegoat thesis was the Nazi policy of murdering Jews. Considering the Nazis' severe manpower shortages, they should have used the Jews as slave laborers. Instead, the Nazis murdered the overwhelming majority of Jews who fell into their hands. Even those few Jews who were used as slave labor were usually so mistreated that they died in a matter of weeks or months. When a Nazi general, Kurt Freiherr von Grienanth, gingerly noted in September 1942 that "the principle should be to eliminate the Jews as promptly as possible without impairing essential war work," he was demoted by Heinrich Himmler, the chief of the Gestapo, who denounced the general's proposal as a subtle effort to support the Jews.[7] To most German military leaders Germany's primary war was against the Allies, but for the Nazis, it was the war against the Jews.

A third fact undermining the scapegoat thesis is that in the early years of the Third Reich, the Nazis did not want the Jews to remain in Germany, where they could have been used as scapegoats; indeed, the Nazis encouraged Jews to leave Germany. In what now reads as incredible, in January 1935, Reinhard Heydrich, head of the SA, issued a directive to the Bavarian political police to cooperate with German Zionists. "The activity of the Zionist oriented youth organizations [in encouraging Jews to emigrate to Palestine] . . . lies in the interest of the National Socialists States' leadership."[8] Two months later the Nazis forbade Jewish organizations from encouraging Jews to stay in Germany. All of this was rather strange behavior toward "scapegoats."

A fourth error in the scapegoat thesis is the premise upon which it rests—that antisemitism was so politically effective in Germany that the Nazis needed to use it to achieve power. On the contrary, the major appeal of the Nazis to the German electorate was not the party's antisemitism, but its promise of economic improvement, its appeals to patriotism, and its promises to avenge Germany's humiliation at the Versailles Conference that followed World War I. While it is true that the people who voted for the Nazis were at best indifferent to the fate of Jews, most of them did not vote for the Nazis because of the Nazis' antisemitism.[9] The most important factor in Nazi success at the polls was the economic situation in Germany.

The final refutation of the scapegoat thesis was delivered by Adolf Hitler himself, in his final message to the German people. Speaking just prior to committing suicide, Hitler spoke of that which was most important to him. The subject that gripped Hitler's attention to the last moments of his life was the Jews. On April 29, 1945, Adolf Hitler addressed his final words to the German people: "*Above all*, I charge the leaders of the nation and those under them to scrupulous observance of the laws of race and to the merciless opposition to the universal poisoner of all peoples, international Jewry" (emphasis ours).[10] Scapegoats to the end?

IDEOLOGICAL ROOTS OF NAZI ANTISEMITISM

Nearly every popular ideology in German history helped provide ideological soil for Nazi antisemitism: Christianity, the Enlightenment, Marxism, nationalism, and racism. The antisemitism of the first three has been discussed in separate chapters. Let us now discuss the antisemitic elements in German nationalism and racism and see how our general thesis applies to them.

German nationalist antisemites argued that German Jews had failed to fulfill their part of the bargain implicit in emancipation—that, in return for citizenship, they cease being a distinct people. As German nationalism intensified, any manifestation of the Jews' national identity increased antisemitism.* In 1879, the leading historian of modern Germany, Heinrich von Treitschke, a man with both a wide scholarly and a political following, published *A Word About Our Jewry.* In this essay, he set forth the conditions under which German Jews could be accepted in Germany. "What we have to demand from our Jewish fellow citizens is simple: That they become Germans, regard themselves simply and justly as Germans." They could continue practicing Judaism, Treitschke wrote, but should restrict it to the private domain, and not try and influence Germany with Jewish values: "We do not want an era of German-Jewish mixed culture to follow after thousands of years of German civilization."[11]

In addition, Treitschke accused the Jews of having contempt for Germans. For example, he accused the leading Jewish historian of the time, Heinrich Graetz, of preaching in his *History of the Jews,* "Deadly hatred . . . of the purest and most powerful exponents of German character, from Luther to Goethe, and Fichte. . . . And this stubborn contempt for the German *goyim* is not at all the attitude of a single fanatic."

Treitschke then cited another "fanatic" Jew, the popular writer Ludwig Borne, who, not having an exclusive German national identity, was a hostile "outsider": "Borne was the first to introduce into our journals the peculiar shameless way of talking about the Fatherland offhand, and without any reverence, like an outsider, as if mocking of Germany did not cut deeply into the heart of every German."

*So strong was this German hostility to Jewish peoplehood that many German Jews decided to drop the national component of Judaism and to identify themselves as "Germans of the Mosaic persuasion," Jews whose one and only national identity was German. Many German Jews so feared accusations of "dual loyalties" that, in 1840, the most important nineteenth-century leader of Reform Judaism in Germany, Abraham Geiger, opposed the intervention of world Jewry on behalf of Jews in Damascus who were victims of a "blood libel."

It was in response to these perceived threats to German values that Treitschke wrote what later became the slogan of the Nazis: "Even in the best educated circles . . . we hear today the cry, as from one mouth 'the Jews are our misfortune.'"

Within a year of *A Word About Our Jewry*'s publication, a German students' association distributed an "Anti-Semites' Petition," which demanded that Bismarck achieve the "emancipation of the German People from a form of Alien domination which it cannot endure for any length of time." The petition demanded major restrictions on Jewish immigration, the exclusion of Jews from government and teaching positions, and the resumption of a Jewish census. It was circulated mainly in Prussia, where the petition received 225,000 signatures. A counter-petition circulated by liberal students did poorly. At the University of Göttingen, for example, the petition demanding an end to equal rights for Jews received more than twice as many signatures as the petition requesting that Jews merely be allowed to retain their equal rights.

Alongside this rising nationalist sentiment in Germany was the racist movement that promulgated a philosophy of German/Aryan superiority and cultural refinement counterpoised against Jewish inferiority and decadence. Its most influential exponent was the English expatriate Houston Stewart Chamberlain, who in 1899 published *Foundations of the Nineteenth Century*, one of the most important racist and antisemitic works in modern history, and one well received by many intellectuals of the day. The *London Times Literary Supplement* (December 1919) called it "unquestionably one of the rare books that really matter."

According to *Foundations*, the future of humanity will be determined by the outcome of the epochal struggle between two "races": the Teutonic ("Aryan") and the Jewish ("Semitic"). The racial thesis of *Foundations* notwithstanding, Chamberlain's real opposition was to the Jews' values and theology, not to their race and biology.

This fact was repeatedly made clear throughout his two-volume work. One would expect a racial antisemite to hate all Jews, but Chamberlain painstakingly disassociated himself from such "crude" antisemitism: he repeatedly denied any "personal animus against individuals belonging to the Jewish nation."[12] In fact, Chamberlain dedicated *Foundations of the Nineteenth Century* to a Jew, Julius Wiesner, once his professor at the University of Vienna.

It was not hatred of the Jews as a race that animated the foremost advocate of racial antisemitism. He hated what the Jews stood for, and their success in overturning others' values: "I cannot help shuddering . . . at the portentous, irremediable mistake the world made in accepting the traditions of this wretched little nation . . . as the basis of its belief."[13] He hated the Jews for their monotheism and moral values, which prevented the natural human being from possessing unrestricted freedom: "The Jew came into our gay world and spoiled everything with his ominous concept of sin, his law, and his cross."[14]

The success of Chamberlain's Aryan versus Jew interpretation of history was remarkable. Within a few years of publication the book went through eight editions and "became the Bible of hundreds of thousands of Germans." Kaiser William II read it aloud to his children and sent it to all the army officers and libraries in Germany. In a letter to Chamberlain, the Kaiser wrote, "You explain what was obscure, you show the way of salvation to Germany and all the rest of mankind."[15]

Throughout the late nineteenth and early twentieth centuries, antisemitic ideologies proliferated in Germany. In addition to traditional Christian sources of antisemitism, anti-Jewish attacks now emanated from virtually all sources, including anti-Christian ones. The latter focused their animus against Judaism for, among other things, bringing forth Christianity. The very creator of the term "anti-Semitism" and founder of the Anti-Semites League, Wilhelm Marr, denounced Christianity as a "disease of the human consciousness" that was but one more manifestation of Judaism.[16] Eugen Dühring, the prominent racist of the late 1800s, argued that "Christianity is itself semitic" and that all monotheistic religions preach hatred of life.[17] Richard Wagner called for a new German religion with no Jewish or Christian influence: "Emancipation from the yoke of Judaism appears to us the foremost necessity."[18]

Hatred of Judaism for subverting pagan values and unleashing Christianity was later expressed in a song of the Hitler Youth: "Pope and Rabbi shall be no more. We want to be pagans once again. No more creeping to Churches. We are the joyous Hitler Youth. We do not need any Christian virtues. Our leader, Adolf Hitler, is our Savior."[19]

Despite such anti-Christian attitudes, there was always a crucial distinction between the racists' anti-Judaism and their anti-Christianity. They held all Jews accountable for alien Jewish values, including non-religious and assimilated Jews. Racists held that Jewish values were embedded in Jewish blood. Christians, however, could cease being Christians and become good German Aryans by adopting an Aryan Christianity with an Aryan Jesus (Chamberlain, for example, claimed that Jesus was an Aryan and completely devoid of Jewish blood), Aryan disciples, and the removal of all Jewish concepts in Christianity, such as monotheism and its universal moral code.

To most contemporary readers, one of the most shocking aspects of the racist campaign against the Jews was the success it achieved in academic and educated circles. Yet the fact is that advocacy of nationalist and racist antisemitism was as widespread among intellectuals as among other Germans. A Jewish writer, B. Segel, described this phenomenon in the early 1920s: "In Berlin I attended meetings which were entirely devoted to the *Protocols* [*of the Elders of Zion*]. The speaker was usually a professor, a teacher, an editor, a lawyer, or someone of that kind. The audience consisted of members of the educated class, civil servants, tradesmen, former officers, ladies, above all students. . . . Passions were whipped up to the boiling point. There in front of one, in the flesh, was the cause of all those ills [the Jews], those who made the war and brought about the defeat and engineered the revolution. . . . I observed the students. A few hours earlier they had perhaps been exerting all their mental energy in a seminar under the guidance of a world famous scholar, in an effort to solve some legal or philosophical or mathematical problem. Now young blood was boiling, eyes flashed, fists clenched, hoarse voices roared applause or vengeance. . . . Whoever dared to express a slight doubt was shouted down, often insulted and threatened. . . . German scholarship allowed belief in the genuineness of the *Protocols* and in the existence of a Jewish world conspiracy to penetrate ever more deeply into all the educated sections of the German population, so that now [1924] it is simply ineradicable. . . . None of the great German scholars (save for the late lamented Strack [a Christian scholar of the Talmud]) rose to unmask the forgery."[20]

Nine years after this typical meeting in Berlin, Adolf Hitler was chancellor of Germany, and soon the Holocaust, the consequence of all these various German and European ideologies, was under way. When the antisemitism of these ideologies, whether Christian, nationalist, universalist Enlightenment, or racist, is understood, the Nazi destruction of European Jewry can no longer be regarded as some psychological aberration, Machiavellian need for scapegoats, or racist eruption, but as a logical consequence of Jew-hatred.

THE NEAR-UNIVERSALITY AND DEPTH OF EUROPEAN ANTISEMITISM

The unique German brew of antisemitic ideologies culminated in Germany's unleashing the "Final Solution" of the "Jewish Problem." But thanks to the virtual universality of antisemitism, the Germans found fertile fields to sow the Holocaust throughout nearly all of Europe. The six million Jews slaughtered by the Nazis came from twenty-one European countries. Hitler's goal was to render at least Europe *judenrein* (free of Jews), and by 1945, he had murdered almost seven out of every ten Jews on the European continent. In some countries, the Germans murdered the overwhelming majority of Jews. To cite the two most extreme examples, in Poland, the Germans murdered 3 million Jews out of a prewar Jewish population of 3.3 million, and in Latvia, Lithuania, and Estonia, 228,000 out of 253,000.

The major reason for the Nazis' success in murdering Europe's Jews was the cooperation they received from citizens of Nazi-occupied countries. Thus, almost everywhere, wherever the local populations refused to cooperate the percentage of Jews murdered was considerably smaller than elsewhere, and in two instances—Denmark and Finland—almost all the Jews were saved.

Concerning Denmark, its prewar Jewish population of eight thousand was mainly composed of Jews well integrated into Danish society.

After the German takeover in April 1940, Himmler and other top German officials repeatedly pressured Denmark to take actions against its Jewish citizens.

Lucy Dawidowicz described the events: "After Denmark came under martial law, Best [the German minister in charge of Denmark] tried to deport the Danish Jews. His plans . . . were reported on September 28 [1943] to Danish Social Democratic leaders. The Germans had scheduled the roundup of the Jews for October 1, 1943, but in an extraordinary operation involving the whole Danish people and the agreement of the Swedish government, nearly all Danish Jews were hidden and then ferried across to Sweden, where they remained in safety until the end of the war. The Germans managed to round up some four hundred Jews, whom they sent to Theresienstadt [a concentration camp in Czechoslovakia]. The internment of the Danish Jews in Theresienstadt agitated the Danish government which repeatedly requested permission to inspect the camp. In June, 1944, such permission was granted, and the visit was made by delegates of the Danish Red Cross. As a consequence of persistent Danish interest in the deported Jews, none was sent to Auschwitz. At the end of the war, fifty-one had died in Theresienstadt of natural causes."[21]

Finland provided a second example of a German-occupied nation being able to save its Jews. When Himmler visited Helsinki in July 1942, he pressured the Finns to deport their Jews to German concentration camps. The Finnish foreign minister, Rolf Witting, simply refused to consider the matter, and no Finnish Jews were murdered.

A third example of a country (in this instance an ally of Germany) where the Nazis encountered stiff resistance to the "Final Solution" from the populace and leadership is Bulgaria. After Bulgaria's leaders halted the deportation of native Bulgarian Jews, though not of Jewish refugees living there, "the Germans continued to exert pressure to deport the Jews, but the counterpressure of Bulgarian opinion, especially the Bulgarian Orthodox Church, restrained the government from compliance. King Boris III, too, was opposed to deporting any but 'Communist elements.'"[22] As a result, 50,000 of the 64,000 Jews in Bulgaria survived the war.

In most countries the Germans occupied, however, they received enormous local support in locating, arresting, and, in Eastern Europe, murdering the Jews. It was this support, offered enthusiastically in countries with large Jewish populations, that enabled the "Final Solution" to achieve its demonic success.

In Poland, with its history of antisemitism and its large Jewish population (10 percent of the population), the Germans were repeatedly aided in their program to murder all Polish Jews. When Poland became independent in 1919, the event was accompanied by a series of pogroms.* During the years between the wars, severe quotas were placed on Jews in universities, and discriminatory economic regulations impoverished many Jews.[23]

The record of Polish support for Nazi actions against the Jews is documented in many sources, nowhere more vividly than in *The Warsaw Diary of Chaim A. Kaplan*.[24] Kaplan, a German-born Jew living in Poland, meticulously recorded Jewish life in Poland under Nazi rule. His published diary runs from September 1, 1939, the day of the German invasion, until Kaplan's own deportation on or about August 4, 1942. Throughout the journal Kaplan wrote of Poles' support for the Nazis' anti-Jewish policies. For example, when the Nazis ordered the confiscation of almost all the Jews' property and money, Jews pleaded with longtime Christian friends to accept sums for safekeeping. But,

*A popular Jewish joke of the interwar period bears witness to the depth of Polish antisemitism. "Ignace J. Paderewski, post-war premier of Poland, was discussing his country's affairs with the late President Wilson. 'If all our demands are not granted at the peace conference,' said Mr. Paderewski, 'I can foresee serious trouble in my country. Why, my people will be so irritated that many of them will go out and massacre the Jews.' 'And what will happen if your demands are granted?' asked Mr. Wilson. Replied Paderewski, 'Why, my people will be so happy that many of them will get drunk and go out and massacre the Jews.'" (S. Felix Mendelsohn, *The Jew Laughs*, p. 46) It would be unfair, however, not to also acknowledge both that the country with the largest number of non-Jewish rescuers of Jews honored at Yad Vashem (Israel's Holocaust memorial center) are from Poland and that the punishment for hiding Jews in Poland could be death, which was not generally the case in France or Italy, for example.

wrote Kaplan, "the Christian 'friends' refused, because their merchants association had forbidden its members to give assistance to Jews in any form whatsoever" (October 16, 1939).

The depth of Polish Jew-hatred was particularly evident in Kaplan's description of the expulsion of the Jewish community of Pultusk. The entire community, including "old men with canes and sick people on the point of death" was exiled to Poplawy. "The rabbi went with the exiles. . . . That night the Polish inhabitants of the village attacked the rabbi, beat him up, and stole his last pennies. They stole the money from the rest of the exiles as they were leaving the village. The crowd cheered them all and emptied their pockets" (October 26, 1939). Another example: Kaplan noted that in the early days of the occupation, before the Nazis had ghettoized the Jews and when Jews and Poles waited on bread lines for food, the Poles, "even though . . . they do not know German . . . have nevertheless learned to say *'Ein Jude'* in order to get [a Jew] thrown out of line" (October 5, 1939).

But what may most reveal the depth of Polish antisemitism is that most of the Poles in the anti-Nazi underground refused to help Polish Jews even during the Jews' revolt in the Warsaw Ghetto. And a few months after the revolt's failure, on September 15, 1943, General Tadeusz Bor-Komorowski of the Armia Krajowa, the main Polish underground force, ordered that Jewish anti-Nazi fighters be liquidated.[25] Though many moving individual instances of Poles risking their lives to save Jews are recorded, such as the seven Poles who smuggled arms into the Warsaw Ghetto and several thousand Poles who hid Jews, Poles overwhelmingly reacted to the Nazi genocide of the Jews with, at best, indifference, and often, support. Only with Polish cooperation could the Nazis have murdered over 90 percent of the more than three million Jews of Poland. And it was not coincidental that the major Nazi death camps were located in Poland.

Hitler's actions against the Jews were also abetted by his ally from 1939 to 1941, Joseph Stalin. When German Foreign Minister Joachim von Ribbentrop met with Stalin to discuss the Soviet-German partition of Poland, they also addressed Germany's treatment of Polish Jews. Von Ribbentrop reported Stalin's response: "The Polish national problem might be dealt with as Germany sees fit," a statement that the Germans understood as supportive of their anti-Jewish actions.[26]

Though Stalin knew about German persecution of Polish Jews from 1939 on, he kept this information secret. As a consequence, when the Germans broke their alliance with the Soviets and invaded the USSR in 1941, Soviet Jews had no idea that the Germans intended to murder them. The effects of this Communist-induced ignorance were catastrophic. Oblivious to Nazi designs, the Jews in occupied Soviet territories at first made no attempt to resist the German army or even to flee. When the Germans ordered local Jewish leaders to gather all the Jews for resettlement to a "Jewish region," the Jews obeyed. When the Jews did gather, *Einsatzgruppen*, Nazi mobile killing units, together with "local Ukrainian, White Russian, or Latvian militia would transport the Jews outside the town and murder them all—men, women, and children—by machine-gun fire within abandoned dugouts and ravines."[27]

The Germans relied on local support of this kind throughout Eastern Europe. As soon as they captured Kovno, Lithuania, gangs of Lithuanians murdered 3,800 Jews on June 25–26, 1941. Upon capturing Lvov, in Soviet Ukraine, the Germans immediately organized a Ukrainian militia that murdered 7,000 Jews on July 2–3. The historian Shmuel Ettinger noted that the actions of the Ukrainians were so immediate and precipitate that "the murders were halted by order of the Germans," who wished to bring greater order to the genocide campaign. That fall, at the end of September 1941, on Yom Kippur, Germans and Ukrainians murdered at least 34,000 Jews in Babi Yar, a ravine near Kiev.

Romanians also participated in the murder of their Jews. On June 28, 1941, bloody pogroms were carried out there, and 7,000 Jews were murdered. Later, the Romanians established concentration camps for the Jews. By the war's end 300,000 Romanian Jews had been murdered through the joint efforts of Germans and Romanians.

In the German puppet state of Slovakia in March 1942, the leader of the Slovak People's Party, Father Josef Tiso, a Catholic priest, agreed to expel the Jews. After his Fascist Hlinka Guard conducted massive manhunts for Jews, 35,000 were sent eastward to be murdered in the death camps. A Slovak rabbi went to Archbishop Kametko and asked

him to influence his former private secretary, Tiso, to stop the expulsions. The archbishop responded: "This is no mere expulsion. There you
will not die of hunger and pestilence; there they will slaughter you all,
old and young, women and children, in one day. This is your punishment for the death of our Redeemer. There is only one hope for you—
to convert all to our religion. Then I shall effect the annulling of this
decree."[28]

In the fall of 1944, Rabbi M. D. Weissmandel escaped while en
route to a concentration camp and ultimately met with the papal nuncio,
describing for him the horrors of the Jews in temporary camps awaiting deportation to Auschwitz. He begged the papal nuncio to intervene
with Tiso. The papal nuncio answered: "This, being a Sunday, is a holy
day for us. Neither I nor Father Tiso occupy ourselves with profane
matters on this day."

Weissmandel persisted, arguing that the lives of innocent human
beings, including infants and children, were not a profane matter. The
papal nuncio responded: "There is no innocent blood of Jewish children
in the world. All Jewish blood is guilty. You have to die. This is the punishment that has been awaiting you because of that sin" [the death of
Jesus].

Shmuel Ettinger summarized the support given by the people of
Eastern Europe in the Nazi war against the Jews: "The most active
accomplices of the Germans in these acts of extermination were the
Ukrainians and Lithuanians, but they had many helpers among the Cro-
atians, Rumanians, Hungarians and Slovaks. . . . Their police personnel
were willing to search tirelessly for days and even weeks in order to hunt
down one concealed Jewish child. Though Poland was notorious for her
antisemitism, it is a fact that the number of Jews hidden and saved there
by the local population was many times higher than in Soviet Ukraine
and Soviet White Russia. . . . [But] it is not by chance that Poland was
chosen as the country of extermination. The Polish people . . . [did not]
lift a finger to help the Jews, even in the worst days of mass murder, or
during the Warsaw ghetto uprising. There were many Poles who handed
escaping Jews over to the Nazis. Nevertheless, there were some Poles,
mainly in the monasteries, who were shocked at the brutal murders,

and particularly the slaughter of young children, and attempted to save them. Through them several thousand Jewish children were saved in Poland."[29]

There is no question that in Western Europe the Germans took greater care in carrying out the "Final Solution," knowing that anti-Jewish feelings were less intense there. As a result, except for Holland, the percentage of Jews murdered in Western Europe was considerably less than in Eastern Europe. Nonetheless, the Germans were also extended extensive cooperation in Western Europe. In France, for example, the Nazis required French cooperation to carry out deportation of Jews, since they lacked the manpower to do it alone.

On June 11, 1941, the Nazis formulated plans to round up all Jews between the ages of sixteen and forty. Pierre Laval, vice prime minister in Vichy, unoccupied France, informed the Germans that he would not use French police to round up Jews who were French citizens. But he did order the French police to turn over to the Germans the 64,070 Jewish refugees in Paris, including children under sixteen years of age. By mid-July, French police had delivered 4,051 Jewish children under the age of sixteen into the hands of the Nazis—Jews whom the Nazis themselves had not ordered rounded up. These children were subsequently sent to Auschwitz.[30]

Virtually every secular and religious ideology and nationality in Europe had been saturated with Jew-hatred by the time the Nazis developed the Final Solution. Over the preceding decades and centuries major elements of Christianity, Marxism and socialism, nationalism, and Enlightenment and post-Enlightenment thought had come to view the existence of Jews as a distinctive people with a distinctive Jewish identity as intolerable. In the final analysis, they all would have opposed what Hitler did, but without them, Hitler could not have done it.

THIRTEEN

Anti-Zionist Antisemitism

U NTIL THE HOLOCAUST, ENEMIES OF THE JEWS—whether pagan, Christian, Muslim, men of the Enlightenment, Leftist, or Nazi—proudly and publicly espoused their Jew-hatred.[1] With the revelations of the Nazi crimes, it became taboo to call oneself an opponent of the Jews, and so, for the first time in history, most antisemites denied that they were antisemites. In fact, post-Holocaust antisemites have often gone further and insisted that they actually like Jews. Soviet leaders, for example, heads of one of the most antisemitic governments and societies in the world, not only denied being antisemitic, they actually boasted of being the only society to have actually eliminated antisemitism. The USSR also claimed to be the only country to have outlawed antisemitism in its constitution, an act initiated by the well-known "patron" of the Jews, Joseph Stalin. Similarly, many of the Arabs whose proclaimed policy is to destroy the Jewish state virulently deny being antisemitic. If one were to take such people at their word, there are almost no more antisemites on earth. Since the revelations of the Holocaust, the most hated people in history no longer have enemies.

Clearly, only a change in rhetoric has taken place among antisemites. Hitler and Eichmann rendered the term "antisemite" almost universally ugly and therefore unusable, at least for the time being. Those who, prior to the Holocaust, would have called themselves, and certainly would have been called by others, antisemites now utilize the term "anti-Zionist." Thus the Soviets, when they jailed Jews for Jewish activities, claimed to be only "anti-Zionist," and those who seek to destroy the Jewish state and deny the Jews their national identity likewise call themselves only anti-Zionist. They deny hating all Jews, only those Jews who insist upon retaining their Jewish national beliefs and a Jewish state.*

Yet this claim of anti-Zionists that they do not hate all Jews is not new to anti-Zionists. Virtually all modern antisemites have claimed that they oppose only Jews who affirm Jewish nationhood. Only Hitler and the Nazis, among modern antisemites, have hated all Jews. Unless the Nazis are to be considered the only antisemites in modern history, anti-Zionists are as antisemitic as every other type of antisemite. Like all other antisemites, anti-Zionists are at war with nearly every identifying Jew.

Anti-Zionism is unique in only one way: it is the first form of Jew-hatred to deny that it hates Jews. Accordingly, any discussion of anti-Zionism must begin by explaining why it is antisemitism.

ANTI-ZIONISM AS ANTISEMITISM IN THEORY

Can someone deny that Italians are a nation, work to destroy Italy, and all the while claim that he is not an enemy of the Italian people because he does not hate all Italians? The question is obviously absurd. If you deny Italian nationhood and any Italian rights to their homeland, and seek to destroy Italy, no matter how sincerely you may claim to love some Italians, you are an enemy of the Italian people. The same holds true for those who deny Jewish nationhood and the Jews' right to their

---

*The Jews have always been both a nation and a religion, but to legitimize their denial of the Jews' right to Israel, anti-Zionists deny that the Jews are a nation or a people, and assert that they are members only of a religion. A typical such denial of Jewish peoplehood is this statement from the charter of the Palestine Liberation Organization: "Judaism, in its character as a religion, is not a nationality with an independent existence. Likewise the Jews are not one people." (Article 20 of the Palestine National Covenant)

state, and who advocate the destruction of Israel. Such people are enemies of the Jewish people, and the term for their attitudes, even when
espoused by people who sincerely like some Jews, is antisemitism.

An anti-Zionist would likely respond that the analogy between
Italy and Israel is invalid, because Italian has meaning as a nationality,
while Judaism has meaning only as a religion. And since Judaism is only
a religion and Zionism is a national movement, one can oppose Zionism
without being an enemy of the Jews or Judaism.

In addition to reasons already presented, this argument is false on
four scores.

First, it makes the extraordinary assumption that non-Jews can tell
Jews what it means to be Jewish. As a prominent Orthodox Jewish theologian Rabbi Emanuel Rackman wrote: "I am a Jew and a Zionist. For
me the two commitments are one. Furthermore, I hold this to be the
position of historic Judaism. . . . I must firmly ask [non-Jews] to respect
my religious convictions as I see them and not as they see them."[2]

Throughout its long history, Judaism has held that Jewish nationhood is, along with God and Torah and chosenness, a pillar of Judaism.
In the words of an ancient Jewish text, "God, Torah and Israel are one."
The Jews' self-definition as a nation with a homeland in Israel is not
some new political belief of contemporary Jews but the essence of Judaism since biblical times.

Second, the contention that anti-Zionists are not enemies of the
Jews, despite their advocacy of policies that would lead to the mass
murder of Jews, is, to put it as generously as possible, disingenuous.
If anti-Zionism succeeded in its goal of destroying Israel, nearly all of
Israel's more than six million Jews plus an untold number of non-Israeli
Jews would die in their effort to maintain Israel. Both the Israelis and
their Arab enemies know this. Arab leaders, some Western-oriented
propaganda notwithstanding, have repeatedly called for the destruction
of the Jews in Israel during a war with Israel. The Israelis, for their part,
would fight to the last, both to keep Israel alive and because they have
reason to believe that death is a preferable fate to capture by their Arab
enemies. In the words of the Israeli *leftist* writer Amos Kenan, written in
the aftermath of the Six-Day War: "Shukairy [the head of the Palestine

Liberation Organization before Yasir Arafat] used to say that the Jews should be driven into the sea. After the 1967 defeat, it became apparent that a slogan of this sort was not good public relations for the Arab cause. So today, only the Zionists are to be thrown into the sea. The only trouble is that when the Arabs get through pushing all the Zionists into the sea, there won't be a Jew left in Israel. For not a single Jew in Israel will agree to less than political and national sovereignty."[3]

Given, then, that if anti-Zionism realized its goal, another Jewish holocaust would take place, attempts to draw distinctions between anti-Zionism and antisemitism are simply meant to fool the naive.

Third, it was possible before the establishment of Israel in 1948 to oppose the Zionist movement and not be an enemy of the Jews, just as prior to 1776, one could have opposed American statehood without being an enemy of Americans. Once the United States was established, however, anyone advocating its destruction would obviously be considered an enemy of Americans. So, too, once Israel was established, anyone advocating its destruction is an enemy of the Jews.

Fourth, anti-Zionists would be hard put to find any affirmatively identifying Jew who would not view them as mortal enemies. Studies and opinion polls have shown that over 95 percent of American Jewry identifies with the right of Jews to the Jewish state.[4] For the overwhelming majority of religious Jews, as we have seen, Israel and Jewish nationhood are part of their religious creed. An anti-Zionist is therefore an enemy of religious Jews.[5] As for secular Jews, anti-Zionists oppose the one aspect of Judaism that they most affirm—Israel.

ANTI-ZIONISM AS ANTISEMITISM IN PRACTICE

Though they constantly deny being antisemites, in their writings and speeches anti-Zionists rarely draw distinctions between Zionists and Jews.

To hide their antisemitism, enemies of the Jews nearly always use the word "Zionist" when they mean Jew. This substitution often has been ludicrous. As noted earlier, on October 21, 1973, the Soviet ambassador to the United Nations, Yakov Malik, declared: "The Zionists have come forward with the theory of the Chosen People, an absurd ideology." This was a typical example of antisemitism masquerading as anti-Zionism. An attack on Jewish chosenness is not an attack on Zionism: chosenness plays no role in Zionism. Rather, it is a basic doctrine of Judaism. Malik's attack was consistent with Soviet, Arab, and leftist opponents of the Jews who disguise their attacks on Jews and Judaism as attacks on Zionism. In the USSR Museum of Religion and Atheism in Leningrad (St. Petersburg), an exhibit about Zionism and Israel designated the following as anti-Soviet *Zionist* material: Jewish prayer shawls, tefillin (phylacteries), and Passover Haggadahs, all *religious* items used by Jews for thousands of years.[6]

A similar and characteristic use of anti-Zionism to disguise antisemitism was made in the *Black Panther* (August 25, 1970), the newspaper of that late radical black organization. Writing about the trials of Panther leader Huey Newton and of the "Chicago Eight," the paper concluded: "It was a Zionist judge, Judge Freedman, who sentenced Huey P. Newton to fifteen years in jail. It was a Zionist judge, Judge Hoffman, who allowed the other Zionists to go free but has kept Bobby Seale in jail. . . . The other Zionists in the Conspiracy 8 trial were willing and did sacrifice Bobby Seale. . . . Once again we condemn Zionism as a racist doctrine." The men denounced as Zionists include Jerry Rubin, Abbie Hoffman, and William Kunstler, people who could best be described as "non-Jewish Jews." The *Black Panther* attacked them because they were Jews by birth, not because they were Zionists.[7]

Such thinking goes on. In September 2002, Amira Baraka (the former LeRoi Jones), the official poet laureate of New Jersey, recited his poem "Somebody Blew Up America," at the renowned Dodge Poetry Festival in Waterloo, New Jersey. The poem asks:

Who knew the World Trade Center was going to get bombed?
Who told 4,000 Israeli workers at the Twin Towers to stay home that day?
Why did Sharon stay away?

Baraka, who, in earlier years, wrote verses calling for "dagger poems in the slimy bellies of their owner-jews," has long claimed that he no longer is antisemitic, only opposed to Zionism and to Israel's right to exist. But in spreading the Islamist libel that Jews and Israel had advance knowledge, which it withheld, of the 9/11 attacks, Baraka writes of "4,000 Israeli workers" who were warned to stay away from the World Trade Center that day. But, of course, 4,000 Israelis never worked at the World Trade Center; 4,000 or more Jews did, and about 400 of them died. In line with other anti-Zionist antisemites, Baraka speaks of Israel, Jews, and Zionists as indistinguishable.[8]

In Italy, in 2002, the liberal daily *La Stampa*, in a cartoon supposedly directed against Israel (but actually intended to arouse hatred against all Jews), harked back to the most damaging canard of Christian antisemitism: deicide. The cartoon showed the infant Jesus looking up from his manger at an Israeli tank and pleading: "Don't tell me they want to kill me again."[9] In England, at about the same time, A. N. Wilson, the highly regarded British novelist and biographer, accused the Israeli army of "poisoning the water supplies" on the West Bank, a lie that obviously intended to put people in mind of the medieval libel that Jews caused the Black Death by poisoning the wells of Europe.[10]

In the Arab world, "anti-Zionists" have long adopted the calumnies of antisemitism and now spread them under the guise of anti-Zionism. The late president of Egypt, and the then leading political figure in the Arab world, Gamal Abdel Nasser, repeatedly cited the *Protocols of the Elders of Zion* to document his charge that three hundred Zionists rule the world.

Muhammad Baghdadi, the cowriter of a forty-one–episode Egyptian television series based on *The Protocols of the Elders of Zion*, insisted that the series respected Judaism as a religion: "We only criticize the Zionists," he told a *New York Times* reporter (Dec. 26, 2002). Among those depicted in the series as a villain is a Jew in a black hat, with side curls and a long beard. Since ultra-Orthodox Jews have overwhelmingly been non-Zionists, clearly it was the intention of the series to depict all Jews as evil and as enemies. In early 2000, *Al-Jadida*, the Palestinian Authority's official newspaper, ran a cartoon depicting an old man labeled "the 20th century," and a young man "the 21st century." Between them stands a dwarf wearing a Jewish skullcap and a Star of David; he is labeled "the disease of the century."[11]

Moral leaders of various faiths have repeatedly warned that anti-Zionism is antisemitism in practice. Dr. Martin Luther King Jr., upon hearing a black student at Harvard launch a tirade against Zionists, said: "When people criticize Zionists, they mean Jews. You're talking antisemitism."[12]

In a similar vein, the president of the United Church of Christ, Dr. Robert Moss, commented on the anti-Zionist resolution passed by the UN General Assembly in 1975: "We should not be deceived by the use of the term Zionism. The sponsors of this resolution mean by it Jews and Judaism as well as the state of Israel." The UN delegate from Costa Rica noted that the resolution was an invitation to genocide against the Jewish people.[13]

Whether the destruction of the Jewish national movement and the Jewish state, a holocaust of the six million Jews of Israel, and the subsequent abandonment of world Jewry to the goodwill of the world with no refuge of its own are carried out in the name of anti-Zionism or antisemitism is quite irrelevant to Jews. That the people who want to do these things now call themselves anti-Zionists instead of antisemites is an interesting historical fact. There may be some differences in what aspects of Jewish life anti-Zionists and antisemites hate, but these differences are of interest only to historians. For Jews the consequences are identical.

FOURTEEN

Eight Lies About Israel

I N THE MEDIEVAL WORLD, millions of Christians believed that Jews murdered non-Jews and drank their blood (see pages 81–85), and a century ago, tens of millions of people believed in *The Protocols of the Elders of Zion*, a forgery that depicted world Jewry as engaged in an international plot to take over the world and that became Adolf Hitler's "warrant for genocide" against the Jews (see pages 202–203). Today, tens, and quite possibly, hundreds of millions of Muslims accept the blood libel as true; and the *Protocols of the Elders of Zion* is one of the best-selling books throughout the Arab world (see pages 110–111).

The Western world, in which both these libels originated, is at this point not willing to reaccept them as true. But other, newer lies about Jews, specifically about the Jewish state and those Jews who support it, have achieved widespread acceptance. So once again Jews are forced to legitimize their existence by combating lies about them.

LIE: *It is Israel that is the cause of Middle East tensions because of its refusal to make compromises for peace.*
TRUTH: In 1967, immediately following the Six-Day War, Israel offered to return almost all the land it had won in that war of self-defense in

160

exchange for peace.[1] The Arab world responded to this offer in September 1967 with the three famous "No's" of Khartoum; "no peace with," "no negotiations with," and "no recognition of" Israel. As Israeli Foreign Minister Abba Eban commented: "This is the first war in history which has ended with the victors suing for peace, and the vanquished calling for unconditional surrender."*

More than a decade later, when Egyptian President Anwar as-Sadat promised that his country would recognize Israel's right to exist and establish diplomatic relations if it returned the Sinai Peninsula to Egypt, Israel, under the leadership of the right-wing prime minister Menachem Begin returned the Sinai in its entirety. That territory alone, three times as large as Israel, made up 91 percent of the land the Jewish state had captured in the Six-Day War. As part of handing over land that served as a potential protective buffer in case of war with Egypt, Israel also gave up the oil fields it had developed in Sinai, which would have saved Israel billions of dollars each year on oil and enabled it to become largely energy independent.

And this was only one of many times Israel was willing to make compromises for peace. At Camp David in the summer of 2000, Israeli Prime Minister Ehud Barak offered Palestinian Authority Chairman Yasir Arafat and the Palestinians 92 percent of the West Bank and part of Israel proper (to make up for part of the percentage of the West Bank it was not returning) in which to establish a Palestinian state. Arafat not only rejected the offer, but Palestinians then launched the second *intifada*, during which the Jews of Israel, civilians especially, were targeted for death by suicide/homicide bombers.†

Thus, in Israel's often desperate pursuit of peace, it has returned, or

---

*In fact, Israel's willingness to compromise preceded Israel's existence as an independent state. In 1947, the Jewish population of Palestine supported the UN partition plan to divide the land into a Jewish and Arab state, with Jerusalem (where Jews were a majority) to be internationalized. The Arabs rejected the proposal, initiated attacks on the Jewish community in Palestine and, upon Israel's creation in May 1948, launched a war to destroy it.

†The families of the killers were given large payments of money by Iraq and Saudi Arabia. In addition, the bombers themselves were promised that as a reward for mur-

offered to return, more than 97 percent of the land captured in 1967 (in addition to much of the West Bank, the Golan Heights, lost by Syria in its war with Israel, remains in Israel's hands). So much for the charge that Israel has not been willing to make compromises for peace.

One final thought: When discussing Israel's security needs, few of its opponents, and even many of its supporters, are aware of just how small the country is. Israel's area is about the same as New Jersey's. In 1869, Mark Twain, after a visit to the Holy Land, wrote: "The word Palestine always brought to my mind a vague suggestion of a country as large as the United States. . . . I could not conceive of a small country having so large a history."[2]

In fact, Israel occupies less than one-six hundredth of the land occupied by the twenty-one Arab states.* Thus, its willingness to cede more than 97 percent of the land it captured in a war of self-defense is truly remarkable.

LIE: *Israel stole the land from the Palestinians.*

TRUTH: In the more than three thousand–year-long-history of the land of Israel as a political entity, only three independent states have ever existed there, and each one has been Jewish: the state established in the aftermath of the Jewish exodus from Egypt, and later ruled for more than four centuries by King David and his descendants; the commonwealth established during the Second Temple, and destroyed by the Romans; and the modern state of Israel, established in 1948.

At all other times, when the Jews did not have a state in the land of Israel, no other country, ethnic group, nation, or religious group did. Thus, in the late 1800s, when the Zionist movement began, and Jews started migrating to Palestine in significant numbers, the area was controlled by the Turkish Ottoman Empire. (Throughout history, there had always been smaller Jewish migrations to the geographic area known as

---

dering Israelis and other Jews, they would immediately ascend to a high place in heaven where they would be served by seventy-two virgins.

*The Arab states occupy 5,414,000 square miles, compared with 8,290 for Israel in its pre-1967 borders, and a little over 10,000 square miles if one includes the West Bank.

Palestine, since the Jews never relinquished their claim to Israel, even after being forcibly removed.) The area of Palestine was regarded by its Turkish rulers and by its Arab residents as a part of Syria, southern Syria to be precise. Even after Israel's creation, Ahmed Shukairy, the founding head of the PLO and Arafat's predecessor, told the UN Security Council, "It is common knowledge that Palestine is nothing but southern Syria."

Those who speak of the Jews of Israel as having stolen the land from the Arabs living there might believe that hundreds of thousands, if not millions, of Arabs had their lands confiscated and taken away by Jews, but that was not the case. In the late nineteenth century, at the time of the rise of Zionism, the Arab population in Palestine was under 250,000, and "the great majority of the Arab population . . . were comparative newcomers—either late immigrants or descendants of persons who had immigrated into Palestine in the previous 70 years."[3]

Furthermore, few of the quarter of a million residents were landowners. Eighty percent of the Arabs living in Palestine were debt-ridden peasants, seminomads, and Bedouins.[4] Turkey held ownership of about 72 percent of the land; most of the rest was owned by absentee landlords who lived in Cairo, Damascus, and Beirut. Sovereignty over the land was transferred to England after Turkey's defeat in World War I, and ownership passed to Israel, under international law, when it became a state in 1948.[5] Of the remaining land, 8.6 percent was owned by Jews, 3.3 percent by Arabs who lived in Israel, and 16.5 percent by Arabs who had left the country, many of them many years earlier.[6]

The land that the Jews had acquired prior to the 1948 war was purchased, often at exorbitant prices: "In 1944, Jews paid between $1,000 and $1,100 dollars an acre in Palestine, mostly for arid and semiarid land; in the same year, rich, black soil in Iowa was selling for about $110 per acre."[7] These purchases were made mainly from large landowners, including the Arab mayors of Jerusalem, Gaza City, and Jaffa.

The 1947 UN partition resolution offered the Arabs living in Palestine a state alongside the Jewish one. The Arabs of Palestine and the surrounding countries rejected the UN offer, and on May 14, 1948 (the day of Israel's establishment), five Arab nations invaded in an effort to destroy the Jewish state. Thus, it was not Israel that tried to steal the land from the Palestinians; rather, it was the Palestinians and five Arab countries that tried, by destroying the Jewish state, to steal the land from the Jews.

LIE: *Israel has a moral obligation to allow the Palestinian refugees who fled in 1948, and their descendants, to return to Israel.*

TRUTH: The objective of those who wish to see Arab refugees and their several million descendants go and live in Israel is to destroy Israel. This is not cynical conjecture on our part but the oft-stated explanation offered by Arab leaders themselves for over half a century. In October 1949, just a year after Israel's creation, Egyptian Foreign Minister Salah al-Din said, "It is well-known and understood that the Arabs, in demanding the return of the refugees to Palestine, mean their return as masters of the Homeland, and not as slaves. With a greater clarity, they mean the liquidation of Israel." Eight years later, the 1957 Arab Refugee Conference in Homs, Syria, passed a resolution stating: "Any discussion aimed at a solution of the Palestine problem which will not be based on ensuring the refugees' right to annihilate Israel will be regarded as a desecration of the Arab people and an act of treason." Four years later, Gamal Abdel Nasser, Egypt's president, declared (September 1, 1961), "If the refugees return to Israel, Israel will cease to exist."

Once one understands that the goal of repatriating the refugees is to destroy the Jewish state, it becomes increasingly easy to understand why the Arab world has treated the 650,000 Palestinian refugees and their descendants so miserably. Since the end of World War II, there have been over 50 million refugees from dozens of countries, the overwhelming majority of whom have been successfully resettled. This number includes the approximately 800,000 Jewish refugees expelled from the Arab countries since 1948. In contradistinction to the Arab treatment of the Arab refugees, world Jewry made sure that every one of the Jewish refugees from Arab countries was given a place to live, money to begin a new life, and citizenship in the country to which he or she fled (including 586,000 in Israel).

The Arab world (with the exception of Jordan) refused to allow Palestinian refugees to become citizens of any Arab country. Driven by its hatred of Israel, the Arab world had a policy of keeping these people homeless and in refugee camps. Otherwise, this problem would have been solved long ago. As Dr. Elfan Rees, an adviser on refugees to the World Council of Churches, noted: "The Arab refugee problem is by far the easiest post-war refugee problem. By faith, by language, by race, and by social organization, they are indistinguishable from their fellows of the host country." In a surprisingly direct statement by a UN representative, Ralph Garroway, the former director of UNRWA, the United Nations Relief and Works Agency for Palestinian Refugees, said in August 1958: "The Arab states . . . want to keep [the refugee problem] as an open sore, as an affront to the United Nations and as a weapon against Israel. Arab leaders don't give a damn whether the refugees live or die."

It must also be emphasized that the Arab states created the refugee crisis by imposing a war on Israel. Had the Arabs not launched this war in 1948, or simply treated Palestinians in the aftermath of 1948 as human beings deserving of homes and citizenship (just as Israel absorbed over 600,000 Jews forced out of the Arab world), there would be no refugee crisis—then or today. It is hard to imagine why Israel should be expected to pay for the consequences of a war that others launched against it more than fifty years ago. Nevertheless, Israel has repeatedly offered to play a significant role in resolving the issues involving the refugees within the context of a Palestinian/Israeli agreement.

But still, if the refugees once lived in the area that now comprises Israel, shouldn't they be allowed to return? In a 1967 editorial, the *New York Times* noted the naïveté of such an argument: "The readmission of the refugees would be the equivalent to the admission to the United States of nearly 70,000,000 sworn enemies of the nation."

The *Times*'s argument brings to mind an episode from American history. In the early 1780s, Benjamin Franklin was negotiating an end to the Revolutionary War, when British diplomats suddenly issued a demand that the United States take back individuals who had supported England in its war against the colonists. Franklin responded: "Your ministers require that we should receive again into our bosom those who have been our bitterest enemies and restore their properties who have destroyed ours; and this while the wounds they have given us are still bleeding."[8]

An additional myth about the refugees needs to be exposed. Many people in the West believe that the Palestinians had all lived in Palestine for centuries, until they were suddenly, and against their will, displaced during the 1948 Arab war to destroy Israel. In fact, many of these people had come to Palestine only a few years before Israel's creation. However, the United Nations, under Arab prodding, defined Palestinian refugees in a manner unlike its definition of every other refugee group: any Arab living in Palestine for two years prior to 1948 could qualify as a "refugee." Many of these so-called refugees had not lived in Palestine for generations, but had just recently migrated there, often to take advantage of the prosperity generated in Palestine by the Jews. That is why during the period of the British Mandate (1917–48), the Arab population gains were primarily in Jewish areas of residence, e.g., 216 percent in Haifa, 134 percent in Jaffa, and not in Arab areas (e.g., only 40 percent in Jenin and 32 percent in Bethlehem).

In addition, many of these refugees were not chased out by Israel (some were), but chose to leave, calculating that the Arab armies would quickly destroy Israel and, that since it would be dangerous to be there while fighting was going on, they would return once Israel was defeated.

In short, those who argue that, if Israel would allow the refugees to return, the Arab-Israeli conflict would end, are right only insofar as destroying Israel would end the Israeli/Arab conflict.

LIE: *Jerusalem is as holy to Muslims as it is to Jews.*
TRUTH: At the Camp David conference in the summer of 2000, Chairman Arafat told President Clinton that Palestinian archaeologists could prove that there never had been a Jewish temple on the Temple Mount in Jerusalem. This statement alone, a flagrant lie, should have been the immediate indication that Arafat had no intention of reaching an agreement with Israel at Camp David. (People who wish to make peace don't start a meeting by denying the most basic truths about their opponent's history.)

The Temple Mount has been the leading Jewish holy site since shortly after it came under Jewish sovereignty during the reign of King David more than three thousand years ago, and sixteen hundred years before Islam came into existence.

Arafat's statement about Jerusalem is part of a widespread Arab campaign to deny the Jews' historical connection to the land of Israel and to Jerusalem in particular. For example, *Al-Hayat Al-Jadida*, the Palestinian Authority newspaper, quoted on October 15, 2000, the statement of Sheik Ikrama Sabri, the mufti of Jerusalem (the highest Islamic religious official in that city): "There is not a single stone in Palestine that proves the [historical] Jewish existence [in the land]."

In fact, ever since King David captured Jerusalem around 1000 B.C.E., the city has been the Jewish people's spiritual capital at all times, and political capital during the three periods when the Jews had a state (for four hundred years after King David, during the time of the Second Temple, and since 1948). No other country or religion over the last three thousand years has ever claimed Jerusalem as a capital or as its most important city. Perhaps that is why Winston Churchill argued as early as 1955: "You ought to let the Jews have Jerusalem; it was they who made it famous."

In contrast to Judaism, Islam claims Jerusalem as its third holiest city. But even that claim exaggerates Jerusalem's significance to Muslims. After all, the city was never regarded as particularly important to Muslims when it was under Arab rule; it became so only when it came under Jewish rule. For example, between 1948 and 1967, Jordan occupied East Jerusalem and treated the city, as did the rest of the Arab world, as a backwater. During the nineteen years Jordan controlled Jerusalem, only one Arab leader, King Hassan of Morocco, ever visited there.

Jerusalem is mentioned 667 times in the Hebrew Bible; it is never mentioned in the Koran. Later Islamic teachings, formulated after the death of Muhammad, claimed that he had ascended to heaven from Jerusalem. After the Arab world conquered the territory that comprises Israel during the seventh century, Arab rulers erected two mosques on the site of what had once been the Jewish temple. Aside from these

mosques, one of which is the Dome of the Rock (from where Muhammad's ascent to heaven is said to have occurred), there are no other sites
of major significance to Islam in Jerusalem (unlike the holy cities of
Mecca and Medina, which, in the words of the late British historian
Christopher Sykes, "are holy places containing holy sites").

It is widely known that Jerusalem is holy to the Jews, but many
people believe that the Jews abandoned Jerusalem until the rise of Zionism. Like many other anti-Israel claims, this, too, is false. Jews have
been the largest religious group in Jerusalem since at least 1844 (when
the first generally accurate census was conducted). At the time, Jews
outnumbered Muslims by 40 percent (7,120 to an estimated 5,000)
and were twice as large as the Christian community (which numbered
3,390). In all the years since, and in nine succeeding censuses, the Jews
have always been the largest group residing there, and the majority since
1864.

Jerusalem's holiness in Jewish life is apparent in many ways. Whenever Jews pray, they face Jerusalem.* The city is mentioned in all three of
the Jewish daily prayer services. The Western Wall is the holiest site in
Jewish life, where both secular and religious Jews go to pray and insert
written petitions to God in the Wall's crevices. For thousands of years,
Jews have commemorated, with the fast day of Tishah-b'Ab (the ninth
of Ab), the destruction of the Temple in Jerusalem by the Babylonians in
586 B.C.E., and the Second Temple by the Romans in 70 C.E. Throughout history, Jews have arranged to have earth from Israel, particularly
from Jerusalem, poured into their graves when they die. In addition, the
smashing of a glass at the conclusion of every Jewish wedding is meant
to remind all those present of the verse from Psalms: "If I forget thee, O
Jerusalem, let my right hand fail" (Psalms 137:5).

For these reasons, the attempt by the Palestinian Authority's late
Chairman Arafat to deny the Jewish connection to Jerusalem is as
preposterous as it is mendacious. Unfortunately, the blood libel, *The
Protocols of the Elders of Zion,* and the Islamist claim that Jews knew in

---

*In contrast, when Muslims pray, they face Mecca.

advance about the 9/11 terrorist attacks on America and therefore four thousand Jewish workers stayed home that day make it clear that, to those who hate Jews, truth is also their enemy.

LIE: *Anti-Zionists are distinct from antisemites.*
TRUTH: There is only one possible reason people isolate Israel of all the countries in the world to deny its right to existence. That is because Israel is the one Jewish state. Anti-Zionism is antisemitism, and for an extended analysis of why there is no difference between anti-Zionism and antisemitism, see Chapter 13.

LIE: *Jews and Christians were well treated under Islamic rule.*
TRUTH: Christians suffered so badly under Muslim rule that most Christian communities in the Arab world gave up their religion and became Muslims; this was the only way for them to avoid the terrible discrimination that the Islamic world practiced against non-Muslims. Jews in the orbit of Islam usually fared better than did Jews in Europe, but that is only because medieval European antisemitism was so harsh. In truth, under Islam, Jews usually suffered a life of degradation and insecurity, and often much worse. At times, they were well treated, but they never had anything remotely approaching equal rights. For a fuller account of the suffering of Jews and Christians under Islam, see Chapter 9.

LIE: *Israel illegally occupies the West Bank.*
TRUTH: Israel captured the West Bank during the Six-Day War of 1967, a war of self-defense. In the days preceding the war, Hafiz al-Assad, the Syrian defense minister and later president, declared: "I, as a military man, believe that the time has come to enter into a battle of annihilation." A week later, on May 27, 1967, President Gamal Abdel Nasser of Egypt proclaimed: "Our basic objective will be the destruction of Israel." Three days after Nasser's speech, Jordan, which ruled over the West Bank, signed a defense pact with Egypt to join in a war explicitly aimed at destroying Israel.

Knowing that it would have to fight against both Egypt and Syria, and desperate to avoid going to war on a third front, Israel sent a message to Jordan's King Hussein assuring him that it would make no move against Jordan unless Jordan attacked Israel first. Shortly after the war began, the king, told by Nasser that the Arabs were winning, ordered his army to begin shelling Israel. It was only then that Israel fought back and took control of East Jerusalem and the West Bank.

Is Israel therefore *morally* required to return the West Bank? Why should it be? If someone tries to kill you with a gun, and you succeed in wresting the weapon away, are you then obliged to return the weapon to your assailant? Jordan and the Palestinians used the strategic highlands of the West Bank and Jerusalem as staging grounds in a war to destroy Israel. As Israeli Prime Minister Benjamin Netanyahu expressed it: "What kind of moral position is it to say that the failed aggressor should be given back all the territory from which he launched his attack?"[9]*

Does Israel then have a legal, if not a moral, obligation to return the West Bank?

No. Although Israel seized the West Bank from Jordan, Jordan itself had no right to this land. King Hussein's grandfather, King Abdullah, had occupied the West Bank during the Arab war to destroy Israel in 1948. After the war's conclusion, Abdullah annexed this territory to Jordan, an act that only two countries, Pakistan and England, recognized as legal. In the eyes of the rest of the world, Jordan had no legal claim to the West Bank. As Stephen Schwebel, the former head of the International Court of Justice in The Hague, wrote in 1970 regarding Israel's case: "Where the prior holder of territory had seized the territory unlawfully, the state which subsequently takes the territory in the lawful exercise of self-defense has, against that prior holder, better title."[11]

---

*But what about the widely accepted belief in "the inadmissibility of the acquisition of territory by war" (as cited, for example, in UN Resolution 242)? This belief, as Mitchell Bard, the author of *Myths and Facts: A Guide to the Arab/Israeli Conflict*, points out, obviously makes sense only when applied to an offensive war. Otherwise, insisting that it is impermissible to acquire territory by war would actually provide an incentive for aggression: "Aggressors would have little to lose because they would be insured against the main consequence of defeat."[10]

In November 1947, when the United Nations passed a partition plan, it designated the West Bank as part of what was to comprise a Palestinian state. However, the Arab residents of the West Bank, along with the rest of the Arab world, rejected this UN plan (because it also allotted land for a Jewish state). Moreover, during the nineteen years the West Bank was under Jordanian rule, both the Arab world and the residents of the West Bank made no effort to establish a Palestinian state there.

For these and other reasons U.S. Ambassador to the UN Madeleine Albright announced in March 1994: "We simply do not support the description of the territories occupied by Israel in the 1967 War as occupied Palestinian territory."

Now, what about the argument that Israel has no right to the West Bank in light of UN Security Resolution 242, which Israel accepted and which demands that Israel return land it captured during the Six-Day War? In truth, the UN resolution spoke of Israel's returning "territories" captured during the war. The resolution deliberately omitted the words "all the" territories, or even "the" territories. This omission was specifically intended to emphasize that Israel was not obliged to return *all* the territory it had captured. As Lord Caradon, Britain's then ambassador to the United Nations, explained: "It would have been wrong to demand that Israel return to its positions of June 4, 1967, because those positions were undesirable and artificial."

Another clause in the resolution called for "the acknowledgement of the sovereignty and territorial integrity of every state in the area and their right to live in peace within secure and recognized boundaries free from threats or acts of force." To this day, these conditions, essential to the resolution, remain unmet. Therefore, to call these territories "occupied," as notes William Safire, the Pulitzer Prize–winning columnist, "reveals a prejudice against Israel's right to what are supposed to be 'secure' defensible borders" (*New York Times*, March 25, 2002).

Because of a long-standing anti-Israel campaign conducted by Arab propagandists, it is widely believed in the West today that Israel has flouted Resolution 242's demand that it return the territories captured in 1967. Yet if one actually reads the resolution, it becomes apparent that its primary concern is a call for peace and for recognition of Israel's right to exist; and that only once that has occurred is Israel obliged to return much, but not all, of the captured territory. Resolution 242 was expressly meant to be implemented as part of a negotiated solution between the parties. There was never an expectation that Israel should withdraw from the territories *prior* to the signing of peace agreements.

Dr. Dore Gold, Israel's former ambassador to the United Nations, notes: "It would be far more accurate to describe the West Bank and the Gaza Strip as 'disputed territories' to which both Israelis and Palestinians have claims."[12]

Finally, given that Israel does not occupy the West Bank immorally or illegally, does it follow that Israel should hold on to all this land forever? Again the answer is no. We believe that Israel should help establish a Palestinian state in the Gaza Strip and on the largest part of the West Bank, but only after it is clear that the Palestinian state will

- accept in word (i.e., in what Arab leaders say to their people in Arabic, and not what they say to Westerners in English) and deed Israel's right to exist;
- relinquish Palestinian claims to any part of Israel;
- end its dissemination of antisemitic hate;
- settle the refugee problem without "resettlement" in Israel;
- stop terrorism against Israel and severely punish those who plan or perpetrate it.
- agree that the Palestinian state will be demilitarized, acquiring weapons for its police forces but not offensive weapons.

Until then, Israel has the right to maintain control over the West Bank. To give it up without these conditions being met is potentially suicidal—which is why Israel's enemies insist that it do so.

LIE: *Palestinians turned to violence against Israel out of desperation.*
TRUTH: If the issue were desperation, then why would the Palestinians have turned against Israel in 2000 after it offered to create a Palestinian state on more than 95 percent of the West Bank and Gaza? And why would they have launched a campaign of suicide bombings—in which

nine hundred Israelis, the large majority of them civilians, including children, have been murdered—during the time of the most dovish, most accommodating government (that of Prime Minister Ehud Barak) in Israel's history?

Despite the aim of many Arabs of destroying Israel, it is assumed among many in the West that the suicide bombings in Israel were driven by desperation and hopelessness, not antisemitism and religious extremism. As Cherie Blair, wife of British Prime Minister Tony Blair, expressed it: "As long as young people feel they have got no hope but to blow themselves up, you are never going to make progress."

To some of Israel's harshest critics, Arab "desperation" is seen not only as understandable, but acceptable and, for some, even praiseworthy. Juergen Moelleman, an official of Germany's Free Democrats, speaking about Palestinian terrorism, declared: "I would resist too and use force to do so . . . not just in my country, but in the aggressor's country as well." Claire Rayner, president of the British Humanist Association, stated in April 2002 that the idea of Israel as a Jewish homeland was "a load of crap," and therefore there was nothing wrong with targeting Israeli restaurants and buses: "If you treat a group of people the way Palestinians have been treated, they will use the only weapon they have, which is their individual lives."[13]

The ultimate statement of defense for the "suicide" killers was provided by Jose Saramago, the Portuguese Nobel laureate in literature: "We can compare what is happening in the Palestinian territories with Auschwitz."[14]

Aside from the fact that resistance fighters in far more desperate circumstances than the Palestinians (who actually enjoy more rights than do Arabs in Saddam Hussein's Iraq, Syria, Libya, and other countries) have not targeted civilians (e.g., anti-Nazi resistance fighters), it is clear from the families of the terrorists themselves that what drives the terrorists is religious passion. In the dozens of interviews with mothers of "suicide" bombers, one never hears mention of poverty. Rather, as one proud mother characteristically put it: "I am a compassionate mother to my children. Because I love my son, I encouraged him to die a martyr's death for the sake of Allah . . . Jihad is a religious obligation incumbent upon us, and we must carry it out. I sacrificed Muhammad as part of my obligation. This is an easy thing. There is no disagreement [among religious scholars] on such matters. The happiness in this world is an incomplete happiness, eternal happiness is life in the world to come, through martyrdom. Allah be praised, my son has attained this happiness . . . I prayed from the depths of my heart that Allah would cause the success of his operation. I asked Allah to give me 10 [Israelis] for Muhammad, and Allah granted my request and Muhammad made his dream come true, killing 10 Israeli settlers and soldiers. Our God honored him even more in that there were many Israelis wounded. [When his brothers informed me of his martyrdom], I began to cry, 'Allah is the greatest,' and prayed and thanked Allah for the success of the operation. I began to utter cries of joy and we declared that we were happy. The young people began to fire into the air out of joy over the success of his operation, as this is what we had hoped for him."

Likewise, the nineteen terrorists who murdered some three thousand Americans on September 11, 2001, came from affluent, in most cases particularly affluent, backgrounds. Fifteen, after all, were Saudis.

Islamic terrorists murder and maim Jews because of ideology. They believe it is God's will to do so. Only Westerners trained to believe that evil always comes from desperate socioeconomic circumstances believe otherwise.

PART THREE

WHAT IS TO BE DONE?

FIFTEEN

What Is to Be Done?

WHAT IS TO BE DONE?

Jew-hatred has existed for thousands of years, from Hellenic and Roman society to the leaders of the Enlightenment, throughout Christendom and Islam, in Communist and Fascist societies, from ancient times until today. There is no reason to suppose that antisemitism, humanity's most enduring hatred, will soon disappear.

What then is to be done? What, if anything, can Jews do to eradicate, diminish, or at the very least individually avoid antisemitism?

One possible response to antisemitism is assimilation. If one is no longer a Jew, in most cases he will no longer suffer antisemitism.

A second option for a Jew is to leave the antisemitism of non-Jewish society and go to live among Jews in the Jewish state, Israel.

A third possible way to help prevent antisemitism is to convert many non-Jews to Judaism. The great German-Jewish leader Rabbi Leo Baeck noted after World War II that, had many Germans had Jewish relatives (meaning Germans who had converted to Judaism), the Holocaust might never have occurred.

A fourth, and the most obvious, Jewish response to antisemitism is to fight it whenever it manifests itself—through all appropriate means from political to physical.

A fifth response to antisemitism is for Jews to influence non-Jews to live according to moral values consonant with those of Judaism.

ASSIMILATION

A Jew who wants to cease suffering Jew-hatred can often do so by the logical device of ceasing to be a Jew. Such a decision is tragic from the perspective of the Jewish people, but for a Jew unconcerned with Jewish survival it is neither illogical nor unworkable. For such Jews antisemitism makes a powerful case on behalf of assimilation.

Many Jews deny that assimilation is possible, recalling that the Nazis checked for "Jewish blood" and murdered assimilated Jews as readily as they murdered identifying Jews.

As true as these facts about Nazi Germany are, however, they ignore the fact that millions of Jews have assimilated in the past, many of them since the second half of the eighteenth century, and that assimilation is possible for a Jew today. The Nazis were unique in their rejection of Jews who adopted the non-Jewish majority's identity. Throughout Jewish history Jews who assimilated escaped antisemitic persecution. Even most Jews forcibly converted have eventually assimilated successfully. Over a hundred thousand Jews forcibly converted to Catholicism during the Spanish Inquisition in the fifteenth century have disappeared as Jews.

Hitler was alone among the major antisemites of history in denying that Jews could become non-Jews. The argument that Hitler "proves" that Jews cannot assimilate is simply wrong. What people who hold this view really mean is that under a racial antisemite like Hitler, assimilation is impossible. But unless one posits that in the coming generation a Hitlerian antisemite will come to power and attempt to murder all of a country's Jews, including, for example, Christian children of Jews who converted to Christianity, pointing to Hitler to deny the possibility of a Jew assimilating is pointless.

The Holocaust can lead to precisely the opposite conclusion. That antisemitic violence will one day be unleashed against one's children is an eloquent argument *for* attempting to assimilate today. Many marginal Jews would sooner try assimilation than bequeath to their children or grandchildren a possible fate of torture and murder. The Soviet poet Boris Pasternak, recipient of the Nobel Prize in literature and a Jew who converted to Russian Orthodoxy, eloquently made this case in his novel, *Dr. Zhivago:* "In whose interests is this voluntary martyrdom? . . . Dismiss this army which is forever fighting and being massacred, nobody knows for what. . . . Say to them: That's enough. Don't hold on to your identity. Don't all get together in a crowd. Disperse! Be with all the rest."[1]

The fact is that a native-born American or French or Uruguayan Jew can assimilate and virtually assure that his/her children do. Of course, full assimilation usually necessitates converting to the majority's religion and may also involve changing one's name and perhaps even one's residence, but it can be accomplished, as it is every day throughout the world. One must not ignore the first step, however. Most Jews who abandon their Jewish identity do not convert to the majority religion, and in the eyes of non-Jews they remain Jews.

Two factors, however, invalidate assimilation as a solution to antisemitism. First, it is applicable only to individuals, not to the Jewish people as a whole. Many Jews will never assimilate, which alone invalidates assimilation as a solution to antisemitism. Moreover, even if all the Jews of some nation would try to assimilate at one time, it is doubtful they would be fully accepted. Many Jewish individuals, perhaps even an entire Jewish community, could assimilate over the course of generations, but it is unlikely that an entire community could at one time. Second, no matter how successful, assimilation could never be considered a solution to antisemitism. A solution to antisemitism must by definition include the survival of Jewry, just as a solution to an illness must by definition include the survival of the patient. We seek solutions to antisemitism that enable Jews to live as Jews.

Nevertheless, it bears repeating that while tragic from Jewry's perspective and a victory for antisemitism, assimilation is a rational and viable way for individual Jews to escape antisemitism.

ZIONISM

A second response, and one that has offered itself as a solution to antisemitism, is Zionism, the return of the Jews to their own land in Israel. Zionism affords Jews the opportunity to cease being minorities everywhere, and to live in the one state wherein they cannot be persecuted by fellow citizens for being Jews. Zionism is, at least in theory, an ideal solution to antisemitism.

Theodor Herzl founded the modern Zionist movement first and foremost as a solution to antisemitism.[2] Herzl, an assimilated Hungarian Jew, had at first advocated Jewish assimilation, including conversion to Christianity, as the solution to the Jewish question. Only when Herzl concluded that the Jewish people could not assimilate into the European nations did he formulate the Zionist solution to antisemitism. What reinforced Herzl in that conclusion was the Dreyfus trial in 1894. After witnessing the virulent antisemitism that accompanied the trial in supposedly enlightened France, Herzl concluded that the only solution to antisemitism was for the Jews to cease living among non-Jews. The Jews must live in their own state.

The founders of Zionism held that the fundamental cause of antisemitism is the Jews' uniquely unnatural position as a "nation within a nation," whereby the Jews' commitment to Jewish peoplehood is often viewed as a challenge or disloyalty to the nationalism of the non-Jews among whom Jews live. Only by living in their own nation can the Jews become like other nations and no longer cause Jew-hatred.

Zionism thus offers entire Jewish communities as well as individual Jews a possible solution to antisemitism. Should all the Jews of a given country make *aliyah* (move to Israel), there will obviously be no more Jews in that country to suffer antisemitism. If that country then continues to oppose Jews, that opposition will focus on Israel, which is in an immeasurably superior position to defend itself than are persecuted Jews in a hostile non-Jewish society.

And that is not all. In addition to providing Jews with a haven from Jew-hatred and potentially reducing antisemitism through "normalizing" the Jews' situation, Zionism also helps to protect Diaspora Jewish communities against antisemitic outbreaks. The establishment of Israel has meant that Jews who continue to live among non-Jews now have a country to help defend their rights and to which they may flee if necessary. Israel has served both functions for Jews in Arab countries, the Soviet Union, Ethiopia, and elsewhere.

These facts notwithstanding, Zionism alone cannot solve antisemitism. Like assimilation, *aliyah* can solve antisemitism for individual Jews and for some Jewish communities, but not for the Jewish people as a whole. First, there is simply no prospect of all the Jews making *aliyah*. More important, even if every Jew in the world moved to Israel, there is no reason to assume that Jew-hatred would disappear.

Contrary to the theoretical bases and great hopes of Zionism, the creation of Israel has not reduced antisemitism—neither for world Jewry nor even for Israeli Jewry. The Jewish state has actually exacerbated antisemitism. In addition to having to suffer traditional antisemitism, Diaspora Jews now have to contend with Israel's mortal enemies, who hate Jews everywhere who affirm Jewish nationhood; and they now have to endure the new antisemitic charge that Diaspora Jewry's commitment to Israel means that Jews are disloyal citizens of the countries they inhabit. As for Israel itself, it has become the focus of intense worldwide hatred. Although few Jews in the world are as secure to express their Jewish identity as the Jews of Israel, few Jews in the world—indeed, few people in the world—are as isolated and despised as the Jews of Israel.

Zionism, whose major aim was to end Jew-hatred through the establishment of the Jewish state, has produced the most hated state in the world. This development would have shocked the secular founders of Zionism, who regarded the Jews as being different from other nations primarily in their not having their own state; who regarded Jew-hatred as basically a reaction to this one abnormality of the Jews; and who accordingly regarded the end of this abnormality, through the Jews living in their own state, as the solution to antisemitism.

But for those who understand that the Jews, because of their chosenness, are different from other nations in ways far deeper than their not having their own state, and who understand why Jew-hatred has been humanity's deepest hatred, it was to be expected that the Jewish state would be as hated among states as Jews have been among peoples.

Theodor Herzl founded Zionism to end antisemitism. Since its creation in 1948, Israel has given Jewry a self-respect it had not known in nearly two thousand years; it has afforded Jews the one place where they can lead a fully integrated Jewish life; it has been a haven for hundreds of thousands of Holocaust survivors and other oppressed Jews of various lands; it has given Jews hope after Auschwitz. It has, in short, done virtually everything for the Jewish people except the one thing Zionism's founders expected it to do: end antisemitism.

SEEKING CONVERTS

A third possible way to decrease antisemitism, particularly in the United States today, is to increase the number of Jews through converting many non-Jews to Judaism. This helps prevent antisemitism in four ways. First, by increasing the number of Jews, the Jews become stronger and less likely to be attacked. Second, it ensures that many non-Jews have Jewish relatives. Third, serious conversions ideally spread Jewish values. And fourth, by making it known that Jews welcome converts, Jews can help destroy such antisemitic beliefs as that Jews think they are an inherently superior race, or that Jews are ethnic chauvinists.

Such an approach to helping prevent antisemitism has rarely been suggested. This, too, has a number of reasons. First, Jews have rarely lived in societies where they were unharassed, let alone free to convert non-Jews to Judaism. Second, many Jews have come to believe that seeking converts would provoke antisemitism. And third, many Jews believe that Judaism does not seek converts.

The first problem does not exist for American Jews, for they are free to advocate Judaism. As for the fear of incurring antisemitism, we are not speaking here of converting Christians, but rather of reaching out to the tens of millions of unchurched non-Jews in the United States. Nor does seeking converts imply missionizing in the traditional Christian sense since Judaism does not hold that it is the only way to God. Rather, we are for making it known that Jews accept and desire converts, and for educating the general public about Judaism with its distinctive values and way of life.

Such an approach to seeking converts would not only not increase antisemitism, it would decrease it, for a major source of hostility to Jewry emanates from the perception that Jews consider themselves a superior race and constitute a closed ethnic club.

Now the only question remaining is, does Judaism seek converts?

The answer is yes. This surprises most Jews, who for so long have believed that Judaism discourages people from converting. But the reasons for this Jewish policy are historical, not theological, and they were brought about by non-Jews. For nearly fifteen hundred years Jews lived in Christian and Muslim societies that often made conversion to Judaism a capital offense—both for the convert and for the Jews involved in the conversion. It was only for this reason that Jews adopted their policy of discouraging conversion. *Judaism desires converts*, and when Jews were free to do so they actively encouraged would-be converts.

In the Talmud, Rabbi Eleazar ben Pedat went so far as to claim that the exile of the Jews from Israel, the most destructive event in ancient Jewish history, had one constructive purpose: "The Holy One, praised be He, exiled Israel among the nations for the purpose of gaining converts" (Pesachim 87b). In fact, of several dozen statements in the Talmud concerning converts and seeking converts, all but four are highly positive.[3] The *Avot de Rabbi Nathan* (chap. 12), an early rabbinic work, encouraged Jews to emulate Abraham, who alone with his wife, Sarah, spread the monotheist ideal: "Every Jew should endeavor to actively bring men under the wing of God's presence even as Abraham did." The model of Abraham was used not only to encourage Jews to seek converts, but also to encourage potential Gentile converts: "If a man wishes to convert to Judaism, but says, 'I am too old to convert,' let him learn from Abraham, who when he was ninety-nine years old, entered God's covenant" (the rabbinic text, Tanhuma B, Lekh Lekha 40). Some rabbis went so far as to proclaim that converts were the greatest of Jews: "Said Resh Lakish: the convert is dearer than the Jews who stood before Mount Sinai. Why? Because had they [the Jews] not seen the thunder and the lightning and the mountains quaking and the sounds of the horn, they would not have accepted the Torah. But this one, who saw none of these things, came, surrendered himself to the Holy One and accepted upon himself the kingdom of heaven. Could any be dearer than he?" (Tanhuma B, Lekh Lekha 6)

In espousing these beliefs about Jews influencing non-Jews, the rabbis were faithfully reflecting the Hebrew Bible's attitude. The prophet Isaiah dreamed of the day when all the nations of the world would declare: "Come, let us go up to the Mount of the Lord, to the House of the God of Jacob; that he may instruct us in His ways and that we may walk in His path. For out of Zion shall go forth the Torah, and the word of God from Jerusalem" (Isaiah 2:3).

Judaism bestowed what may be considered its highest honor upon a convert. Jewish tradition holds that the Messiah will be of the family of Ruth (ancestress of King David), a woman who converted to Judaism and for whom a book of the Bible is named.

That Jews attempted to implement Judaism's wish to seek converts is recorded in non-Jewish and Jewish sources. The New Testament states that in the Roman Empire the Jews would "sail the seas and cross whole countries to win one convert" (Matthew 23:15). Judaism had become so popular among segments of the Roman intelligentsia that Juvenal, the great Roman writer, wrote a satire about Roman fathers who eat no pork, observe the Sabbath, and worship only the heavenly God, and whose sons undergo circumcision, despise Roman laws, and study the Jews' Torah. The Jewish historian Josephus wrote in the first century: "The masses have long since shown a keen desire to adopt our religious observances; and there is not one city, Greek or barbarian, nor a single nation, to which our customs of abstaining from work on the seventh day has not spread, and where the fasts and lighting of [Sabbath] lamps and many of our prohibitions in the matter of food are not observed" (Contra Apion 2:39).

When the Roman Empire became Christian, however, the situation was altered radically. Conversion to Judaism became a crime, soon a capital one, for both the convert and the Jews involved in the conversion.[4]

One would expect the Jews, now faced with capital punishment, to have ceased their efforts to spread Judaism. Yet in general they did not; and this persistence constitutes the most convincing evidence of how powerful was the Jews' desire to gain converts. As George Foot Moore, the Harvard historian of religions, wrote: "Against all such attempts of pagan or Christian rulers to shut up Judaism in itself and prevent its spread, the Jews persisted in their missionary efforts to make the religion God had revealed to their fathers the religion of all mankind."[5]

Nevertheless, as the persecution of the Jewish community increased, the price for accepting converts became increasingly onerous. Often, whole communities would be punished for one Christian's conversion to Judaism. To cite but one example: in 1012, a German priest, Vicilinus of Mainz, became a Jew and then wrote essays in which he used the Bible to demonstrate the continuing validity of Judaism. Within a few months Emperor Henry II expelled the entire Jewish population of Mainz.

The Jews therefore had no choice but to change their attitudes toward encouraging conversion to Judaism. The point cannot be overemphasized that Jews stopped seeking converts to Judaism only because they were forced to, and only then did vigorous discouragement of would-be converts become the official Jewish policy. In the words of Rabbi Solomon Luria (1510–1573), perhaps the leading European Talmud scholar of the sixteenth century: "Under the present conditions, when we live in a country that is not ours, like slaves under the rod of a master, if a Jew encourages someone to become a proselyte he becomes a rebel against the government, subject to the death penalty. . . . Therefore, I caution anyone against being a party to such activity when the law of the state forbids it, for he thereby forfeits his life."[6]

Jewish reluctance to seek converts under such conditions was highly understandable. But why have Jews been reluctant to seek converts in a society such as the United States, where converts and Jews who facilitate conversions are not made to suffer at all? One reason is inertia. A communal attitude nearly one thousand years old is not easily broken. A second reason is that over the last century and a half much of the Jewish community has become secular and ethnic. Obviously such Jews are unable to encourage conversion to a religion that they do not practice, and whose beliefs they do not hold. A characteristic example of the inability of secular Jews to advocate Judaism is offered in the widely praised book *Letters to an American Jewish Friend: A Zionist's Polemic* by Hillel Halkin, a secular Jew. Halkin relates the following: "A Jewish girl whom I knew was thinking of marrying a non-Jewish boy and wanted him to become a Jew. She asked me if I would talk to him; I agreed. . . . His first question was, 'tell me, apart from my future mother-in-law's feelings, why should I become a Jew?' . . . And there wasn't a single reason I could think of. . . . This encounter happened with a non-Jew, but had it been with an assimilated Jew or with a Jew who wished to know why he should feel more committed to his Jewishness than he did, I could not have answered any differently. I don't know why one should be a Jew."[7]

A third reason why Jews do not encourage converts is that some unfortunately still believe that a convert to Judaism is not "really" Jewish (thus unwittingly disqualifying Abraham, the first Jew, and Ruth, the ancestress of King David and the Messiah). Fourth, even religious Jews generally lack the ability to articulate Judaism to non-Jews, or for that matter, to irreligious Jews. Finally, some conversions devoid of meaning have given conversions to Judaism a bad name. We are referring here to hasty, pro forma "conversions" made more to alleviate the bad feelings of anxious in-laws than to help create a new committed Jew. While Jews must enthusiastically welcome converts to Judaism, such sign-on-the-dotted-line conversions are not the way.

There are then any number of obstacles to overcome in beginning a program to seek converts to Judaism. But there is little question that among other benefits to Jewry, and to society at large, more converts would be an effective tool in the fight against antisemitism.

COMBATING OUTBREAKS OF ANTISEMITISM

By far the most common Jewish response to antisemitism is to fight it whenever it erupts and attempt to identify and suppress its sources before it erupts. Since the Holocaust, Jews, particularly those living in democracies, have effectively prevented major antisemitic attacks in their countries and have achieved a success, unparalleled by any other religious or ethnic group, in helping their fellow Jews in nondemocratic countries, particularly the former USSR.

In the United States, for example, groups such as the Anti-Defamation League (ADL), the American Jewish Committee, and the Simon Wiesenthal Center have vigilantly monitored the far Right and Left for signs of antisemitism and have generally effectively silenced Jew-haters through public exposure. Other Jewish groups helped lead the fight against Soviet antisemitism, and against the persecution of Jews in Ethiopia, Syria, and elsewhere.

With regard to combating antisemitism and its anti-Zionist incarnation, American Jewry has functioned since the Holocaust like a finely tuned watch. Jews have learned how to use media effectively, petition public officials, demonstrate, and work to elect candidates sympathetic to the fight against domestic and international enemies of the Jews. In a world that revolves to a substantial extent around power and public persuasion, the access to power of Jews and non-Jews committed to fighting antisemitism has been of great importance to Jewish survival. And even so, antisemitism and anti-Zionism, particularly in the Arab world, Europe, and Africa, have thrived.

Given the success of Jewish groups in helping to combat outbreaks of antisemitism in the United States, we only wish to add the following points.

First, the case against antisemitism and anti-Zionism must be made before all Americans, not only in Washington. The struggle for America's continuing support for Israel will ultimately be won or lost back in the home districts of congressmen, not in Washington alone. American Jews must earn the support of their fellow Americans for Israel's security and other Jewish causes by taking their case directly to the American people. For this, Jewry needs not only good lobbyists who can effectively make Jewry's case before policymakers and legislators, but eloquent spokesmen in leadership positions who can engender goodwill directly from the American people.

Second, American Jews must understand their stake in modern politics, and should not, both for their sake and for America's, identify with only one brand of politics. Third, American Jews should not equate the death of religion with Jewish security. That some American Jews and some Jewish institutions have been among the leaders against virtually any public manifestation of religion in the United States may ultimately backfire against Jewish, not to mention American society's, better interests. A secular government is in everyone's best interests, a secular society is not. Religious America, not secular Europe, is Jewry's best friend.

Finally, as all Jews must recognize, virtually all their efforts to combat antisemitic outbreaks deal with the symptoms rather than the causes of Jew-hatred. This is why no matter how effective these efforts, they cannot solve antisemitism. These efforts are important and effective—but only in a society relatively free of antisemitism. When a Jewish group publicly condemns someone for antisemitism, that condemnation is effective only if the society has values that hold antisemitism contemptible. Thus, the only *solution* to antisemitism is for Jewish Jews to affect society's values. All other attempts to end antisemitism are doomed to failure. They only buy time until the next eruption.

A SOLUTION TO ANTISEMITISM

Zionism, seeking converts to Judaism, and combating antisemitism when it arises are each critically important and together could help prevent, or at least minimize, future antisemitic outbreaks. But if the goal is to put an end to antisemitism, then Jews must also attempt to influence the moral values of non-Jews so that no aspect of Judaism any longer threatens the non-Jews' values. If the Holocaust taught anything, it is that to prevent another one, the Jews have no choice but to influence their neighbors' moral values.

Jews must therefore resume their original task of spreading ethical monotheism. The Jewish role is to bring humankind not to Judaism but to universal, God-based morality. *It is the exquisite irony of Jewish history that this task, which has been the ultimate cause of antisemitism, must be fulfilled to end antisemitism.*

This means in essence that the Jews must make the world aware of two basic principles: ethics need God, and God demands ethics. The Jewish people, in the tradition of ethical monotheism's greatest advocates, the Jewish Prophets, must therefore oppose religionists who advocate God without depicting goodness along with faith as the major concern of God, and likewise oppose secularists who advocate a value system devoid of religious moral values. In the first case, God is rendered morally irrelevant and religion becomes either a superstitious refuge from the moral demands of this world or a proponent of evil. It is not a coincidence that the last words heard by victims of Islamist terrorism (such as the passengers on the planes that were crashed into the World Trade Center and the Pentagon) were *Allahu Akhbar*, "God is great." In the second instance (i.e., a value system without God), ethics become relative, rarely transcending personal taste. God without ethics has led to religious massacres from Crusaders to Osama bin Laden; values and ideologies without God have led to the secular massacres of the Gulag and Auschwitz.

While many secular Jews may find this prospect most unappealing, there is really little choice. For even these Jews recognize that if antisemitism is a moral failing, only the moral values of non-Jews can prevent antisemitism. The only questions regarding antisemitism over which Jews might then differ is not whether Jews ought to influence the moral values of others but through which values. In the United States Jews have tended to push secular liberal values, trusting that these would constitute a bulwark against antisemitism. Jewish history has taught Jews well the dangers of reactionary religious and political ideologies, and the need for pluralism and a nondogmatic approach to religious beliefs. But American Jews are increasingly aware of the dangers on the Left. The breakdown of many traditional moral values and of a sense of obligation and accountability to a moral God poses as great a threat to the Jews' well-being as has the extreme Right. Indeed, in America, the greatest threat to Jewish security now emanates from the secular Left (e.g., the universities and the intellectual Left). Thus secular values, as indispensable as they are to the proper functioning of *government*, are not enough to ensure the moral vitality of the *society*, and only a morally strong society will not be hostile to Jews and Israel.

The time may be uniquely ripe for Jews, especially in the United States and Israel, to influence the world by communicating not only humanist, liberal, or conservative but Jewish and ethical monotheist values. As we have seen, leftist, rightist, secularist, socialist, and even humanist ideologies emanating from the Enlightenment have often been saturated with antisemitism. For Jews to attempt to eliminate antisemitism through ideologies that themselves have easily led to antisemitism is obviously an exercise in self-destruction.

Israel and America offer contemporary Jews unique opportunities to reduce antisemitism and to "repair the world under the rule of God." As thousands of years of Jew-hatred have shown, *the tasks are identical.* As Jews have believed since antisemitism began, only in a world guided by ethical monotheism will Jews be able to live in peace.

It is not the purpose of this book to delineate these values or how to communicate them. Those are critical subjects worthy of their own extended analysis.[8] Our concern has been only to show that Jewish religious and moral values are both the ultimate cause of and solution to antisemitism.

"The Jews," said the great modern Jewish thinker Abraham Joshua Heschel, "are a messenger who forgot his message." For the Jews' sake, as well as for humanity's, Jews need to remember that message.

The Meaning of Antisemitism for Non-Jews

A NTISEMITISM IS A JEWISH PROBLEM, but non-Jews make a most self-destructive error when they dismiss it as only the Jews' problem. For reasons explained in this book, treatment of the Jews has served as one of humanity's moral barometers. Watch how a nation, religion, or political movement treats Jews, and you have an early and deadly accurate picture of that group's intentions toward others.

Moral non-Jews who fail to act against antisemites will very likely end up suffering from them. Nothing about Jew-hatred is clearer than this. Jew-haters begin with Jews but never end with them, as antisemitism is ultimately a hatred of higher standards. The antisemites first wish to destroy the perceived embodiment of that higher call to the good, the Jews. But they do not hate the Jews alone. They hate whatever and whoever represents higher values and moral achievement. Whoever sees antisemitism as only some aberrational hatred on the part of an otherwise morally acceptable group does not understand antisemitism. So long as there are good people and decent societies, the Jews will never be the only targets of antisemites.

The clearest contemporary example of such a target is the United States. Those who hate the Jewish nation are usually those who are most likely to hate America as well. Almost as consistently as Jew-hatred, America-hatred has become a moral litmus test of nations, regimes, and ideologies. America represents freedom, a higher quality of life, and a willingness to fight for its values. These qualities are despised by regimes characterized by tyranny and socioeconomic failure, and by individuals in the West who support such regimes or who wish to denigrate America for reasons akin to those of antisemites in their denigration of Jews. With all its flaws, America alone stands between liberty and the ascent of tyranny throughout the world.

Thus, it is small surprise that among tyrannical regimes and their defenders, America and Israel are so often identified as the same enemy. This is not merely a consequence of America's standing all too often alone, or almost alone, behind Israel; the United States has aided various Arab countries very generously, and it has on some critical occasions backed Arab regimes (such as Nasser's Egypt in 1956 and Saudi Arabia in 1981) against Israel. This hostility is aroused largely because America and Israel represent democracy (epitomized by political, personal, and economic liberty), equal rights for women, a generally higher quality of life, and a willingness to confront despotism. That is why the two countries that are most hated by radical Islamists are Israel and the United States.

Likewise, within the West itself, so often the individuals who most vilify America do the same to Israel. For example, in the 1980s, the *Village Voice*'s Alexander Cockburn, a leftist columnist known for his scathing attacks on America, compared Israel in Lebanon to the Nazis in Poland.[1] Similarly, as noted, Professor Noam Chomsky—revered on the Left for his anti-American writings and speeches (see pages 49, 53)—in his book *The Fateful Triangle: The United States, Israel, and the Palestinians*, makes twelve references to Hitler, and all twelve references are made in order to liken Israel and/or Zionism to Hitler.[2] There clearly is a desire among opponents of Israel (and America), in the eloquent words of the *New Republic*'s longtime editor and publisher, Martin Peretz, "to try to establish a parity of immorality" between Israel and its enemies (though in actuality, the United States and Israel are usually depicted as worse).[3] The reason for this is that the Jewish nation (again, like America) has offered itself, and is perceived, as a moral beacon; hence many individuals wish to portray it as negatively as possible.

Yet despite all this hatred, America remains the dreamed-for haven of the world's oppressed; and Israel remains an embattled democracy in the midst of authoritarian states, and the birthplace of the kibbutz to which tens of thousands of youth from around the world have long turned for a living lesson in human equality,* and at the same time, the only country in the world targeted for annihilation.

America, with all its imperfections, has similarly represented a model of something better, and has led the world's fights against evil— and in so doing constitutes a moral challenge to others. But the Jews have played this role for millennia. The Jews might be described as humanity's miner's canary. Just as the death of canaries warns miners of noxious fumes, so the death of Jews warns civilized nations of noxious moral fumes. But despite these universal ramifications of Jew-hatred, few heed these warnings. Examples abound.

Many in the Western democracies dismissed the Nazis' antisemitism as a bad feature of people who otherwise could be lived with. Among those was Arthur Hays Sulzberger, who became the *New York Times*'s publisher in 1935. Sulzberger, a nominally identifying Jew, felt that the threat of Nazi antisemitism was being used by some Jews to arouse pro-Zionist feelings—he regarded himself as an anti-Zionist—among Jews and non-Jews. He, therefore, instructed his city editor not to give "too much space" to the efforts of groups such as the American Jewish Committee (AJC) to aid the Jews of Europe. Even before Sulzberger's appointment as pub-

*There is another parallel between Jew-hatred and America-hatred. Both are often perceived as emanating from antagonism to Jews' and Americans' wealth. We have seen how this perception is false regarding Jew-hatred. It is also false as regards America-hatred. Were wealth the major reason for hating a nation, Switzerland ought to be at least as deeply hated as America, and certainly the Arab oil-exporting nations, whose wealth increased in direct proportion to a decrease in Third World wealth, should be particularly hated. Yet America, like Israel and the Jews, is hated far more than are these countries. It is what America represents, not merely its wealth, that is loathed.

lisher, the paper had instituted a ban on letters-to-the-editor concerning Hitler (during the years the Nazis were coming to power), out of fear that the *Times*, widely known to be owned by the Ochs and Sulzberger families, would be perceived as being a "Jewish newspaper." Thus, the *Times*'s policy during the Nazi era—a policy for which the paper has since apologized—was to underplay Hitler's and the Nazi's antisemitism. Harvard professor Ruth Wisse has recently written on the extraordinarily damaging effects of such a policy. What might have happened, she speculates, if

the publishers of *The New York Times* had acted truly without bias. They would then have responded to Hitler's virulent antisemitism as signaling a broader danger to everything precious to themselves and to America. They would have assiduously gathered information about Hitler's program of rearmament, as Winston Churchill tried to do once he became convinced that Hitler was planning to attack the West. They would have drawn daily attention to Germany's abuses of democratic freedoms, its perversions of law, its abrogation of civil liberties. And they would have registered the way that Nazi antisemitism cloaked darker and anti-democratic purposes behind an enmity directed against the Jews alone.[4]

In short, had the West perceived the antisemitism of Hitler and the Nazis to be the evil it was, and had Hitler and the Nazis, therefore, been perceived to be the evil they were, free nations would have then opposed Hitler earlier and saved not only six million Jews but tens of millions of others.

The Soviet Union was another example of a state whose hostility to Jews (and to Israel as time went on) was both an indicator of its immoral nature and a warning of the threat it posed to societies that held liberty and justice as primary values. Those in the West who regarded the Soviet Jewish problem as solely a Jewish problem did a serious disservice to other Soviet religious groups and nationalities in the Soviet Union whose plights were not as publicized as that of Soviet Jews; and they did the West a disservice by hampering efforts to confront, or even acknowledge, the evil nature of the Soviet regime.

A particularly telling example of the refusal to take antisemitism seriously took place in Africa in the 1970s. Before the Ugandan dictator Idi Amin began to slaughter a half million Ugandans, he had already announced his hatred of Israel and his admiration for Hitler's "Final Solution." But only Jews, and America, whose ambassador protested, listened; the rest of the world ignored Amin's antisemitism and anti-Zionism—that was the Jews' problem. But as then U.S. ambassador to the United Nations Daniel Patrick Moynihan pointed out: "It is no accident" that the "racist murderer" Idi Amin called for the extinction of Israel. "For Israel is a democracy and it is simply the fact that despotisms will seek whatever opportunities come to hand to destroy that which threatens them most, which is democracy."[5] Amin went on to live in peace and tranquility in Saudi Arabia.

One of the first acts of the Ayatollah Ruholla Khomeini after assuming power in Iran was the takeover of the Israeli embassy in Tehran. That too was dismissed as the Jews' problem—until the Iranians did the same thing to the American embassy.

Hatred of Israel and Jews as indicators of the haters' evil continues. Too bad the world ignored, or even dismissed, Palestinian Muslim suicide bombings against Israelis as Israel's problem (or even fault, see pages 172–174). Had the civilized world condemned and confronted the atrocities, perhaps other Islamists might have thought twice about engaging in terror. Instead, radical Islamists were inspired by Palestinian terror. And 9/11 and what has followed since are history. Now, innocents are terrorized in many parts of the world—and none as much as Muslims themselves, so many of whom supported Palestinian terror against Israeli civilians.

As Thomas Friedman, the foreign affairs columnist of the *New York Times* and a man who has often voiced sharp criticism of Israel, prophesied as early as 2002: "If suicide bombing is allowed to work in Israel, then, like hijacking and airplane bombing [earlier innovative tactics of Palestinian terrorists], it will be copied and will eventually lead to a bomber strapped with a nuclear device threatening entire nations. That is why the whole world must see this Palestinian suicide strategy defeated."

That is why it is such a grievous error to dismiss Arab and Muslim hatred of Israel as a Jewish problem that ultimately reveals little about the moral state of many Arab and other Muslim societies. It has gradually become clear that the hatred of Israel is a moral indicator of some precision. As the Christians of Lebanon, who have suffered far more from Muslim hatred than the Jews of Israel, have learned, Arab leaders who call for wars to annihilate Zionism are not otherwise tolerant, democracy-loving gentlemen. There is often a direct correlation between the ferocity of a Muslim leader's hatred of the Jewish state and his hatred of democracy and other Western values. Syria's Assad, Iran's Khomeini, Libya's Gadhafi, Iraq's Hussein, and Osama bin Laden are five such examples.

As Professor Wisse reminds us: "We know from the past that the West paid dearly for ignoring Hitler's war against the Jews. One can only hope that it will not pay as dearly for having ignored or underestimated for so long the Arab war against Israel and the Jews."[6] (Conversely, Arab and other Middle Eastern Muslim societies less characterized by despotism and wanton cruelty, such as Tunisia, are also characterized by a greater tolerance of the Jews.)

Jew-hatred and its latest incarnation, Israel-hatred, are the price Jews pay for their role in history. They pay it often unwillingly and they live the role, for the most part, unwittingly. But the eminent French Catholic theologian Jacques Maritain understood it. "Israel," he wrote, "is to be found at the very heart of the world's structure, stimulating it, exasperating it, moving it. Like an alien body, like an activating ferment injected into the mass, it gives the world no peace, it bars slumber, it teaches the world to be discontented and restless as long as the world has not God, it stimulates the movement of history. . . . It is the vocation of Israel which the world hates."[7]

Moral non-Jews who do not heed the universal implications of this hatred are destined to be its victims.

ACKNOWLEDGMENTS (for original 1983 edition)

W E WISH TO EXPRESS OUR GRATITUDE to Dr. Max Vorspan,
professor of history at the University of Judaism of the Jewish Theological Seminary of America; to Dr. William Brin-
ner, professor of Near Eastern Studies at the University of California,
Berkeley; and to Dr. Gilbert Graff. Each of these scholars has given us
very valuable advice and criticisms. We also wish to thank David Lehrer
and Mildred Marcus of the Los Angeles office of the Anti-Defamation
League. Needless to say, we take all responsibility for any errors of fact
or interpretation that remain.

Our editor, Fred Hills, senior vice president of Simon & Schuster,
deserves special recognition for his simply indispensable advice and constant encouragement. His faith in the significance of this book made it
possible.

To Kathy Phipps, wherever she is in Oregon, go our thanks for her
patient and excellent typing of the manuscript.

This book was written during our seven years as director and education director, respectively, of the Brandeis-Bardin Institute. To the
thousands of the institute's members and BCI alumni, thank you for
your support and encouragement. We are particularly grateful to David
Woznica and Pat Havins.

This book was written in California: at Brandeis-Bardin, in Los Angeles, Mammoth Lakes, and Palm Springs. We are especially indebted to Romy and Flora Rosman for the use of their idyllic retreat in Palm Springs, and to Ira and Betty Weiner for their beautiful cottage in Mammoth Lakes. All writers should be blessed with such settings in which to think and write.

August 2003: We would like to thank Jeff Helmreich for his advice and suggestions for Chapter 14, "Eight Lies About Israel," and Kelly Gionti, Fred Hills's assistant, for her insightful criticisms and suggestions that ensured a tighter manuscript.

Dennis Prager and Joseph Telushkin

NOTES

PART ONE: WHY THE JEWS? THE EXPLANATION

One: Why Jew-Hatred Is Unique

1. The term "anti-Semitism" was coined in 1879 by Wilheim Marr, an anti-Jewish spokesman in Germany, as a euphemistic substitute for *Judenhass*, Jew-hatred. The term is a misnomer, of course, since it has nothing to do with Semites. Therefore, to avoid any confusion we have adopted the approach of the distinguished historian James Parkes, who has suggested that "antisemitism" be written as one word. Emil Fackenheim, the Jewish philosopher, has also adopted this spelling, explaining "the spelling ought to be antisemitism without the hyphen, dispelling the notion that there is an entity 'Semitism' which 'anti-Semitism' opposes" (Emil Fackenheim, "Post-Holocaust Anti-Jewishness, Jewish Identity and the Centrality of Israel," in *World Jewry and the State of Israel*, ed. Moshe Davis, p. 11, n. 2).

2. *Pogrom* is not the only word bequeathed by antisemitism to the contemporary vocabulary. Other terms include *genocide*, stemming from the Nazi attempt to murder all Jews; *Holocaust*, the Nazi murder of six million Jews between 1939 and 1945; and *ghetto*, the name given to the enclosed areas where Jews were forced to live in parts of European cities

until the twentieth century. (See "The Origin of the Ghetto," in Cecil Roth's *Personalities and Events in Jewish History*, pp. 226–36).

3. The Russian expression was *"Byay Zhidov Spassai Rossiyu"* (Beat the Zhids and save Russia). This phrase is so well known among the Russians that Yevgeny Yevtushenko quoted it in his most famous poem, "Babi Yar," written in protest against contemporary Soviet antisemitism.

4. The lack of documentation in Egyptian and Persian sources in no way disproves that such anti-Jewish campaigns were conducted. These countries might well have been embarrassed by their ineffectual efforts to wipe out the Jews. Even today, despite the vast amount of pictorial and eyewitness proofs, the testimony of tens of thousands of survivors, and the confessions of thousands of perpetrators, dozens of books, pamphlets, and articles have been published denying the Germans' attempt to annihilate the Jews.

5. We do not use the commonly utilized term *exterminate* in referring to Hitler's murder of the Jews, as this word was used by the Nazis in order to equate the murder of Jews with the extermination of vermin.

6. N. Hanover, *Yeven Mezulah,* pp. 31–32, cited in H. H. Ben-Sasson et al., *A History of the Jewish People,* p. 656.

7. Bernard Glassman, *Anti-Semitic Stereotypes Without Jews: Images of the Jews in England, 1290–1700.* See particularly pp. 37–40 and 67–70.

8. See Paul Lendvai, *Anti-Semitism Without Jews.*

9. Salo Baron, *The Russian Jew Under Tsars and Soviets,* pp. 49–50.

Two: Antisemitism: The Hatred of Judaism and Ethical Monotheism

1. *New York Times,* November 30, 1974.

2. Ernest van den Haag, *The Jewish Mystique,* pp. 60–61.

3. Reported by the first-century Egyptian Jewish philosopher Philo, and cited in Vamberto Marais, *A Short History of Anti-Semitism,* p. 28.

4. Quoted from a personal conversation with Hitler by Hermann Rauschning in *The Ten Commandments,* ed. Armin Robinson, pp. ix–xiii.

5. Cited in Ernst Christian Helmreich's *The German Churches Under Hitler,* p. 201.

6. See Maimonides, *The Commandments,* vol. 1, Positive Commandments, no. 9, pp. 12–13, in the translation of Charles B. Chavel. Regarding the other laws of monotheism, see Maimonides' *Sefer ha-Mada (Book of*

Knowledge), introduction to "Fundamentals of the Torah" and "Idolatry and Heathenism."

7. In the two biblical depictions of Utopia, the Garden of Eden, and the messianic days, all creatures are depicted as herbivorous (Genesis 1:27–29; Isaiah II:6,7,9). In addition, the Talmud (Sanhedrin 59b) explicitly states that human beings are allowed to eat meat only as a concession to man's lust for meat.

8. For a fuller explanation of Kashrut, see Dennis Prager and Joseph Telushkin, *The Nine Questions People Ask About Judaism*, pp. 57–64.

9. The Talmud records one telling exception to the prohibition on attending public events on the Sabbath, which also illustrates the moral gulf that existed between Jewish and Roman law and society. The rabbis permitted Jews to attend gladiator fights on Sabbaths and any other day so that they could vote at the end of each fight to spare the life of the defeated gladiator (Tosefta, Avodah Zarah).

10. This seems to have departed from the views of Jesus. Jesus is cited in the New Testament as stressing the need to observe Jewish law: "Do not imagine that I have come to abolish the law or the prophets. I tell you solemnly, till heaven and earth disappear, not one dot, not one little stroke, shall disappear from the law until its purpose is achieved. Therefore, the man who infringes even the least of these commandments and teaches others to do the same will be considered the least in the kingdom of heaven; but the man who keeps them and teaches them will be considered great in the kingdom of heaven" (Matt. 5:17–19). According to the New Testament, Jesus' early disciples observed Jewish law. Acts 10:14 records Peter's observance of Kashrut; Acts 15:1 records that "some men came down from Judea" to teach followers of Jesus that "unless you have yourselves been circumcised in the tradition of Moses, you cannot be saved." In Acts 21:24, James (Jesus' brother) says to Paul, "Let everyone know that there is no truth in the reports that they have heard about you, and that you still regularly observe the law."

11. Cited in Rosemary Reuther, *Faith and Fratricide*, p. 150.

12. The name Israel, which literally means "wrestle with God," was given to the patriarch Jacob (Gen. 32:29). Hence the term "children of Israel" is the biblical term for the Jewish nation.

13. Reform Judaism, begun in Germany, was characterized in its early period as much by its dropping of Jewish nationhood as by its dropping

of much of Jewish law. The first major Reform prayer book, published in Breslau in 1818, deleted all prayers for the coming of the Messiah and for the return of the Jews to Israel, on the grounds that the Jews needed neither. They were fully content as Germans and could fulfill all their national aspirations as Germans in Germany. The Reform abandonment of Jewish peoplehood spread to the United States. The 1885 convention of the American Reform rabbinate declared: "Judaism is only a religion. We Jews are not a nation." Reform Judaism has since returned to the normative Jewish view of Judaism, and today affirms the national component at least as strongly as the other components.

14. That the Jews are a nation defined by religion is acknowledged by both secular and religious Jews. This was demonstrated by a 1963 Israeli Supreme Court case. Daniel Rufeisen, a German Jew who converted to Catholicism, applied for Israeli citizenship under Israel's Law of Return, which offers any Jew immediate citizenship upon arrival and application in Israel. He contended that being born into the Jewish nation rendered his religious identity irrelevant; just as one could be a German of any faith, one could be a Jew of any faith. The secular Supreme Court of Israel ruled against Rufeisen, ruling that a Jew who adopts another *religion* automatically leaves the Jewish *nation*. (This explains why Jews regard fringe groups such as "Jews for Jesus" as having left the Jewish people.)

15. Clermont-Tonnerre's speech is reprinted in *The Jew in the Modern World*, ed. Paul R. Mendes-Flohr and Jehuda Reinharz, pp. 103–5.

Three: The Chosen People Idea as a Cause of Antisemitism

1. The Malik statement is a prime example of anti-Judaism hiding behind the cover of anti-Zionism (see chap. 13). The attack on chosenness is purely an attack on a basic Jewish religious belief: chosenness is not a component of the secular Zionist movement.

2. The study appears in Gertrude Selznick and Stephen Steinberg, *The Tenacity of Prejudice*, p. 6.

3. The story of this document that claims to outline the program of a Jewish world conspiracy is recounted in an important work of scholarship, *Warrant for Genocide: The Jewish World Conspiracy and the Protocols of the Elders of Zion*, by Norman Cohn. Though the *Protocols* had been definitively proven to be a forgery by the *London Times* in 1921, it continued to be utilized by antisemites and believed by millions of people. In the

United States, Henry Ford had tens of millions of copies rewritten under the title *The International Jew* and distributed through his newspaper, the *Dearborn Independent*. Although Ford eventually apologized to the Jewish community, his antisemitic publications were used by Adolf Hitler throughout the Nazi era. During the 1960s the *Protocols* were republished by President Gamal Abdel Nasser of Egypt, and they were distributed by King Faisal of Saudi Arabia in the 1970s. As of 2003 the *Protocols* have been published in more than 60 editions throughout the Arab world.

4. For a discussion of Shaw's hostility to the doctrine of chosenness, see Hayim Greenberg's essay, "The Universalism of the Chosen People," reprinted in the *Hayim Greenberg Anthology*, ed. Marie Syrkin.

5. *Religion in Life*, Summer 1971, p. 279.

6. *Sabbath Prayer Book*, Jewish Reconstructionist Foundation, p. xxiv.

7. See Mordecai Kaplan's essay in *The Condition of Jewish Belief*, ed. Milton Himmelfarb, p. 121.

8. The implication by Rabbi Jacob Agus, ibid., pp. 13–14 that historically the Jews did see themselves as superior to the nations surrounding them is misleading. The Jews saw their superiority as an existential fact, not a theological premise, as Jewish lifestyle, not Jewish chosenness. They saw—how could they not?—that they lived a morally better life than did the societies around them (see chap. 4). In a comparable manner, Paul and his disciples thought that they were living morally superior lives to most of the Romans around them.

9. Louis Jacobs, *A Jewish Theology*, p. 274.

Four: The Higher Quality of Jewish Life as a Cause of Antisemitism

1. Thomas Sowell, *Ethnic America: A History*, p. 94.

2. The church, in fact, long discouraged Catholics from reading the Bible on their own. It was only Martin Luther's fifteenth-century translation of the Bible into German that widely popularized Bible study among literate Germans.

3. Talmud Bava Bathra, 21a.

4. Moses Maimonides, *Laws of Torah Study* I:1–10 (emphasis ours).

5. Cited in Beryl Smalley, *The Study of the Bible in the Middle Ages*, p. 52.

6. Cited in S. D. Goitein, *Methods of Education*, p. 66. Cited in *A History of the Jewish People*, ed. H. H. Ben-Sasson, p. 521.

7. *A History of the Jewish People,* ed. H. H. Ben-Sasson, p. 521.

8. Abraham Joshua Heschel, *The Earth Is the Lord's,* p. 46.

9. See the discussion of the extremely high Jewish representation in the status professions in Ernest van den Haag, *The Jewish Mystique,* chaps. 10–11. This was the source for the above-stated statistics.

10. In the 1970s the following percentages of different religious groups attended college: Baptists 28 percent, Methodists 45 percent, Episcopalians 65 percent, and Jews 88 percent. Cited in Andrew Greeley, *The American Catholic: A Social Portrait,* p. 41.

11. By the mid-1950s the enrollment of Jews in the Ivy League schools was 23 percent: Nathan Glazer and Daniel P. Moynihan, *Beyond the Melting Pot,* 2d ed. rev., p. 157. In 1981, with the Jews composing only 2.6 percent of the American population, the Jewish percentage at Harvard was estimated at between 28 to 40 percent, Richard Reeves, *American Journey,* p. 280.

12. U.S. Bureau of Census and the National Jewish Population Survey, cited in Sowell, *Ethnic America,* p. 5.

13. Raphael Patai, *The Jewish Mind,* p. 441.

14. Charles R. Snyder, *Alcohol and the Jews,* p. 4.

15. Hosea 4:11, Isaiah 5:11 and 28:7; Proverbs 20:1, 21:17, 23:19–21, and 23:29–35, 31:4–5.

16. The material contained herein is drawn, unless otherwise noted, from Raphael Patai, *The Jewish Mind,* pp. 433–47.

17. Snyder, *Alcohol and the Jews,* pp. 85, 92, 98, 101.

18. Stephen D. Isaacs, *Jews and American Politics,* pp. 6, 119–20.

19. Israel Abrahams, *Jewish Life in the Middle Ages,* pp. 325ff.

20. Chaim Bermant, *The Jews,* p. 243.

21. Lancelot Addison, *The Present State of the Jews* (London, 1675), chap. 25; cited in Abrahams, *Jewish Life,* p. 307.

22. Moses Maimonides, *Code of Jewish Law, Gifts to the Poor,* chap. 7; *Jewish Encyclopedia* 3:669–70 and *Encyclopedia Judaica,* 8:281–86.

23. *Plutarch's Lives,* "Lycurgus," p. 61.

24. Diogenes Laertius, *Lives of Eminent Philosophers,* 2 vols. (Cambridge, Mass.: Harvard University Press, n.d.), VI, 72; VII, 33 and 131.

25. Abba Hillel Silver, *Where Judaism Differed,* pp. 48–49.

26. 1 Corinthians 7:1–2; 6–7.

27. Origen's statement is cited in Silver, *Judaism Differed,* p. 221.

28. Shabbat 31A, Kiddushin 20B, Yoma 1:1.

29. Gershom Scholem, *Major Trends in Jewish Mysticism,* pp. 105–6.
30. Patai, *Jewish Mind,* pp. 493–94.
31. See Glazer and Moynihan, *Melting Pot,* p. 165; and T. P. Monaham and W. Kephart, "Divorce and Desertion by Religious and Mixed Religious Groups," *American Journal of Sociology* 50, no. 5 (March 1954): 454–65.
32. The studies are cited in Marshall Sklare, *America's Jews,* p. 95.
33. Glazer and Moynihan, *Melting Pot,* p. 165.

Five: Non-Jewish Jews and Antisemitism

1. The term "non-Jewish Jew" is taken from Isaac Deutscher's autobiographical essay, *The Non-Jewish Jew.* In the essay, the noted Marxist historian described his abandonment of God, law, and Jewish nationhood, and his subsequent identification with "humanity" rather than with any particular people or country.
2. It is true that Marx converted to Christianity at the age of six. But this was a pro forma conversion done by his father to avoid Prussian anti-Jewish legislation. Marx was an atheist and opponent of religion who did not consider himself a Christian, and was regarded by his opponents, both in his own time and until today, as a Jew.
3. Ernest van den Haag, *The Jewish Mystique,* pp. 96–97.
4. As regards the heritage of the Jewish mission, the modern historian Walter Laqueur writes: "One explanation of the Jewish inclination toward left-wing radicalism . . . is that it is an outgrowth of Jewish messianism" (*Out of the Ruins of Europe,* p. 478). And concerning the distorted moral passion, George Mosse, one of the foremost scholars of modern German history, writes: "Jewish monotheism meant a social conscience imbued with personal responsibility and a love for one's fellow man. . . . For many young Jews this commitment to a left-wing idealism provided a new religion" (*Germans and Jews,* p. 206).
5. See Stanley Rothman and S. Robert Lichter, *Roots of Radicalism: Jews, Christians, and the New Left,* p. 81.
6. Seymour Martin Lipset, "The Left, the Jews and Israel," *Encounter,* December 1969.
7. Peter G. J. Pulzer, *The Rise of Political Anti-Semitism in Germany and Austria,* p. 261.
8. Radical Jews "yearn to bleach away their past and become men without, or above, a country" (Irving Howe, *World of Our Fathers,* p. 93).

9. Cited in Robert Wistrich, *Revolutionary Jews from Marx to Trotsky*, p. 189.

10. Cited in Rothman and Lichter, *Roots of Radicalism*, p. 111.

11. Ibid., p. 93.

12. Ibid., p. 89.

13. Istvan Deak, *Weimar Germany's Left-Wing Intellectuals: A Political History of the Weltbühne and Its Circle*, p. 24.

14. In the words of the Columbia professor and historian of the period, Fritz R. Stern, the leftist intellectuals who attacked the foundations of Weimar Germany "were not concerned with compromise . . . they sought to destroy the present" (*The Politics of Cultural Despair: A Study in the Rise of Germanic Ideology*, p. 268).

15. Kurt Tucholsky, *Gesammelte Werke*, 2:1086. Cited in Deak, *Weimar Germany's*, p. 43.

16. Deak, p. 43.

17. Masse, *Germans and Jews*, p. 214.

18. *Die Weltbühne*, May 31, 1932, p. 835. Cited in George Mosse, *Masses and Man*, p. 311.

19. Mosse, ibid., p. 310.

20. Rothman and Lichter, *Roots of Radicalism*, pp. 81–82.

21. Simon Karlinsky, "Dostoevsky as Rorschach Test," *New York Times Book Review*, June 13, 1971.

22. Noam Chomsky, *Towards a New Cold War*, p. 254.

23. The quote is from Chomsky's article "On Resistance," *New York Review of Books*, December 1967.

24. Martin Peretz, *The New Republic*, January 3–10, 1981, p. 38. See also Nadine Fresco, "The Denial of the Dead: The Faurisson Affair—and Noam Chomsky," *Dissent* (Fall 1981): 467–83.

25. *Commentary*, October 1968.

26. Quoted in Philip Nobile, *Intellectual Skywriting*, p. 96.

27. Ibid., p. 98.

28. In conversation with Philip Nobile, ibid., p. 145.

29. *New York Review of Books*, August 2, 1967.

30. *Commentary*, September 1967.

31. Ben Stein, *The View from Sunset Boulevard*, pp. 39, 126–27.

32. Norman Mailer, *The Presidential Papers*, pp. 69–70.

33. The essay is contained in Laqueur's book *Out of the Ruins of Europe*.

34. *Commentary*, December 1981.
35. Werner Cohn, *Partners in Hate*, p. 125.

Six: Other Theories of Antisemitism

1. A recent example of an attempt to dejudaize the Jewish experience, though the subject was not antisemitism, was supplied by a Jewish academic, Stephen Steinberg, professor of sociology at Queens College, New York. His book, *The Ethnic Myth*, concentrates on the Jews in order to debunk the "myth" that "there are ethnic reasons for ethnic success, and the causes are to be found within the groups themselves." The biggest myth of all, according to Steinberg, is that there are Jewish reasons for the Jews' success. The notion that specifically Jewish values may be at the root of Jewish achievements in America repulses Professor Steinberg. Thus, he reduces the Jews' achievements in America to a series of fortuitous socioeconomic circumstances. This even includes the Jews' commitment to education: "But were these values [on education] distinctively part of a religious and cultural heritage, or were they merely cultural responses of a group that had acquired the economic prerequisites for educational mobility at a time when educational opportunities abounded?" (p. 137).

2. Maurice Samuel, *The Great Hatred*, p. 48.

3. That economic factors do not cause Jew-hatred does not mean that they do not cause some ethnic rivalry or some resentment of Jews. But such feelings of resentment are one thing and Jew-hatred is quite another. This book is concerned with the Jew-hatred that has existed for over two thousand years, and that has not been caused by Jews who lead lives of conspicuous consumption.

4. Hannah Arendt, *The Origins of Totalitarianism*, p. 4.

5. Arthur Hertzberg, *The French Enlightenment and the Jews*, p. 7.

6. Ibid.

7. T. W. Adorno, Else Frenkel-Brunswick, Daniel J. Levinson, and R. Nevitt Sanford, *The Authoritarian Personality*.

8. From the Max Horkheimer preface to *The Authoritarian Personality*, p. ix.

9. Gordon Allport, *The Nature of Prejudice*, pp. xv–xvi.

10. Adorno et al., *Authoritarian Personality*, p. 1.

11. Originally published as *Réflexions sur la Question Juive* (Paris: Paul Morihein, 1946), the book was translated and published in the United States in 1948 by Schocken. It is currently in its *thirteenth* printing as a Schocken paperback. Citations are from that edition.

12. Sartre, *Anti-Semite,* p. 54.

13. Ibid., p. 53.

14. Ibid., pp. 13, 67, 91.

15. Ibid., p. 135.

PART TWO: THE HISTORICAL EVIDENCE

Seven: Antisemitism in the Ancient World

1. Philostratus, *The Life of Apollonius of Tyana,* translated by F. G. Conybeare; cited in Menachem Stern, *Greek and Latin Authors on Jews and Judaism,* 2:341.

2. Yizhak Heinemann in *Anti-Semitism* (Jerusalem: Keter, 1974), p. 3.

3. Josephus, *Against Apion,* 2:65.

4. Cited in Josephus, *Against Apion* 1, 304–11.

5. The Jews' successful revolt against Antiochus's attempt to destroy Judaism is commemorated by the holiday of Chanukah.

6. Victor Tcherikover, *Hellenistic Civilization and the Jews,* p. 478, n. 39; see also pp. 195–96, 199.

7. Josephus, *Against Apion* 1, 91–96.

8. Tacitus's extensive writings on the Jews, the most detailed account of Judaism and Jewish history in classical Latin literature, have been collected in *Greek and Latin Authors on Jews and Judaism,* edited with introductions, translations, and commentary by Menachem Stern, 2:1–93. Concerning the impact on Tacitus's description of the Jews, Stern notes: "Since this description is found in the works of the greatest historian of Rome, its subsequent influence, especially after the revival of interest in Tacitus in the sixteenth century, may be considered out of all proportions to its inherent merits" (p. 1).

9. See Philo, *Embassy to Gaius,* Loeb edition, vols. 9–10, trans. F. H. Colson. Cited in Vamberto Morais, *A Short History of Anti-Semitism,* p. 28.

10. A discussion of the Jewish population in the Roman Empire is in Salo Baron, *A Social and Religious History of the Jews,* 1:370–72.

11. Cited in Stern, *Greek and Latin Authors,* 1:431.

12. Josephus, *Antiquities*, vol. 20.5 1–3 and *The Jewish War*, 2.12.2.
13. Stern, *Greek and Latin Authors*, 2:26.
14. Baron, *Social and Religious History*, 1:194.
15. Rosemary Reuther, *Faith and Fratricide*, pp. 24–25.
16. This dislike was not motivated by my distinctive Jewish economic status. Historians Marcel Simon in *Versus Israel* and J. Juster in *Les Juifs dans L'Empire Romain* have both documented that the pagan world did not associate the Jews with distinctive economic roles or with wealth. See Edward Flannery, *The Anguish of the Jews*, chap. 1.

Eight: Christian Antisemitism

1. See note on p. 93. See also Hyam Maccoby, *Revolution in Judaea,* for a full discussion of Jesus the Jew.
2. Whereas other Gospel writers had usually attacked Jewish authority figures, John uses the term "the Jews" almost exclusively (some sixty times) for his condemnation (see Rosemary Reuther, *Faith and Fratricide*, pp. 115–16).
3. See R. S. Storrs, *Bernard of Clairvaux* (New York: Gordon Press, n.d.), p. 357, and J. H. Newman, *Historical Sketches* (Westminster, Md.: Christian Classics, 1970), 2:234. Both these works are cited by the Catholic historian Malcolm Hay in his *Europe and the Jews*, p. 27.
4. Citations from the speeches and writings of St. John Chrysostom are in Hay, *Europe*, pp. 26–31.
5. Ibid., pp. 30–31.
6. St. Ambrose wrote two accounts of this, one sent as a letter to the emperor, the other as a letter to his sister. Both are in Jacob Marcus, *The Jew in the Medieval World*, pp. 107–10.
7. The facts and contemporary chronicles of the Crusades are in Leon Poliakov, *The History of Anti-Semitism: From the Time of Christ to the Court Jews*, pp. 41–56. The complete Jewish chronicles from the Crusader period have been translated and edited by Professor Shlomo Eidelberg in *The Jews and the Crusaders: The Hebrew Chronicles of the First and Second Crusades*.
8. Poliakov, *Time of Christ to the Court Jews*, p. 45.
9. Ibid., p. 47, n. 6.
10. Ibid., p. 48.

11. See Hay, *Europe*, pp. 127–28; for methods of torture used, see pp. 132–33.

12. We are indebted in this section to a remarkable work of contemporary scholarship, *The Devil and the Jews: The Medieval Conception of the Jew and Its Relation to Modern Antisemitism*, by Joshua Trachtenberg. The relevant pages of Trachtenberg's book are pp. 97–155.

13. Trachtenberg, *Devil and the Jews*, p. 130.

14. Ibid., p. 131.

15. Charles Lamb, "Imperfect Sympathies," *Essays of Elia*. Cited in Hay, *Europe*, p. 126.

16. In F. J. Child's *The English and Scottish Popular Ballads* (Magnolia, Mass.: Peter Smith, 1965), the compiler quotes twenty-one versions of the ballad about Hugh of Lincoln. See Marcus, *Jew in the Medieval World*, p. 126.

17. Trachtenberg, *Devil and the Jews*, p. 135.

18. Haim Hillel Ben-Sasson, *Trial and Achievement. Currents in Jewish History*, p. 247.

19. James Parkes, *The Foundations of Judaism and Christianity*, p. 247. Malcolm Hay places much of the blame for the continued popularity of the blood libel in modern times on a faction in the Vatican: "Although Pope Innocent IV in the 13th century had decreed that no one was to accuse the Jews of using human blood in the religious rites, this prohibition did not prevent the publication of the old calumnies by the semi-official journal of the Vatican, *La-Cruila Cattolica*, in a series of articles . . . [that] appeared between February, 1881 and December, 1882. Characteristic of its articles is this selection from the March 4, 1882, issue: 'Every practicing Hebrew worthy of that name is obliged even now, in conscience, to use in food, in drink, in circumcision, and in various other rites of his religious and civil life the fresh or dried blood of a Christian child, under pain of infringing his laws and passing among his acquaintances for a bad Hebrew . . . all this is still true and faithfully observed in the present century'" (*Europe*, pp. 311–12).

20. The blood libel had been introduced into the Muslim world by Christian missionaries in the nineteenth century. See Hay, *Europe*, p. 310.

21. Professor Jacob Milgrom of the University of California at Berkeley has noted: "This prohibition is not found anywhere else in the ancient Near East. . . . That none of Israel's neighbors possess this absolute and universal binding prohibition means that it cannot be a vestige of a

primitive taboo, but the result of a deliberate reasoned enactment. This is clear from the rationale appended to the law: "blood is life" (Leviticus 17:11, 14 and Deuteronomy 12:23. Milgrom's conclusion appears in the *Encyclopedia Judaica*, 4:1115).

22. Ahad Ha-Am, *Selected Essays*, pp. 203–4.
23. James Parkes, *The Jew in the Medieval Community*, p. 50.
24. Trachtenberg, *Devil and the Jews*, p. 97.
25. Ibid.
26. Trachtenberg, *Devil and the Jews*, p. 99.
27. Ben-Sasson, *Trial and Achievement*, pp. 254–55.
28. Trachtenberg, *Devil and the Jews*, p. 114.
29. Raul Hilberg, *The Destruction of the European Jews*, p. 4.
30. Hilberg, *Destruction*, pp. 4–6. In each instance, we have cited only the first date on which any given law was enacted. Most of the laws were reinforced many times.
31. Cited in Hilberg, *Destruction*, p. 12.
32. See A. Roy Eckhardt, *Your People, My People*, p. 24.
33. *Mein Kampf*, p. 213.
34. Cited in Friedrich Heer, *God's First Love*, p. 286.
35. Hay, *Europe*, p. 286.
36. This pamphlet is reprinted in *The Jew in the Medieval World*, ed. Jacob Marcus, pp. 167–69.
37. See Eliezer Berkovits, *Faith After the Holocaust* (New York: Ktav, 1973), for a scathing and brilliant assessment of Christian responsibility for the Holocaust.
38. Cited in Heer, *God's First Love*, after dedication page.

Nine: Islamic Antisemitism

1. Salo Baron, *A Social and Religious History of the Jews*, 3:94.
2. S. D. Goitein, *Jews and Arabs*, p. 84. Goitein's book is the best survey of Jews under the Arabs and Islam. *The Jews of Arab Lands*, by Norman A. Stillman, complements Goitein's work, with over three hundred pages of documents from Jewish life in the Islamic world.
3. Goitein, *Jews and Arabs*, pp. 58–59.
4. The translations used in this chapter are taken from the Koran, translated by the noted Arab scholar N. J. Dawood (New York: Penguin, 1964).

5. Walter Kaufmann, *Religions; in Four Dimensions*, p. 186.

6. Ibid.

7. Goitein, *Jews and Arabs*, p. 64.

8. Christians, too, were accused of omitting from the New Testament a prophecy of Jesus relating to Muhammad: "And of Jesus, who said to the Israelites: 'I am sent forth to you by Allah to confirm the Torah already revealed and to give news of an apostle that will come after me whose name is Ahmed [another name of Muhammad's]'" (61:6).

9. See Joel Kraemer, "War, Conquest and the Treatment of Religious Minorities in Medieval Islam," in *Violence and Defense in the Jewish Experience*, ed. Salo Baron and George Wise, p. 150.

10. Ibid., pp. 151–52.

11. The complete text of the Pact of Umar is printed in *Islam*, vol. 2: *Religion and Society*, ed. and trans. Bernard Lewis, pp. 217–19.

12. Goitein, *Jews and Arabs*, pp. 67–68.

13. Both the regulation and the quote from Baron are in Baron, *Social and Religious History*, 3:167.

14. Ibid., p. 168. Baron noted that this procedure was regarded as so degrading that when Muslims imposed this on Christians in Jerusalem in 758, many Christians fled to Byzantium.

15. Ibid., p. 171.

16. Kraemer, "Treatment of Religious Minorities," p. 153.

17. See Raul Hilberg, *The Destruction of the European Jews*, p. 5.

18. Baron, *Social and Religious History*, 3:141.

19. Ibid., p. 140.

20. This description of Jewish life in Yemen is taken from Goitein, *Jews and Arabs*, pp. 74–78.

21. The quotation appears in Lane, *An Account of the Manners and Customs of the Modern Egyptians* (Magnolia, Mass.: Peter Smith, n.d.), pp. 512–13, and is cited in Shimon Shamir, "Muslim-Arab Attitudes Towards Jews in the Ottoman and Modern Periods," in *Violence and Defense in the Jewish Experience*, ed. Salo Baron and George Wise, p. 195.

22. See *A History of the Jewish People*, ed. H. H. Ben-Sasson, pp. 847–48.

23. See Shamir, "Muslim-Arab Attitudes," p. 195.

24. See "Palestine Before the Zionists" by the Harvard historian David Landes, *Commentary*, February 1976, pp. 47–56.

25. James Finn, *Stirring Times*, 1:118–19.

26. Albert Memmi, *Jews and Arabs*, pp. 32–33.

27. Ibid., p. 33.

28. Yehoshafat Harkabi, *Arab Attitudes to Israel*, p. 221.

29. Cited in Elias Cooper, "Forgotten Palestinian: The Nazi Mufti," *American Zionist*, March-April 1973, p. 26.

30. Among the war criminals welcomed to Nasser's Egypt were Leopold Gleim, head of the Gestapo in Poland; Hans Eichler, who served in Buchenwald; Heinrich Willerman, a doctor who experimented on human guinea pigs in Dachau; and Alois Moser, who took part in the massacre of hundreds of thousands of Jews in Soviet Ukraine. In Syria, the Nazis include Franz Rademacher, head of the German foreign office department dealing with Jews, and Otto Ernst Remer, the former military governor of Berlin. The Egyptians also employed several hundred Nazi technicians to develop its missile and aircraft industry, while the Syrians used Nazis to develop their secret police and assist in producing anti-Jewish propaganda. (See Julian J. Landau, *Israel and the Arabs*, p. 173.)

31. Cited in Landau, ibid., p. 175.

32. Cited in Harkabi, *Arab Attitudes*, p. 279.

33. See Moshe Ma'oz, "The Image of the Jew in Official Arab Literature and Communications Media," in *World Jewry and the State of Israel*, ed. Moshe Davis, p. 45.

34. Cited in Landau, *Israel and the Arabs*, p. 177.

35. Cited in Ma'oz, "Image of the Jew," p. 46.

36. Andrew Sullivan, "Washington Diarist," in *New Republic*, November 5, 2001, back page.

37. Cited in Gabriel Schoenfeld, "Israel and the Anti-Semites," *Commentary*, June 2002, p. 15.

38. See Ma'oz, "Image of the Jew," p. 38.

39. Cited by Landau, *Israel and the Arabs*, p. 40.

40. Ma'oz, "Image of the Jew," p. 44. In Cairo in 1974, Dennis Prager saw Arab translations of *The Protocols* in nearly every bookstore he visited.

41. See Robert Wistrich, *Intifida II: The Arab Campaign to Destroy Israel*, American Jewish Committee website, www.ajc.org.

42. Andrew Sullivan, "Washington Diarist."

43. Harkabi, *Arab Attitudes*, p. 241.

Ten: Secular Antisemitism: The Enlightenment

1. Except where otherwise noted, the quotations from the *Dictionnaire Philosophique* are cited in Leon Poliakov's *The History of Anti-Semitism: From Voltaire to Wagner*, pp. 88–89. Poliakov has, in the main, relied on the J. Benda. Naves edition of 1936, which follows the 1769 edition of the *Dictionnaire*.

2. From the entry on "Jew" in the *Dictionnaire*, 1756 edition, cited in *A History of the Jewish People*, ed. H. H. Ben-Sasson, p. 745.

3. Poliakov, *From Voltaire to Wagner*, p. 87.

4. Peter Gay, a professor at Yale University, has authored the following volumes on the Enlightenment: *The Enlightenment: vol. 1: The Rise of Modern Paganism; vol. 2: The Science of Freedom*. Also *The Party of Humanity: Essays in the French Enlightenment*, and *The Enlightenment: An Anthology*.

5. Gay, *Party of Humanity*, pp. 103, 105.

6. Ibid., pp. 44, 53.

7. Arthur Hertzberg's *The French Enlightenment and the Jews*, pp. 286, 287, 288, 289–90. We are indebted to Professor Hertzberg's work for documenting the profound influence of eighteenth-century Enlightenment thinking on modern antisemitism.

8. Gay, *Enlightenment: Anthology*, p. 746.

9. Cited in Hertzberg, *French Enlightenment*, p. 284.

10. Poliakov, *From Voltaire to Wagner*, p. 491, n. 38.

11. Hertzberg, *French Enlightenment*, pp. 297, 300, 301.

12. Ibid., p. 10.

13. Ibid., p. 299.

14. Poliakov, *From Voltaire to Wagner*, p. 119.

15. The material cited from d'Holbach comes from Poliakov, ibid., pp. 120–24.

16. Montesquieu, *L'Esprit des lois*, XXV, 13: "A Most Humble Remonstrance to the Inquisitors of Spain and Portugal." Cited in Poliakov, *ibid.*, p. 82.

17. Ben-Sasson, *History of the Jewish People*, p. 745.

18. Cited in Ben-Sasson, ibid., p. 746.

19. Cited in Ben-Sasson, ibid., p. 742.

20. Hertzberg, *French Enlightenment*, pp. 38–39.

21. Shmuel Ettinger, "The Origins of Modern Anti-Semitism," in *The Catastrophe of European Jewry*, ed. Yisrael Gutman and Livia Rothkirchen, p. 12.

Eleven: Leftist Antisemitism

1. "Almost all the rabbis of Trier from the sixteenth century onwards were ancestors of Marx," notes the Marx biographer David McLellan, *Karl Marx: His Life and Thought*, p. 3.
2. Quoted in Nathan Rotenstreich, "For and Against Emancipation: The Bruno Bauer Controversy," in *Yearbook IV* of the Leo Baeck Institute, pp. 7–8.
3. *On the Jewish Question* appears in Karl Marx's *Early Writings*, ed. Quintin Hoare, and trans. Rodney Livingston and Gregor Benton, pp. 211–41. The quote is on p. 241.
4. Robert Wistrich, *Revolutionary Jews from Marx to Trotsky*, p. 33.
5. *On the Jewish Question*, p. 236.
6. Ibid., p. 239.
7. "The social emancipation of the Jews is the emancipation of society from Judaism." Ibid., p. 241.
8. Cited in Julius Carlebach, *Karl Marx and the Radical Critique of Judaism*, pp. 355–56.
9. Max Geltman, "On Socialist Anti-Semitism," *Midstream* 23, no. 3 (March 1977): 25. The earlier citations in the paragraph are on pp. 24–25.
10. Written in a letter to Friedrich Engels on May 10, 1861. In this letter, Marx attacked his political opponent Ferdinand Lasalle as being a descendant of one of these leprous Jews.
11. Cited in Edmund Silberner's "Inaugural Lecture," delivered at the Hebrew University on January 4, 1953, and subsequently reprinted under the title *The Anti-Semitic Tradition in Modern Socialism*.
12. In recent years, Arnold Kunzli has attempted a posthumous psychoanalysis of Marx's antisemitism. Kunzli concludes that Marx's identification of Jews and Judaism with capitalism was a way of distancing himself from Jews. We know, in fact, that Marx virulently reacted against any mention of his Jewish origins. This desire to distance himself would also explain why he ignored the Jewish working class, and

why he took no notice of socialist movements among Jewish workers. "Marx must, therefore, have experienced the emergence of a Jewish socialism as a vexation, for thereby the legitimacy of his system, into which he had . . . forced Judaism was made questionable, and his alibi destroyed and he himself again brought into association with his Judaism." (See Arnold Kunzli, *Karl Marx-Eine Psychographie*, p. 209, cited in Leon Poliakov, *The History of Anti-Semitism: From Voltaire to Wagner*, p. 556, n. 148. See also Chap. 5 of this book, on revolutionary non-Jewish Jews.)

13. Edmund Silberner, "Was Marx an Anti-Semite?" *Historica Judaica*, April 1949, p. 52.

14. Nora Levin, *While Messiah Tarried*, pp. 100–101.

15. The most important assessment of the French socialists' attitudes toward the Jews was written by Lichtheim in the essay "Socialism and the Jews," reprinted in his *Collected Essays*, pp. 413–47.

16. Cited in Jacob Katz, *From Prejudice to Destruction: Anti-Semitism, 1700–1933*, p. 121.

17. Alphonse Toussenel, *Les Juifs, rois de l'époque* (1845), pp. 73–74. Cited in Lichtheim, "Socialism and the Jews," p. 422.

18. Lichtheim, ibid., p. 424.

19. *Carnets de P. J. Proudhon: Texte inédit et intégral*, ed. Pierre Haubtmann, 2: 337–38. Quoted in Lichtheim, p. 425.

20. Lichtheim, ibid., p. 426.

21. Jean Juarès subsequently had a change of heart, and argued that socialists should protest this injustice. See Edmund Silberner, "French Socialists and the Jews," *Historica Judaica*, April 1957, pp. 13–14.

22. *Jewish Social Studies*, January 1947.

23. In 1972, the Politburo of the North Vietnamese Communist party hailed the Black September (a wing of the Palestine Liberation Organization) murder of the Israeli athletes at the Olympics in Munich.

24. See Bernard Weinryb, "Antisemitism in Soviet Russia," in *The Jews in Soviet Russia Since 1917*, ed. Lionel Kochan, p. 326. Kochan's book and William Korey's *The Soviet Cage: Anti-Semitism in Russia* are the two most comprehensive works on Soviet antisemitism.

25. Quoted in Zev Katz, "After the Six-Day War," in Kochan, *Jews in Soviet Russia*, p. 335.

26. Witnessed by Dennis Prager, who speaks Russian, in 1972.

27. George Will, *Los Angeles Times*, October 9, 1979.

28. *Pravda*, July 6, 1967. Cited in Kochan, *Jews in Soviet Russia*, p. 347.

29. *American Jewish Year Book 1976*, vol. 76, ed. Morris Fine and Milton Himmelfarb, pp. 93–94.

30. *Intercontinental Press*, September 6, 1971. Cited in *Facts*, November 1972, p. 550.

31. Ibid., p. 551.

32. Cited in Arnold Foster and Benjamin Epstein, *The New Antisemitism*, p. 147.

33. Marie Syrkin, "Redwashing Terrorism," in *The State of the Jews*, p. 210. Syrkin notes that before its showing in the United States some of the PLO's and Redgrave's more extreme antisemitic positions were censored. In the original version of the movie, for example, PLO leader Yasir Arafat declared: "The only solution to the Middle East problem is the liquidation of the state of Israel." To which Redgrave responds, "Certainly" (p. 211).

34. See Alan Dershowitz, "Now Jews Must Overcome," *ADL Bulletin*, April 1981, p. 10.

35. Ibid., p. 8.

36. See the article by Father Leo Rudloff, "Capucci, Terrorism and the Vatican," *ADL Bulletin*, November 1981.

37. Cited in *ADL Bulletin*, October 1981, p. 7.

Twelve: Nazi Antisemitism

1. "There were Gypsy tribes that were murdered and there were others that were protected. Individual Gypsies living among the rest of the population were not ferreted out and many even served in the Nazi army. It appears that the Nazis were ambivalent about what to do with them, but those who were murdered were the victims more of a campaign against so-called 'asocials' than against the Gypsy people as such." Yehuda Bauer, *The Holocaust in Historical Perspective*, p. 36.

2. Adolf Hitler, *Mein Kampf*, p. 312.

3. Cited in Lucy Dawidowicz, *The War Against the Jews*, p. 86.

4. Cited in Dawidowicz, ibid., p. 84.

5. Dawidowicz, ibid., p. 4.

6. Ibid., pp. 141–42.

7. Lucy Dawidowicz, *A Holocaust Reader*, p. 85.

8. Cited in Dawidowicz, *War Against the Jews*, p. 191.

9. "Regional analyses of the Nazi party have appeared which trace in detail its evolution from a fringe group to a mass movement. They have focused primarily upon the novel structure and propaganda techniques of the party, and have in several cases cast strong doubts upon the significance of antisemitism in drawing recruits to the party and in attracting voters after 1929. In the case of Northeim, for example, historian W. A. Allen has argued that many who flocked to National Socialism just 'ignored or rationalized' its hatred of Jews; similarly, in . . . Bavaria." Geoffrey G. Field, *Evangelist of Race: The Germanic Vision of Houston Stewart Chamberlain*, p. 457.

10. Cited in Dawidowicz, *War Against the Jews*, p. 22.

11. Treitschke's account is in *Modern Jewish History: A Source Reader*, ed. Robert Chazan and Marc Lee Raphael, pp. 80–84.

12. Cited in Field, *Evangelist of Race*, p. 186.

13. Letter to Harriet Chamberlain, June 7, 1896, cited in ibid., p. 107.

14. Cited in Will Herberg, *Judaism and Modern Man*, p. 274.

15. Poliakov, *The Aryan Myth*, p. 319.

16. Quoted in Uriel Tal, "Anti-Christian Anti-Semitism," in *The Catastrophe of European Jewry*, ed. Yisrael Gutman and Livia Rothkirchen, p. 94.

17. Ibid., p. 95.

18. Cited in Dawidowicz, *War Against the Jews*, pp. 32–33.

19. Cited in Carl Friedrich, "Anti-Semitism: Challenge to Christian Culture," in *Jews in a Gentile World: The Problem of Anti-Semitism*, ed. Isacque Graeber and Steuart Henderson Britt, p. 8.

20. Cited in Norman Cohn, *Warrant for Genocide*, pp. 136–37.

21. Dawidowicz, *War Against the Jews*, pp. 373–74.

22. Ibid.

23. Celia Heller's *On the Edge of Destruction* details the sufferings of Polish Jewry between the two world wars.

24. *The Warsaw Diary of Chaim A. Kaplan* has been translated and edited by Abraham I. Katsh.

25. Yehuda Bauer, *A History of the Holocaust*, p. 285.

26. John Toland, *Adolf Hitler*, p. 797.

27. Shmuel Ettinger, "The Modern Period," in *A History of the Jewish People*, ed. H. H. Ben-Sasson, p. 1025. Unless otherwise noted all the fac-

tual evidence about Eastern European cooperation with the Nazis comes from pp. 1023–35.

28. Both this and the following instance are told in Rabbi M. D. Weissmandel's autobiographical account of the Holocaust years, *Min Hamezar*, pp. 24–25, and are cited in Eliezer Berkovits, *Faith After the Holocaust*, pp. 16–17.
29. Shmuel Ettinger, "Modern Period," p. 1034.
30. Raul Hilberg, ed., *Documents of Destruction: Germany and Jewry, 1933–1945*, pp. 152–53.

Thirteen: Anti-Zionist Antisemitism

1. An earlier version of this chapter appeared in chap. 6 in *The Nine Questions People Ask About Judaism*, by Dennis Prager and Joseph Telushkin.
2. *American Zionist*, March 1971.
3. Amos Kenan, "New Left Go Home," in *The New Left and the Jews*, ed. Mordecai S. Chertoff, p. 311.
4. See Norman Podhoretz, "Now, Instant Zionism," in *New York Times Magazine*, February 3, 1974, p. 39.
5. There is a fringe group of several hundred ultra-Orthodox Jews in Israel, known as the *neturei karta*, who are well-known enemies of Israel and of Zionism. At first, one might think that their positions are consistent with anti-Zionists'. But this is not so. These Jews believe that the Jews are a nation (Am Yisrael) and there should be a Jewish state. They insist, however, that this state should not come into existence until the Messiah personally establishes it, and since this was not the case with Israel (and furthermore, since the leaders of the state do not abide by the religious practices of the *neturei karta*), they do not recognize the current state of Israel. In any case, the *neturei karta* Jews are as representative of Jews as the snake-handling sects are of Christians.
6. Cited in William Korey's "Updating the Protocols," *Midstream*, May 1970, p. 17.
7. While the Left's antisemitism generally masquerades under the guise of anti-Zionism, the anti-Jewish writings of the Fascist Right usually acknowledge their animosity toward the Jews, seeing Zionism correctly as a manifestation of Judaism. The late Gerald L. K. Smith, the major disseminator of antisemitic writings in the United States over the past

four decades, wrote in the *Gerald L. K. Smith Newsletter* of April 19, 1973: "The enemies of Christ are determined to capture the world—not through the United Nations, not through what people call a World Government, but through the manipulating, financial and military power of World Zionism."

8. *New York Times,* September 28, 2002, B1.
9. Cited in Gabriel Schoenfeld, "Israel and the Anti-Semites," *Commentary,* June 2002, p. 16.
10. Ibid., p. 17.
11. See Charles Krauthammer, "Peace of the Antisemites," in *Washington Post,* January 7, 2000.
12. See Seymour Martin Lipset, "The Socialism of Fools: The Left, the Jews and Israel," in Chertoff's *New Left,* p. 104.
13. See Sidney Liskofsky, "U.N. Resolution on Zionism," in the *American Jewish Year Book, 1977,* vol. 77, ed. Morris Fine and Milton Himmelfarb, p. 109.

Fourteen: Eight Lies About Israel

1. Michael Oren, *Six Days of War: June 1967 and the Making of the Modern Middle East,* pp. 313–14.
2. Mark Twain, *The Innocents Abroad,* pp. 385, 398.
3. Aharon Cohen, *Israel and the Arab World,* p. 238.
4. Moshe Aumann, *Land Ownership in Palestine 1880–1948,* p. 5; cited in Mitchell Bard, *Myths and Facts,* p. 44.
5. Leonard David, *Myths and Facts—1985,* p. 12.
6. Ibid.
7. Cited in Bard, *Myths and Facts,* p. 52, n. 28.
8. Bard, *Myths and Facts,* p. 180.
9. Benjamin Netanyahu, *A Place Among the Nations,* p. 292.
10. Bard, *Myths and Facts,* p. 96.
11. Cited in Dr. Dore Gold, "Occupied Territories or Disputed Territories?" *Jerusalem Issue Brief,* p. 2.
12. Ibid., pp. 3–4.
13. Cited in Gabriel Schoenfeld, "Israel and the Anti-Semites," Commentary, June 2002, p. 16.
14. Ibid.

15. David Horowitz, "Know the Enemy and What He Believes," *Jewish World Review* (a website), June 24, 2002.

PART THREE: WHAT IS TO BE DONE?

Fifteen: What Is to Be Done?

1. Boris Pasternak, *Dr. Zhivago*, pp. 117–18.
2. We say *modern* Zionist movement because the Jews' goal of returning to Zion (Israel) is as old as the Jews' exile (starting in 586 B.C.E.).
3. The four statements reflect annoyance with converts whose motives for conversion were insincere, or disappointment with converts who deserted the Jewish community during periods of persecution.
4. See George Foot Moore, *Judaism in the First Centuries of the Christian Era*, I:352–53; and Andrew Sharf, *Byzantine Jewry from Justinian to the Fourth Crusade*, pp. 19ff.
5. Moore, ibid.
6. Commentary to Yevamot 49A; cited in Ben-Zion Bokser, *Jews, Judaism and the State of Israel*, p. 134.
7. Hillel Halkin, *Letters to an American Jewish Friend*, pp. 239–40.
8. See, for example, Dennis Prager and Joseph Telushkin, *The Nine Questions People Ask About Judaism*.

Epilogue: The Meaning of Antisemitism for Non-Jews

1. *Wall Street Journal*, July 22, 1982.
2. See Werner Cohn, *Partners in Hate*, p. 125.
3. *New Republic*, August 2, 1982.
4. Ruth Wisse, "On Ignoring Anti-Semitism," *Commentary*, October 2002, p. 31.
5. Cited in *Midstream*, May 1976, p. 21.
6. Ruth Wisse, "On Ignoring Antisemitism," p. 33.
7. Jacques Maritain, *A Christian Looks at the Jewish Question*, pp. 29–30.

Abrahams, Israel. *Jewish Life in the Middle Ages*. Philadelphia: Jewish Publication Society, 1896; New York: Atheneum (pbk.), 1969.

Adorno, T. W., Else Frenkel-Brunswick, Daniel J. Levinson, and R. Nevitt Sanford. *The Authoritarian Personality*. New York: Norton (pbk.), 1969.

Allport, Gordon W. *The Nature of Prejudice*. Reading, Mass.: Addison-Wesley (pbk.), 1979.

Arendt, Hannah. *The Origins of Totalitarianism*. New York: Harcourt Brace Jovanovich, Harvest Books, 1973.

Aumann, Moshe. *Land Ownership in Palestine 1880–1948*. Jerusalem: Academic Committee on the Middle East, 1976.

Bard, Mitchell G., *Myths and Facts: A Guide to the Arab/Israeli Conflict*. Chevy Chase, Md.: American-Israeli Cooperative Enterprise, 2001.

Baron, Salo. *The Russian Jew Under Tsars and Soviets*. New York: Macmillan, 1976.

———. *A Social and Religious History of the Jews*. 2d ed. New York: Columbia University Press, vol. 1: 1952; vol. 3: 1957.

———, and George Wise. *Violence and Defense in the Jewish Experience*. Philadelphia: Jewish Publication Society, 1977.

Bauer, Yehuda. *A History of the Holocaust*. New York: Franklin Watts, 1982.

———. *The Holocaust in Historical Perspective*. Seattle: University of Washington Press, 1978.

Ben-Sasson, Haim Hillel, ed. *A History of the Jewish People*. Cambridge, Mass.: Harvard University Press, 1976.

———. "The Middle Ages." In *A History of the Jewish People*, ed. H. H. Ben-Sasson. Cambridge, Mass.: Harvard University Press, 1976.

———. *Trial and Achievement: Currents in Jewish History*. Jerusalem: Keter, 1974.

Berkovits, Eliezer. *Faith After the Holocaust*. New York: Ktav, 1973.

Bermant, Chaim. *The Jews*. New York: New York Times Books, 1977.

Bokser, Ben-Zion. *Jews, Judaism and the State of Israel*. New York: Herzl Press, 1973.

Carlebach, Julius. *Karl Marx and the Radical Critique of Judaism*. London: Routledge and Kegan Paul, 1978.

Chertoff, Mordecai S., ed. *The New Left and the Jews*. New York: Pitman, 1971.

Chomsky, Noam. *9-11*. New York: Seven Stories Press, 2001.

———. *Towards a New Cold War*. New York: Pantheon, 1982.

Cohen, Aharon. *Israel and the Arab World*. Boston: Beacon Press, 1976.

Cohn, Norman. *Warrant for Genocide: The Jewish World Conspiracy and the Protocols of the Elders of Zion*. New York: Harper and Row, 1966, 1967.

Cohn, Werner. *Partners in Hate: Noam Chomsky and the Holocaust Deniers*. Cambridge, Mass.: Avukah Press, 1995.

Cooper, Elias. "Forgotten Palestinian: The Nazi Mufti." *American Zionist*, March-April 1973.

Davis, Leonard J. *Myths and Facts 1985: A Concise Record of the Arab-Israeli Conflict*. Washington, D.C.: Near East Report, 1984.

Dawidowicz, Lucy. *A Holocaust Reader*. New York: Behrman House, 1976.

———. *The War Against the Jews*. New York: Holt, Rinehart and Winston, 1975.

Deak, Istvan. *Weimar Germany's Left-Wing Intellectuals: A Political History of the Weltbühne and Its Circle*. Berkeley: University of California Press, 1968.

Dershowitz, Alan. "Now Jews Must Overcome." *ADL Bulletin*, April 1981.

Deutscher, Isaac. *The Non-Jewish Jew and Other Essays*. London: Oxford University Press, 1968.

Eckhardt, A. Roy. *Your People, My People*. New York: Quadrangle, 1974.

Eidelberg, Shlomo. *The Jews and the Crusaders: The Hebrew Chronicles of the First and Second Crusades*. Madison: University of Wisconsin Press, 1977.

Encyclopedia Judaica. 16 vols. Jerusalem: Keter, 1972.

Ettinger, Shmuel. "The Modern Period." In *A History of the Jewish People*, edited by H. H. Sasson, pp. 727–1096. Cambridge, Mass.: Harvard University Press, 1976.

———. "The Origins of Modern Anti-Semitism." In *The Catastrophe of European Jewry*, edited by Yisrael Gutman and Livia Rothkirchen. New York: Ktav, n.d.

Fackenheim, Emil. "Post-Holocaust Anti-Jewishness, Jewish Identity and the Centrality of Israel." In *World Jewry and the State of Israel*, edited by Moshe Davis. New York: Arno Press, 1977.

Field, Geoffrey G. *Evangelist of Race: The Germanic Vision of Houston Stewart Chamberlain*. New York: Columbia University Press, 1981.

Finkelstein, Norman G. *The Holocaust Industry: Reflections on the Exploitation of Jewish Suffering*. New York: Verso, 2000.

Finn, James. *Stirring Times*. London: C. Kegan Paul, 1878.

Flannery, Edward. *The Anguish of the Jews*. New York: Macmillan, 1965.

Flavius, Josephus. *Against Apion, Antiquities*, and *The Jewish War* are all available in the Loeb Classical Library. 9 vols. Translated by H. St. J. Thackeray, Ralph Marcus, and Louis Feldman, 1926–65.

Foster, Arnold, and Benjamin Epstein. *The New Anti-Semitism*. New York: McGraw-Hill, 1974.

Frank, Anne. *The Diary of Anne Frank*. Garden City, N.Y.: Doubleday, 1952; New York: Simon and Schuster, Pocket Books (pbk.), 1963, 1974.

Fresco, Nadine. "The Denial of the Dead: The Faurisson Affair and Noam Chomsky." *Dissent*, Fall 1981.

Friedrich, Carl. "Anti-Semitism: Challenge to Christian Culture." In *Jews in a Gentile World*, edited by Isacque Graeber and Steuart Henderson. New York: Macmillan, 1942.

Gay, Peter. *The Enlightenment*. 2 vols. New York: Knopf, vol. 1, 1966; Vol. 2, 1969.

———. *The Enlightenment: An Anthology*. New York: Simon and Schuster, 1973.

———. *The Party of Humanity: Essays in the French Enlightenment*. Princeton, N.J.: Princeton University Press, 1959; New York: Norton (pbk.), 1971.

Geltman, Max. "On Socialist Anti-Semitism." *Midstream*, March 1977.

Glassman, Bernard. *Anti-Semitic Stereotypes Without Jews: Images of the Jews in England, 1290–1700*. Detroit: Wayne State University Press, 1975.

Glazer, Nathan. *The Social Basis of American Communism*. 1st ed. New York: Harcourt, Brace, 1961.

————, and Daniel Patrick Moynihan. *Beyond the Melting Pot.* 2d ed. rev. Cambridge, Mass.: M.I.T. Press, 1970.

Goitein, S. D. *Jews and Arabs: Their Contacts Through the Ages.* New York: Schocken (pbk.), 1964.

Greeley, Andrew. *The American Catholic: A Social Portrait.* New York: Basic Books, 1977.

Gutman, Yisrael, and Livia Rothkirchen, eds. *The Catastrophe of European Jewry.* New York: Ktav, n.d.

Ha-Am, Ahad. *Selected Essays.* Translated by Leon Simon. New York: Meridian Books, 1962.

Halkin, Hillel. *Letters to an American Jewish Friend.* Philadelphia: Jewish Publication Society, 1977.

Harkabi, Yehoshafat. *Arab Attitudes to Israel.* Jerusalem: Keter, 1972.

Hay, Malcolm. *Europe and the Jews.* Boston: Beacon Press (pbk.), 1961.

Heer, Friedrich. *God's First Love.* New York: Weybright and Talley, 1967.

Heller, Celia. *On the Edge of Destruction.* New York: Columbia University Press, 1977.

Helmrich, Ernst Christian. *The German Churches Under Hitler.* Detroit: Wayne State University Press, 1979.

Herberg, Will. *Judaism and Modern Man.* Philadelphia: Jewish Publication Society, 1951; New York: Atheneum (pbk.), 1970.

Hertzberg, Arthur. *The French Enlightenment and the Jews: The Origins of Modern Anti-Semitism.* New York: Columbia University Press, 1968; New York: Schocken (pbk.), 1970.

Heschel, Abraham Joshua. *The Earth Is the Lord's.* New York: Henry Schuman, 1950; New York: Harper and Row, Harper Torchbook (pbk.), 1966.

Hilberg, Raul. *The Destruction of the European Jews.* New York: Quadrangle, 1961.

————. *Documents of Destruction: Germany and Jewry, 1933–1945.* Chicago: Quadrangle, 1971.

Himmelfarb, Milton. *The Condition of Jewish Belief.* New York: Macmillan, 1969.

Hitler, Adolf. *Mein Kampf.* Translated by Ralph Manheim. Boston: Houghton Mifflin, Sentry Edition, 1971.

Howe, Irving. *World of Our Fathers.* New York: Harcourt Brace Jovanovich, 1976.

Isaacs, Stephen D. *Jews and American Politics.* Garden City, N.Y.: Doubleday, 1974.

Jacobs, Louis. *A Jewish Theology.* New York: Behrman House, 1973.

Jewish Encyclopedia. 12 vols. New York: Funk and Wagnalls, 1901–5.

Katsh, Abraham, trans. and ed. *The Warsaw Diary of Chaim A. Kaplan.* New York: Macmillan, 1965; New York: Collier (pbk.), 1973.

Katz, Jacob. *From Prejudice to Destruction: Anti-Semitism, 1700–1933.* Cambridge, Mass.: Harvard University Press, 1980.

Katz, Zev. "After the Six-Day War." In *The Jews in Soviet Russia Since 1917,* edited by Lionel Kochan. New York: Oxford University Press (pbk.), 1978.

Kaufmann, Walter. *Religions in Four Dimensions.* New York: Reader's Digest Press, 1976.

Kenan, Amos. "New Left Go Home." In *The New Left and the Jews,* edited by Mordecai S. Chertoff. New York: Pitman, 1971.

Kochan, Lionel, ed. *The Jews in Soviet Russia Since 1917.* New York: Oxford University Press (pbk.), 1978.

The Koran. Translated by N. J. Dawood. New York: Penguin Books (pbk.), 1974.

Korey, William. *The Soviet Cage: Anti-Semitism in Russia.* New York: Viking Press, 1973.

————. "Updating Protocols." *Midstream,* May 1976.

————. "Updating the Protocols." *Midstream,* May 1970.

Kraemer, Joel L. "War, Conquest and the Treatment of Religious Minorities in Medieval Islam." In *Violence and Defense in the Jewish Experience,* edited by Salo Baron and George Wise, pp. 143–59. Philadelphia: Jewish Publication Society, 1977.

Landau, Julian J. *Israel and the Arabs.* Jerusalem: Israel Communications, 1971.

Landes, David. "Palestine Before the Zionists." *Commentary,* February 1976, pp. 47–56.

Laqueur, Walter. *Out of the Ruins of Europe.* New York: Library Press, 1971.

Lendvai, Paul. *Anti-Semitism Without Jews: Communist Eastern Europe.* 1st ed. Garden City, N.Y.: Doubleday, 1971.

Levin, Nora. *While Messiah Tarried.* New York: Schocken, 1977.

Lewis, Bernard. *Islam.* Vol. 2, *Religion and Society.* New York: Harper and Row, 1974.

————. *Semites and Anti-Semites: An Inquiry Into Conflict and Prejudice.* New York: Norton, 1999.

Lichtheim, George. *Collected Essays.* New York: Viking (pbk.), 1973.

Lipset, Seymour Martin. "The Left, the Jews and Israel." *Encounter,* December 1969.

————. "The Socialism of Fools: The Left, the Jews and Israel." In *The New Left and the Jews,* edited by Mordecai S. Chertoff. New York: Pitman, 1971.

Lukofsky, Sidney. "U.N. Resolution on Zionism." In *American Jewish Yearbook 1977,* edited by Morris Fine and Milton Himmelfarb. Philadelphia; Jewish Publication Society, 1976.

Maccoby, Hyam. *Revolution in Judaea.* New York: Taplinger, 1980.

McLellan, David. *Karl Marx: His Life and Thought.* New York: Harper and Row, 1973.

Mailer, Norman. *The Presidential Papers.* New York: Putnam, 1963.

Maimonides, Moses. *The Commandments.* Translated by Charles B. Chavel. London: Soncino Press, 1967.

Ma'oz, Moshe. "The Image of the Jew in Official Arab Literature and Communications Media." In *World Jewry and the State of Israel,* edited by Moshe Davis. New York: Arno Press, 1977.

Marcus, Jacob, ed. *The Jew in the Medieval World.* New York: Union of American Hebrew Congregations, 1938; New York: Harper and Row, Harper Torchbooks (pbk.), 1965.

Maritain, Jacques. *A Christian Looks at the Jewish Question.* New York: Longmans, 1939.

Marx, Karl. "On the Jewish Question." In *Early Writings.* Translated by Rodney Livingston and Gregor Benton. New York: Random House, Vintage (pbk.), 1975.

Memmi, Albert. *Jews and Arabs.* Chicago: O'Hara, 1975.

Mendelsohn, S. Felix. *The Jew Laughs.* Chicago: L.M. Stein, 1935.

Mendes-Flohr, Paul R., and Jehuda Reinharz, eds. *The Jew in the Modern World.* New York: Oxford University Press, 1980.

Mitchell, Peter R., and John Schoeffel, eds. *Understanding Power: The Indispensable Chomsky.* New York: New Press, 2002.

Moore, George Foot. *Judaism in the First Centuries of the Christian Era.* 3 vols. Cambridge, Mass.: Harvard University Press, 1927–30.

Morais, Vamberto. *A Short History of Anti-Semitism.* New York: Norton, 1976.

Mosse, George. *Germans and Jews: The Right, the Left, and the Search for a Third Force in Pre-Nazi Germany.* New York: Howard Fertig, 1970.

———. *Masses and Man,* New York: Howard Fertig, 1980.

Netanyahu, Benjamin. *A Place Among the Nations: Israel and the World.* New York. Bantam, 1993.

Nobile, Philip. *Intellectual Skywriting: Literary Politics and The New York Review of Books.* New York: Charterhouse, 1974.

Oren, Michael B. *Six Days of War: June 1967 and the Making of the Modern Middle East.* New York. Oxford University Press, 2002.

Parkes, James. *The Foundations of Judaism and Christianity.* London: Vallentine, Mitchell, 1960.

———. *The Jew in the Medieval Community.* 2d ed. New York: Hermon Press, 1976.

Pasternak, Boris. *Dr. Zhivago.* Translated by Max Hayward and Manya Harari. New York: Pantheon, 1958.

Patai, Raphael. *The Jewish Mind.* New York: Scribner, 1977.

Plutarch. *Plutarch's Lives.* New York: Modern Library, n.d.

Podhoretz, Norman. "Now Instant Zionism." *New York Times Magazine,* February 3, 1974.

Poliakov, Leon. *The Aryan Myth.* New York: Basic Books, 1974.

———. *The History of Anti-Semitism: From the Time of Christ to the Court Jews.* New York: Viking, 1965; New York: Schocken (pbk.), 1974.

———. *The History of Anti-Semitism: From Voltaire to Wagner.* New York: Vanguard, 1975.

Prager, Dennis, and Joseph Telushkin. *The Nine Questions People Ask About Judaism.* New York: Simon and Schuster, 1981.

Pulzer, Peter G. J. *The Rise of Political Anti-Semitism in Germany and Austria.* New York: Wiley (pbk.), 1964.

Rauschning, Hermann. *Hitler Speaks,* London: T. Butterworth, 1939.

Reeves, Richard. *American Journey.* New York: Simon and Schuster, 1982.

Reuther, Rosemary. *Faith and Fratricide.* New York: Seabury Press, 1974.

Robinson, Armin, ed. *The Ten Commandments.* Preface by Herman Rauschning. New York: Simon and Schuster, 1944.

Rotenstreich, Nathan. "For and Against Emancipation: The Bruno Bauer Controversy." *Yearbook IV* of the Leo Baeck Institute, East and West Library, London.

Roth, Cecil. *Essays and Portraits in Anglo-Jewish History.* 1st ed. Philadelphia: Jewish Publication Society, 1962.

———. *Personalities and Events in Jewish History.* Philadelphia: Jewish Publication Society, 1953.

Rothman, Stanley, and S. Robert Lichter. *Roots of Radicalism: Jews, Christians, and the New Left.* New York: Oxford University Press, 1982.

Rudloff, Leo. "Capucci, Terrorism and the Vatican." *ADL Bulletin,* November 1981.

Samuel, Maurice. *The Great Hatred.* New York: Knopf, 1941.

Sartre, Jean-Paul. *Anti-Semite and Jew.* New York: Schocken, 1948; (pbk.), 1965.

Scholem, Gershom. *Major Trends in Jewish Mysticism.* 3d ed. New York: Schocken, 1954.

Selznick, Gertrude, and Stephen Steinberg. *The Tenacity of Prejudice.* New York: Harper and Row, 1969.

Shamir, Shimon. "Muslim Arab Attitudes Toward Jews in the Ottoman Modern Periods." In *Violence and Defense in the Jewish Experience,* edited by Salo Baron and George Wise, pp. 191–203. Philadelphia: Jewish Publication Society, 1977.

Sharf, Andrew. *Byzantine Jewry from Justinian to the Fourth Crusade.* London: Routledge and Kegan Paul, 1971.

Silberner, Edmund. "French Socialists and the Jews." *Historica Judaica,* April 1957.

———. "Was Marx an Anti-Semite?" *Historica Judaica,* April 1949.

Silver, Abba Hillel. *Where Judaism Differed.* New York: Macmillan, 1956; (pbk.), 1972.

Sklare, Marshall. *America's Jews.* New York: Random House, 1971.

Smalley, Beryl. *The Study of the Bible in the Middle Ages.* Notre Dame, Ind.: University of Notre Dame Press (pbk.), 1970.

Snyder, Charles R. *Alcohol and the Jews.* Arcturus (pbk.), 1978. (Reprint of the edition published by Free Press, Glencoe, Illinois, in 1958, issued as number 1 of the monographs of the Yale Center of Alcohol Studies.)

Sowell, Thomas. *Ethnic America: A History.* New York: Basic Books, 1981.

Stein, Ben. *The View from Sunset Boulevard.* New York: Basic Books, 1979.

Steinberg, Stephen. *The Ethnic Myth.* New York: Atheneum, 1981.

Stern, Fritz. *The Politics of Cultural Despair: A Study in the Rise of Germanic Ideology.* Garden City, N.Y.: Doubleday (Anchor Books), 1965.

Stern, Menachem. *Greek and Latin Authors on Jews and Judaism.* Jerusalem: Israel Academy of Sciences and Humanities, vol. 1: 1974; vol. 2: 1980.

Stillman, Norman. *The Jews of Arab Lands.* Philadelphia: Jewish Publication Society, 1979.

Stone, Isidor F. *The Hidden History of the Korean War.* New York: Monthly Review Press, 1969.

Syrkin, Marie, ed. *Hayim Greenberg Anthology.* Detroit: Wayne State University Press, 1968.

———. "Redwashing Terrorism." In her *The State of the Jews.* Washington, D.C.: New Republic Books, 1980.

Szajkowski, Zosa. "The Jewish Saint-Simonians and Socialist Antisemitism in France." *Jewish Social Studies.* January 1947.

Tacitus. *The Histories.* New York: Penguin (pbk.), 1964.

Tal, Uriel. "Anti-Christian Anti-Semitism." In *The Catastrophe of European Jewry,* edited by Yisrael Gutman and Livia Rothkirchen. New York: Ktav, n.d.

Tcherikover, Victor. *Hellenistic Civilization and the Jews.* Philadelphia: Jewish Publication Society, 1959.

Toland, John. *Adolf Hitler.* 1st. ed. Garden City, N.Y.: Doubleday, 1976.

Trachtenberg, Joshua. *The Devil and the Jews: The Medieval Conception of the Jew and Its Relation to Modern Antisemitism.* New Haven, Conn.: Yale University Press, 1943; New York: Meridian Books (pbk.), 1961.

Twain, Mark. *The Innocents Abroad.* New York: Literary Classics of the United States, 1984.

van den Haag, Ernest. *The Jewish Mystique.* 2d ed. New York: Stein and Day, 1977.

von Treitschke, Heinrich. "A Word About Our Jewry." Translated by Robert Chazan and Marc Lee Raphael, eds. In *Modern Jewish History: A Source Reader.* New York: Schocken, 1974.

Wasserstein, Bernard. *Divided Jerusalem: The Struggle for the Holy City,* 2d ed. New Haven, Conn.: Yale University Press, 2001, 2002.

Weinryb, Bernard. "Antisemitism in Soviet Russia." In *The Jews in Soviet Russia Since 1917,* edited by Lionel Kochan. New York: Oxford University Press (pbk.), 1978.

Wistrich, Robert S. *Revolutionary Jews From Marx to Trotsky.* New York: Barnes and Noble Books, 1976.

INDEX

Dennis Prager is one of America's most influential thinkers. He has a nationally syndicated radio show heard in the United States by millions of people on hundreds of stations, and heard internationally on the Internet. He is a *New York Times* bestselling author and syndicated columnist. He is also a classical musician who conducts orchestras in Southern California, including at the Walt Disney Concert Hall; a theologian described in New York's *Jewish Week* as "one of the three most interesting minds in Jewish life today"; a world traveler who has been to 120 countries; and a speaker who has lectured on all seven continents. The *Los Angeles Times* called him "an amazingly gifted man and moralist whose mission in life has been crystallized—'to get people obsessed with what is right and wrong.'" Toastmasters International named him "one of America's five best speakers." Mr. Prager was a Fellow at Columbia University's School of International Affairs, where he did graduate work at the Middle East and Russian Institutes. He taught Russian and Jewish History at Brooklyn College. He has made three short films on values, and a documentary film, *Israel in a Time of Terror*. He is currently completing his lifelong project of writing an extensive explanation and commentary on the Torah in order to make it accessible and relevant to people of every faith and also of no faith. He is the president of the Internet-based Prager University, whose five-minute videos garner nearly one hundred million views a year. His websites are www.dennis prager.com and www.prageruniversity.com.

Joseph Telushkin, named by *Talk* magazine as one of the fifty best speakers in the United States, is the author of *Jewish Literacy: The Most Important Things to Know about the Jewish Religion, Its People, and Its History*. The most widely selling book on Judaism of the past two decades, *Jewish Literacy* has been hailed by leading figures in all the major movements of Judaism. In June 2014, HarperCollins published *Rebbe: The Life and Teachings of Menachem M. Schneerson, the Most Influential Rabbi in Modern History*. Hailed by Ruth Messinger as "an astounding personal biography," and by Dennis Prager as "one of the greatest religious biographies ever written," the book, based on five years of research, tells the story of how Menachem Mendel Schneerson took over a small movement based in Brooklyn in 1951 and turned it into the most dynamic religious movement in modern Jewish history. The book was a *New York Times* bestseller.

In 2006, Bell Tower/Crown published the first volume of his monumental work *A Code of Jewish Ethics: You Shall Be Holy*, a comprehensive presentation of Jewish teachings on the vital topic of personal character and integrity. *A Code of Jewish Ethics* won the National Jewish Book Award as the Jewish Book of the Year. Rabbi Telushkin's earlier book *Words That Hurt, Words That Heal* became the motivating force behind Senators Joseph Lieberman and Connie Mack's 1996 Senate Resolution # 151 to establish a "National Speak No Evil Day" throughout the United States.

He has also written *Jewish Humor: What the Best Jewish Jokes Say about the Jews*. Larry Gelbart, screenwriter of *Mash* and *Tootsie*, said, "I don't know if Jews are really the chosen people, but I think Joseph Telushkin's book makes a strong argument that we're the funniest." His novel *An Eye for an Eye* became the basis for four episodes of David Kelley's Emmy Award–winning ABC TV series, *The Practice*. He also cowrote an episode of the TV series *Touched by an Angel* for Kirk

Douglas, in which Mr. Douglas starred as a man who, after a lifetime of struggle with his faith, returns to God and Judaism.

Rabbi Telushkin was ordained at Yeshiva University in New York, and pursued graduate studies in Jewish history at Columbia University. He resides in New York City with his wife, Dvorah Menashe Telushkin. They have four children.

He lectures throughout the United States, serves as a Senior Associate of CLAL, and is on the Board of Directors of the Jewish Book Council.

Why the Jews?

1. What were your thoughts about the roots and nature of antisemitism before reading the book? Did those thoughts change at all, and if so, how? Which arguments—historic or current—had the greatest impact on your understanding of the situation?

2. Prager and Telushkin write: "Economic depressions do not explain gas chambers." Explain what they mean by this, in a larger sense. Do you agree entirely? How does the book generally deal with the relationship of cause and effect? In what other global conflicts have transparent rationalizations been offered for abhorrent behavior?

3. Discuss the idea of "non-Jewish Jews." How are these Jews defined, and what is their role in the history of antisemitism? Do the authors believe non-Jewish Jews have helped to ease or exacerbate the effects of Jew-hatred? Why?

4. Voltaire, Luther, and Chaucer, among others, are shown to be antisemitic. How surprising is it that these figures—celebrated through time for the achievements of their minds—would harbor such deep feelings of intolerance? Or, as the authors put it, "How could the rational and tolerant Voltaire be so irrational and illiberal when it came to the Jews?" Was this question answered to your satisfaction? How do you personally reconcile the deep flaws of the many who have produced brilliant or moving works throughout history while also voicing such irrational hatreds?

5. It's argued that Voltaire helped foster "the idea that the admission ticket for a Jew into Western society was his willingness to stop being a Jew." This is an obvious contradiction, and an impossible situation for a Jew. Is there any scenario in which you could justify renunciation of personal ideals for social comfort? How reasonable is the idea of Jewish assimilation as a solution to antisemitism?

6. The authors write: "Most modern Jews, themselves secular, have believed that the demise of religion would lead to the end of anti-semitism. Yet the twentieth century, the most secular century in history, has been the most antisemitic." Do you believe increased secularization of society actually increases antisemitism as a general rule? If so, why? If not, what specifically about the 20th century created that correlation?

7. How did the book affect your understanding of the crisis in the Middle East as it stands today? Did your opinion of the troubles there change significantly, and in what way? What argument or evidence caused this shift in your thinking?

8. How are the differences between Nazism and Christian antisemitism approached and defined by the authors? What application do these differences have in illuminating the larger picture?

9. America is offered as an example of one of the only truly Judeo-Christian societies. Why have Jews been able to fit into American culture with relative ease, compared with other countries around the world—even other democracies? How do the authors link the inspiration behind hatred of America and of Israel in certain parts of the world, and is the explanation they offer for this process convincing to you?

10. The book contends that "the further Left one goes" on the political spectrum, "the greater the antisemitism." Did this idea strike you as counterintuitive, and how so? Do you believe it's true, based on the evidence offered?